BARRIERS TO COMPETITION:
THE EVOLUTION OF THE DEBATE

PERSPECTIVES IN ECONOMIC AND SOCIAL HISTORY

Series Editors: Andreas Gestrich
Steven King
Robert E. Wright

TITLES IN THIS SERIES

FORTHCOMING TITLES

BARRIERS TO COMPETITION: THE EVOLUTION OF THE DEBATE

BY

Ana Rosado Cubero

Routledge
Taylor & Francis Group

LONDON AND NEW YORK

First published 2010 by Pickering & Chatto (Publishers) Limited

Published 2016 by Routledge
2 Park Square, Milton Park, Abingdon, Oxfordshire OX14 4RN
711 Third Avenue, New York, NY 10017, USA

First issued in paperback 2015

Routledge is an imprint of the Taylor & Francis Group, an informa business

BRITISH LIBRARY CATALOGUING IN PUBLICATION DATA

Rosado Cubero, Ana.
Barriers to competition: the evolution of the debate. – (Perspectives in economic and social history)
1. Barriers to entry (Industrial organization) 2. Industrial organization (Economic theory) 3. Barriers to entry (Industrial organization) – Econometric models.
I. Title II. Series
338.6'048-dc22

ISBN-13: 978-1-138-66330-5 (pbk)
ISBN-13: 978-1-8519-6644-8 (hbk)
Typeset by Pickering & Chatto (Publishers) Limited

CONTENTS

To my parents

ACKNOWLEDGEMENTS

When I began this research in 2005, I was planning to write a paper about the state of the art of barriers to entry. Four years later this paper has grown into a book. Following this road I discovered a lot of new things about competition and American economic thought and I hope the reader can enjoy this book as much I enjoyed writing it. During this period, several people and institutions have helped me in different ways. The Universidad Complutense de Madrid, Harvard University and the Humboldt Universität zu Berlin deserve a special place in my acknowledgements, both gave me freedom to research as I liked, and supported my work. Within every University a lot of people helped my work, and I appreciate very much their unconditional support of my research and my feelings. A long time ago, in 2004, Julie Mortimer emailed me back, and I consider this email as the beginning of this enquiry, you are in my heart. Richard Caves like the good professor that he is, keeps opening the door of his office to everybody who needs his help, his advice or only to speak to a kind person. Ariel Pakes let me go to Harvard as a visiting researcher offering to me a great opportunity to grow both as a researcher and personally. I have American friends who held my soul together when the road was uphill, Grace Peters, Kimberley Warsett and Henrietta Davis. Spaniards in Somerville kept my spirit safe, thanks to Miguel Vazquez and Noemi Guill.

I spent six months in Berlin at the end of 2008 and the beginning of 2009, with the support of Humboldt Universität, invited by Elmar Wolfstetter. The opportunity to explain my research in the brown bag seminar gives me a great satisfaction, only comparable with the pleasure to listen contributions of my research made by Humboldt scholars. In Berlin and out of the work time Karin Birk, Manfred Schäfers, Reiner Überover and Luke Hu gave me the strength to go on during hard times.

I am honoured to have among my personal friends an irreverent British friend: Professor John Reader who spoke to me for hours about economic theory and barriers to entry; his suggestions have made this book more scientific, not in vain was he Joan Robinson's student in the sixties. The European Society for the History of Economic Thought invited me to speak last four years, and it gave me the opportunity to meet people who provided me new paths to follow in this research, Manuela Mosca and Jose Luis Cardoso deserve special consideration.

In 2004 I got the *Real Colegio Complutense* grant to stay in Harvard and in 2008 I obtained Spain's Ministry of Education grant, *PR2008-0077*, without this support my research adventures would have been much more difficult. Thanks to Department of History and Economic Institutions I, especially Luis Perdices, for its support and for bearing with me for centuries, and for managing every inconvenience in order to let me go.

Other friends in Madrid do not love me less than I love them, Teresa Freire, Pedro Espadas, Rafael León and Itziar Jiménez. My heartfelt thanks to the fifth floor of the Virgen de Sonsoles Hospital in Avila that cared for my father until the end in March 2009. Sylvia Hottinger patiently corrected the original version of this book in English. Every immigrant develops a special skill to make friends wherever they live, some of them became family. I have different families in the world, yet my biological family is the most important one; my parents and Marivi, Santi, Jorge, Jorge and Elena, they respect me even when I pack my luggage. This book has a part of all of them in it but if there are any mistakes only I deserve the blame.

INTRODUCTION

This book is part of a long established sub-discipline of economics, the history of the development of economic ideas and tries to show how the importance of non competitive behaviour of the firms that are analysed through economic models by American researchers, the Federal Trade Commission and the universities, and what economical analysts of Europe should learn about a stimulating American controversy.

The Sherman Law has been in force in the United States since 1890, the main goal of this Law is to outlaw every contract, combination or conspiracy in restraint of trade, as well as to protect industrial markets from monopolization and treat violations of it as crimes. The American Congress gave the federal courts adequate power to distinguish between fair cooperation and illegal agreements. The American courts interpret Section 5 as applicable to anything that is a Sherman Act or Clayton Act violation. The Federal Trade Commission also applies Section 5 to consumer protection issues, such as misleading advertising and fraud.

In the twentieth century no thought on competition had the same meaning for any particular group. Economists and Lawyers speak different languages, and meeting points in the realm of antitrust during the past century have been few. Industrial Organization tried to offer worthwhile tools to judges, courts, defendants and plaintiffs, but there it is necessary to build bridges. At the end of the nineteenth century courts used to work in business jurisprudence, but in the 1950s the traditional custom changed; as did business experts and their reports about what should be defined as competitive and what should be not defined as fair competition. Federal Trade Commission and several academics from faculties of Law and Economics promoted the change.

The Clayton Act and the Federal Trade Commission Act are in force since 1914. The collapse of the American economy in 1929 set the question of the coordination between government and industry. A closed relationship became a special influence on the National Industrial Recovery and other planning experiments of the early New Deal. Within this comfortable new timeframe, antitrust policy receded until the fifties. Supreme Court decisions at this moment which affected to cooperation between firms was fairly lax, for instance, the Court in *Board of Trade of the City of Chicago versus United States* (246 U.S. 231 [1918]) upheld limits that a commodities exchange placed on prices of after-hours trading, saying: 'the restraints should be evaluated through a comprehensive inquiry into their history, purpose, and effect'.[1] In 1920 the Supreme Court of the United States slighted evidence of outright collusion and exonerated the nation's leading steel producer on monopolization charges. In the trial *United States* v. *United States Steel Corp* (251 U.S. 417[1920]) the court credited testimony by the firm's rivals, which let them prosper under a *price umbrella* (thirty years early than Stigler's economic model). The company kept 80 per cent of market share in 1910, (forty years early than Bain considered concentration as a barrier to entry) and 40 per cent in 1920; the court was convinced that market power was eroded by competitors (forty years early than dynamic limit price theory was written). It was to wait until 1925 to fund an economist cited for the Supreme Court, in order to work in an antitrust decision; his name was Harlan Fiske Stone. The influence of economists in antitrust agencies increased during the second half of the past century, and now it is usual to find an economic perspective in law schools, and in extensive and explicit judicial reliance on economic theory.

The consequences of court sentences mean economic cost to the companies. Whenever the behaviour of a firm is considered unfair, the American antitrust, through the Department of Justice but not the (Federal Trade Commission), can impose three types of sanctions: criminal penalties, equitable relief, and monetary damage. Criminal penalties are imposed only for overt price fixing, and it are not relevant for horizontal merger enforcement. Equitable relief entails undoing a wrong that has occurred, or preventing future harm (all antitrust remedies in horizontal merger cases involve equitable relief). It is important to notice that 'The result of such a proceeding, should the plaintiff prevail, is a court issued decree'.[2]

The main argument against regulation was written by Dennis Carlton, he said: 'Antitrust is designed to let markets work when they can work. Regulation is specific, setting rules for prices and quantities'.[3] This is a very important issue, because antitrust is not a kind of regulation, neither is it a complement; under the lens of antitrust: 'Regulation, even well-intentioned, can wind up leading to inefficiencies as regulators set policies designed to please various interest groups'.[4] The other difference is that antitrust is administrated by judges, not by politicians; usually American judges: 'Not beholden to special interests and when guided by economic reasoning, has shown itself to be a valuable tool to promote efficiency'.[5]

In order to illustrate the difference between antitrust and regulation we should consider the 1980s when the political climate in the United States in which economic liberalism predominated hindered the majority of the goals of market control. Antitrust follows the Structure-Conduct-Performance model drawn up in 1984's Guidelines. Antitrust is not regulation even if it gives that impression sometimes; the antitrust authorities followed the mergers and the outlaw agreements between firms, it is not adequate to maintain that they pursued new regulations laws. The field of battle is quite different; antitrust is played out in courts whereas regulation rules are a parliamentary issue. The untoward behaviour of a firm is reported by a competitor and both parties will be defended; attorneys and litigates will be advised by experts; frequently academic professors. It is for this reason that antitrust and deregulation can coexist without problems.

Putting Theory into Practice

Since 1890, the Sherman Law, using antitrust agencies (mainly the Federal Trade Commission), tries to protect customer interests and the free market in order to guarantee equal conditions to the market's agents. Since 1992 the name of the American antitrust regulator has been Agency. To achieve thier goal Agency pursuits every agreement that restricts free trade and competition between firms, mainly cartels and market share; it bans the abusive behaviour of a dominant firm in its market, control of price, tying prices or predatory pricing and so on; also it pays attention to every business activity that could potentially be considered anti-competitive.

The antitrust analysis include two types of rules: the shrinking per se rule and the empty rule of reason using denomination made by Frank Easterbrook; the first responds to the cost, particularly high costs: information and litigation; until 1974 'tying arrangements, boycotts, territorial allocations, and resale price maintenance were unlawful per se'.[6] In the same vein, Mason wrote about the difference between per se and the rule of reason, he said that: 'Is essentially a difference in the detail required of the model in order to permit an inference concerning effects'.[7] The application of per se rules is 'cheap and quick method of enforcing the law',[8] while the rule of reason involves cases, reports and a lot of money. If it is necessary to change to the second rule and then infer economic effects in markets and companies, antitrust must bargain between efficiency and power and the conclusion must be accurate and pertinent, Mason said: 'If efficiency were not a desideratum, along with limitation of market power, no rule of reason would be necessary'.[9]

Several changes happened during the 70s in the field of antitrust, mainly understanding the economic consequences of the practices concerned, antitrust came to follow the second rule: 'We cannot condemn so quickly anymore. What we do not condemn, we must study. The approved method of study is the Rule of Reason'.[10] Rule of Reason could be considered an old controversy in philosophy; economics as a science has to accept a humble achievement; using sophisticated regression analysis and trying to keep away other non-connected effects, economists are able to offer a rule of thumb. Keeping in mind that judges and courts used to refuse economic arguments, the Rule of Reason should be used as guidelines in order to take decisions. In its 2000 guidelines, the Department of Justice assumed that given the great variety of competitor collaborations, Rule of Reason analysis entailed a flexible inquiry and varies in focus and detail depending on the nature of the agreement and market circumstances. Focusing special attention on agreements of a type that always or almost always tends to raise prices or reduce output is *per se* illegal.

Despite the first goal of antitrust, which was created by John Bates Clark in 1914, being to protect the welfare of customers, in practice welfare economics never enjoyed a preferential place among economics' disciplines. Donald Turner pointed out that: 'Economic welfare is significantly served by maintaining a good market for capital assets'.[11] Turner wrote a controversial article in 1965, within eighty-two pages he classified almost every topic concerning antitrust. The debate over his argument in this article still survives. He began his proposal by shedding light on the evidence of concentration of assets in the hands of the largest American business firms, within the most important industries, and describing possible consequences of this behaviour. It is convenient to highlight *predatory pricing* defined as: 'Selling at a lower price than customary profit maximizing considerations would dictate, for the purpose of driving equally or more efficient competitors out of all or the greater part of the market'.[12] In order to expel rivals in the market, his definition of anticompetitive required the existence of high barriers to entry; typically, losses due to a predator add to the resistance of highly established companies, and must cause non-probable performance in firms. It seems better to look at the market structure and its survival over the time. It is interesting to bear in mind that: 'The horizontal merger increases concentration in the market; the conglomerate does not'.[13] Turner said that the likelihood, in a structured industry, of deterrence of entry grows as the number of companies declines, 'Nevertheless, it is virtually impossible to estimate the probabilities of significant adverse effects upon entry'.[14] The cornerstone of Turner's thought was the possibility of giving a rule worthwhile to antimerger policy. He describes three necessary conditions for prohibiting merger:

> 1. - The market concerned must be an oligopoly market: the number of actual sellers must be sufficiently small for them to be able collectively, though not necessarily collusively, to maintain price above competitive levels.
> 2. - The merging firm at the edge of the market must be recognized by those in the market as the most likely entrant or one of a very few likely entrants, with barriers to entry by new companies or by other established firms being significantly higher.

3. - The barrier to entry by the firm in questions must not be so high that the price it must expect to obtain before it would come in is above the price that would maximize the profits of the existing sellers.[15]

Turner could be considered main promoter of guidelines, along with John Bates Clark and Edward Mason; Turner wrote that: 'Antitrust law does not seek directly to compel competition, but rather proceeds negatively by prohibiting certain anticompetitive course of conduct. A firm is free to go out of business and thus eliminate its competitive influence in the market'.[16] Chapters 2, 5 and 6 of this book included a detailed consideration of Guidelines. American antitrust pursuits are boxed in guidelines, including the natural limits of a box when there is handling of particular and peculiar business behaviour. As researchers, we keeping in mind that the line which separates barriers to entry and strategic behaviour is thin and diffuse.

In 1968 the antitrust regulator published the first Merger Guidelines as the regulatory framework within which firms must work. These Guidelines established as their purpose the prevention of the elimination of any company likely to have been a substantial competitive influence in a market, and prevention of subsequent behaviour to obtain a position of dominance in a market. The Guidelines prevent increases of market concentration and established mechanisms to deconcetration.

In order to demonstrate possibilities of unfair competition, such as agreement to share the market through market power, the antitrust regulator undertook to analyse the market of a specific product within the Structure-Conduct-Performance framework, the first consequence should be an overprice in the market higher than the competitive price (or benchmark/shadow price), the other possibility should be an increase of this market price not susceptible to explanation by increase of cost. The Structure-Conduct-Performance paradigm named this price the limit price and defined it as a non-equilibrium price because it included extra profits due to rents generated by market control. The majority of theoretical analyses use Cournot models where two firms share market output and the price is the dependent variable of this share.

The way to exercise market power is to erect barriers to entry, otherwise any rival could be incumbent, attracted by high price and erode extra profits, technically this situation should be happens in the long run, when barriers to entry must be disappearing as every market failure. In the short run, antitrust regulator guards barriers to entry because there is the main way to exercise market power within any kind of market.

The methodological analysis of S-C-P included primarily an accurate knowledge of conditions of supply and demand, market structure, conduct of incumbents in the market and performance in efficiency and welfare.

Defining conditions of supply as:

- Raw materials and their property rights, legislation (domestic or otherwise) concerning the extraction of raw materials.
- Technology and its property rights, legislation and patents.
- Business position in the market, possibilities of survival, and so on.

Defining conditions of demand as:
- Price elasticity of demand measures the sensitivity of quantity demanded by changes in price. Higher price elasticity of demand implies a lot of substitutes.
- Rate of growth of demand, as the higher the growth the more likelihood of rivals entering the market.
- Substitute products, more substitutes allow less market power.
- Marketing type, or selling strategy.
- Purchase method, mainly if the purchase allows customization.

Defining market **structure** as:
- Number of sellers and buyers. As many as possible results in a more competitive market.
- Product differentiation. As many product branches or types of product result in less likelihood of exercise market power by the main companies within a market.
- Cost structure. More sunken costs should be considered as a mechanism of deterrence of rivals.
- Vertical integration. This variable has relevance to the kind of contracts that the companies signed with providers and delivers. The increase of vertical integration in an industry should be considered as a mechanism to keep market power.
- Barriers to entry. Higher barriers of every kind mean that rivals have difficulty entering a market.

Defining firms' **conduct** in their markets in relation with its market structure:
- Pricing behaviour. Rising prices alert the authorities.
- Product strategy. Defined as the way that the company makes and sells its outputs.
- Research and innovation defined as cost supports by the firms.
- Legal tactics. Understanding mainly as capture of state.

The main variables to analyse the firms' **performance** within its market structure are below and all of them rise as competitiveness market improves:
- Production and allocative efficiency
- Progress
- Full employment

- Equity

All of the variables established by Structure-Conduct-Performance in order to test workable competition within the markets are relevant but quite difficult to measure. Also the discrimination by relevance in the analysis became problematic. Some researchers pointed out the difficulty of making a perfect definition of them. But when we are out of the academic field and a scientific economic advantage is used in the real world, for example in a Judge for injuries suffered by a company because the abuse of the dominant position in a market by incumbents, the economy as science must to give tools to help courts. Economic science employs the price as first variable capable to measure the problems in a market. The limit price theory developed by Bain-Sylos Labini-Modigliani at the end of the 1950s allows us to demonstrate when a market is not working in a fair way; at the same time, this economic proposal respects the traditional economic theory. In other words, the limit price theory lacks methodological problems and is a worthwhile tool to lawyers.

In 1984 new Guidelines were published, which are included in Chapter 5, 'Barriers to Entry, the 1980s', keeping in mind that there were defined as consequence as the theoretical analysis of the 70s. 1984 Guidelines defined relevant market as a product of a type and a geographic area in which it is sold by a hypothetical, profit maximizing firm, not subject to price regulation. When companies playing in a market achieve a significant market power, this conduct justifies government intervention. *The Test of Small but Significant and Non-Transitory Increase in Price* is used to define the relevant market in a consistent way. In 1992 the Agency established that this test should be less than 5 per cent in order to keep in an acceptable limit of increase. Critics with Agency said this 5 per cent is not based directly on any explicit model of competition and welfare effects.

The test of small but significant and nontransitory increase in price explained both market characteristics: the likelihood of entry of a rival in this market and the existence of barriers to entry. Since 1975 economic science developed models which measure the likelihood of entry in a market, and since 1984 this theoretical analysis has begun to be considered in antitrust policy. It was necessary to wait until 1992 until the Agencies established how this issue ought to be analysed. Three topics deserve consideration: timelines, likelihood and sufficiency. The timeline was established as two years, because this is a reasonable time in which to enter a market. Likelihood was measured as the minimum viable scale of production in a market, and this must be minor that the average annual level of sales at the premerger entry (or likely sales opportunities available to entrants). Sufficiency is considered as the tangible or intangible assets required for entry. This third point refers to the sunken costs, and a lot of literature has been published about this topic and is the natural evolution of the use of capacity by the incumbents within an industry as barrier to entry and in narrow relationship with economies of scale in the production.

The second relevant point in the 1984 Guidelines was the use of Herfindahl-Hirschman Index of market concentration, calculated by summing the squares of the individual market shares of all the firms included in the market. Since 1992 this index established that 35 per cent is a significant market share in a market able to exercise market power. That means that the companies are interested in raising price and reducing joint output below the sum of their premerger outputs because the lost markups on the foregone sales may be outweighed by the resulting price increase on the merged base of sales.

The 2000 Guidelines included the concept of competitor collaboration: the Agency follows up every illegal agreement among competitors to fix prices or output, share markets and so forth. As the 1984 guidelines included *relevant evidence* the 2000 guidelines included *relevant agreement* both concepts integrated wide-ranging definitions which allow to courts and judges a discretionary use of this concept.

The Book's Structure

This book has six chapters with the intention of shedding light on the economic theory of competition and the political consequences of these improvements, identified as guidelines. Only at the end of the twentieth century is the inclusion of guidelines debate being considered, due to the fact that their theoretical support began a controversy in economic theory, since the point of view of economic thought is a closed circle.

The first part of each chapter in this book exposes the economic theory of competition and the controversy generated as every scientific development. In order to simplify the analysis we classify barriers to entry as belonging to three main types: excess of capacity, industrial concentration and advertising, keeping another epigraph to entry models. During this research, excess of capacity has evolved through the analysis of economies of scale and sunken costs; Industrial concentration since the 80s included the analysis of market power while advertising was a conclusive barrier to entry in the 80s, losing relevance because it evolved into adverse selection models, which are out of the field of the present research. Chapters 2, 5 and 6 included also the use of this economic theory in the drawing up of Guidelines to firms in the United States. The fifth and sixth chapters also debate Guidelines the themselves.

Chapter 1 of this book tries to put in order the competition theories from 1900 to 1956, the year of the publication of *Barriers to New Competition*, the book considered as the inflexion point in the research of non-competitive markets. Perhaps Bain's book could be considered only as the recognition of the old proposals made by Edward Chamberlin in his *The Theory of Monopolistic Competition* as economic tools. Either way this book has the honour of being the origin of the theory of the firm. We consider writing about the ways in which a firm could be included in the old price theory to be interesting. Following this object we take account of several contributions made during the 40s, some of them coming from American Universities and others from the main British Universities. Once every new contribution has been put in order, a group of economists will be considered as the precursors of the theory of firm. Meanwhile the majority of them were changing the old Marginalism and questioning its assumptions. At the same time, behaviourism is making its way as a new branch of economic theory, despite having been present since the beginning. We then follow the behaviourist school until the end of the century because we don't pay attention to their contributions any further. The intent is not to undervalue their role in economy as a science, rather that evaluating behaviourist contributions any further is beyond the scope of this book.

The next paragraph analyses the debate about antitrust control developed at the beginning of the century and centred in the main contributions made by John Bates Clark, Donald Wallace and Edward Mason; both changed the American view of competition and both are the pioneers of pursuing antitrust through guidelines and both attained enough political influence to change the rules. Without the political influence exhibited, principally by Clark, it is possible that the controversy of workable competition would still be dormant.

With regard to industrial organization theory during the first forty years of the twentieth century, the main controversy between lawyers and economists was that according to lawyers, the market share for a single firm should be considered as the firm's market power; for economists the market share is important in relation to the influences of price and market structure. At the end of the 1930s intellectual strength was relevant from Chicago University, Frank Knight, and later George Stigler. They are the champions of free markets and their main idea, that firms' competition is preferable to government regulation, had wide repercussions in both policy makers and academics. Litigants and courts spent more time and money in order to identify main variables and correlations to prove illegal behaviour on the part of a litigant, whereas the controversy between Stigler and Bain produces several papers and articles, and plenty of disagreements along with many intellectual acchievements.

The last pages of the chapter expose the origins of two barriers to entry: excess of capacity and advertising; both are old economic ideas still being developed now. We considered it useful to know the sources of every economic idea developed in this book, into the twentieth century.

Chapter 2 seeks to show how barriers to entry become an important issue in economics. We hope to show how between 1956 and 1970 this idea received more and more attention on the part of economists, sometimes this process takes the form of healthy and occasionally hectic debates, interspersed with periods of neglect. Overall however, the idea survived and flourished.

The first point at issue is whether limit price theory constituted an adequate framework within which to analyse the existence of a barrier to entry during the first twenty years of the debate. I shall begin with an analysis of Joe Bain's early book and articles written before 1970. In this first book, *Barriers to New Competition* (1956), Bain draws up a new classification of barriers to entry. Bain described and analysed different ways used by firms in order to prevent new competitors entering the market. The classifications included economies of scale, brand identity and capital requirements, as well as access to distribution, access to necessary inputs, switching costs, proprietary learning curves, proprietary product differences, government policy, expected retaliation, and so forth.

In order to develop his idea Bain followed three steps. The first step was to clarify the definition of barriers to entry. The second step was to demonstrate how barriers work; Bain's objective was to describe how firms behave within their own market. The third step in Bain's theoretical model was the study of market power. Following the order described above the second step involved developing a successful way of measuring conditions of entry; According to Bain they may be conveniently evaluated in the following terms for limit price theory. This evaluation involves determining the relevant gap between price and minimal cost at which entry may be deterred. The issue should be to establish whether this gap is a successful measure of the existence of a barrier to entry.

Chapter 2 has been written following Bain's work, Sylos Labini's proposals and the contribution of Modigliani. I shall set out the theoretical framework, where the idea of the existence of barriers to entry into an industry is first defined. This model is ultimately derived from a Marshallian partial equilibrium. The chapter then follows the success of the idea of barriers to entry through several key articles published during the period 1956–70, most of which attempt to prove the existence of these barriers using empirical evidence.

The most important political consequence of this theoretical framework of analysis were the 1968 Guidelines, which represented a version this way of thinking. Trying to help courts in antitrust trials the Department of Justice, particularly the antitrust division and the Federal Trade Commission, and with Donald Turner as heard, in 1968 a pack of rules, known as the Guidelines, was published. Since this time, judges, courts, attorneys and lawyers have been handling a cluster of norms with the unique goal of reaching a workable competition in the American markets. Guidelines are not a strict rules but a general mark of actuation, useful to be aware of non-workable competition in any market. Turner's theory agrees with limit price theory, in his words:

> 'The existence of the potential entrant will tend to cause existing sellers to charge a lower price than they otherwise would only if they believe that their current prices will influence the potential entrant's estimation of what the post-entry price and other market conditions are likely to be'.[17]

A higher price could become possible because of the elimination of rivals, but proof, in a judicial sense, is only possible with the analysis of cases. Three years before the implementation of the Guidelines Turner wrote: 'I believe that the courts should demand of Congress that it translate any further directive into something more formidable than sonorous phrases in the pages of the Congressional Record'.[18] In this book we demonstrate that not much has changed; during fifty years change have been restricted to perfection of these Guidelines.

Chapter 3 reviews the controversy between the Harvard School and the Chicago School. In the academic world, perhaps, the importance of the debate on barriers of entry is that it makes up another field of disagreement between those economists brought up in one tradition, and those associated with the other. For Chicago, long-term price equilibrium within markets will ultimately offset the effects of barriers to entry, whereas, according to the Harvard School, the analysis of these barriers remains relevant even in the short term. One of the most stimulating methodological debates within the field of Industrial Organization took place precisely between these two schools of thought, whose main protagonists were Joe Bain and George Stigler. Despite Joe Bain having created the old definition of barriers to entry, the most diffused definition was created by George Stigler in 1968, who defined 'Entry barriers as a cost of producing which must be borne by a firm which seeks to enter an industry but is not borne by firms already in the industry'.[19] Also it means a cost advantage that an incumbent firm enjoys compared to entrants. With such an advantage, the incumbent firm can permanently raise its prices above its costs and thereby earn an extra-competitive return.

Within this controversy, the main authors of the Chicago School always preferred models taken from microeconomics assuming that firms behave within a price system, but not their managements. Thus, according to them, the system works well, resources are allocated efficiently and, in the long run, barriers to entry disappear. Only with imperfect information is risk relevant in the theoretical model. In the Chicago School framework, economic barriers to entry should disappear in the long run, because within a general equilibrium model, they are analysed as market frictions. Institutional barriers to entry, mainly due to the behaviour of lobbies, could survive; in this case, neoclassical economic theory doesn't have the tools to explain how a barrier to entry works.

While the Harvard tradition notes that of barriers to entry make up the point of intersection between microeconomics and business studies, since some barriers might be considered as purely strategic behaviour, the line which separates profit seeking from rent seeking becomes extremely blurred. In business terms, the firm needs to know when there are barriers to entry, because in the majority of developed countries, the proof of the existence of a barrier to entry will lead to a legal judgment and the economic penalization of the firm guilty of such behaviour. Bain considered the need to understand the structure of the specific industry being studied in order to understand its behaviour and set out a theory of how firms perform, since each firm seeks to maintain the status-quo. Actually, Joe Bain has used the rule *per se*, widely disseminated by lawyers which explains how consequences of actions could be determined using logic.

Whereas the Chicago School, with Stigler as its top representative author, developed complex economic models for arguing the benefits of free markets, because of the perfect allocation of resources and fair prices caused by a perfect demand–supply equilibrium. The Harvard School had Joe Bain as its visible head, despite his having worked at Berkeley. Bain believed in imperfect markets, and developed the concept of *barrier to entry* in order to arguing how firms work into their own industries. Therefore barriers to entry as an economic idea was born in 1956. It has survived until today, having switched the bases paradigm from limit price theory to game theory, controversy, however, is far from over. The point was, and still is, to set out a body of empirical data which would demonstrate the existence of barriers to new entrants in an industry. If this can be shown, it would prompt changes in the legal framework or improve the information which allows to courts to dispense justice.

Chapter 4 could be understood as the academics' response to the 1968 Guidelines. As the third chapter shows, the debate about non-competitive market behaviour is open, even now, but during the 70s and 80s the fight was tough. In the cornerstone of this fight are barriers to entry. In order to follow a logical method of analysis, we recognize three groups of entry barriers: excess of capacity, industrial concentration and advertising, devoting a separate paragraph to entry models.

The use of installed capacity in an industry as a barrier to entry, mainly its excess, should be considered as the first entry barrier. Defined as overinvestment in capacity in order to increase the production of the industry in the short term, once the production raise had as consequence that price low, which at the same time, disincentive entry of rivals; the difference between the pre-entry price and the post-entry price after the output incumbents increases don't seem conducive to the entry of new companies to the industry. Several articles were written to demonstrate how this barrier works using empirical evidence. Michael Spence,

Michael Porter and Richard Caves could be considered as the main academics in this field.

Industrial concentration and market power as consequence is the second barrier to entry. To measure concentration of production or sellers in the main companies within an industry and its correlation with the increase of profits is not difficult using statistics. Regardless of whether the correlation is positive there seems that the market price is over the minimum of marginal cost (understood as the benchmark in a competitive market), so appropriation of the customer's exceedance. This market power over the price could include altogether the control of inputs prices and amounts, the manipulation of contracts, and so forth. In this case it seems convenient that authorities antitrust pursue this entry barrier. The weakness of this barrier to entry is connected with economies of scale and competitiveness in a global world.

Advertising deserves deep consideration in this period and each paper about advertising demonstrates that works as a barrier to entry because publicity and propaganda still have a great deal of influence on customers' decisions. In this case, rival firms must expend a lot of money in advertising in order to get clients, or improve their image. Antitrust does not worry about the supervision of advertising, nor does the limit of expenditure appear in Guidelines.

Entry models included a proposal of timing of rival entry as any random variable depending on current price in the industry. Within a limit price model the speed of entry gives a dimension of rivalry. During the 70s this model was only a seed, which grew up in the following decades, as framework useful to understanding market behaviour could be considered as a big improvement of theoretical analysis, the practical application of this model will happen in the 2000 Guidelines.

Chapter 5 is dedicated to the 1980. The chapter structure is quite different because three new methodological branches began to be considered in Industrial Organization theory: competitive strategy, contestable markets and game theory. I begin by introducing each branch, strategy as the expected evolution of Harvard School, using game theory as framework, as natural. Contestable markets could be considered the heir of the legacy of Chicago, 'contestable', in the context of markets, means extremely competitive. Game theory began to be used as theoretical framework in the 80s for the majority of academic works about barriers to entry, whatever the line of thought.

The next paragraphs of this chapter regarding the evolution of the debate of the three branches of barriers to entry defined in the 70s. I recognize entry models independently as usual; this time the inclusion of sequential proposal could be considered the main characteristic of the decade. At this time the use of excess capacity as a barrier to entry began to be questioned by researchers, and began to be considered a strategic decision. In this case, it should be a means of antitrust analysis because in market rules storing over capacity in a factory is expensive, and can drive a company to ruin, at the same time, paying for expensive storage in order to deter entry of competitors can erode profits to the limit of break-down. Industrial concentration as a barrier to entry follows the same path that excess of capacity, researchers began to connect concentration with economies of scale in the production, turning the investigation over a firm decision; market rules show that bad managers rule companies out of the market. This natural evolution drives the analysis from barriers to entry to strategic competitive, they are the two sides of the same coin; even creating a barrier to entry high enough to impede the entry of rivals into a market could be considered a excellent strategic improvement.

The theoretical developments in the analysis of barriers to entry in the 80s are not reflected in the guidelines, in 1984 would be earlier but in the 1992 the argument of excess of capacity could be used to control the price connected directly with the 5 per cent established as the limit of increase of the price in the industry before antitrust intervention. In the same way, industrial concentration continued to be considered as a barrier to entry because the limit of concentration share in a few firms in an industry is 35 per cent of the total.

Advertising remains a barrier to entry, the main development in this field during the 80s was considered as an investment or as a sunken cost. In each case, rivals must to make a detailed analysis if they like to become incumbents in an industry. So, advertising does not deserve consideration in antitrust policy.

Entry models during the 1980s included sequential considerations. This kind of model studied the level of entry deterrence in an industry promoted by incumbents; this is included in a separate paragraph because the others are dedicated to the analysis of a peculiar barrier to entry. When a theoretical model includes a vector of barriers to entry, market conditions, or another special characteristic, there is not an article about excess of capacity, industrial concentration or advertising; being a model of entry barrier is not included in any of these categories. Also, the analysis of entry does not need to be considered as the result of limit price or predatory pricing, I consider that they are other way to research market behaviour. Thus they must be included in the analysis of barriers to competition as they are included in the guidelines to antitrust.

Chapter 5 finishes with the exposition of the main changes included in the 1984 Guidelines, three of them deserve special consideration, firstly market definition, hence market power and the Hirschman-Herfindahl index as the measure of this market power, secondly the consideration of *small but significant and nontransitory* increase in price, and, lastly, likelihood of entry. Over these three pillars the American antitrust policy was built from the 1980s until the present day. Otherwise the guidelines debate began to become relevant at the end of the 80s and therefore deserves consideration in this chapter after the discussion of guidelines.

Chapter 6 respects the classification made for its predecessors, beginning with the evolution of the debate about the three main barriers to entry followed by entry models. One paragraph about 1992, 1997 and 2000 Guidelines and a new paragraph were included due to the debate about Guidelines and its consequences.

Excess of capacity, economies of scale and sunken cost should be considered as the natural evolution of the debate about this barrier to entry, and consequently the utilization of game theory is the expected theoretical framework. Industrial concentration maintains the suspicion that a few companies are controlling a market, keeping the intuition that this behaviour never has been profitable for customers. The main advance in this field occurs in analysis of every market, abandoning the idea of building a standard of behaviour in every industry. Now case analysis is predominant, at the same time that every different trial follows the silent rule of making particular reports respectful to special markets characteristics. We have to keep in mind that we are analysing antitrust, and the machinery began to work only when a company denounces another because of unfair competition; or when The United States, through the Federal Trade Commission, denounces the behaviour of a firm which the customer interests.

The end of the past century and the beginning of the twenty-first century could be considered as the blossom of entry models; they allow the application of game theory at will. They allow creativity, looking to for new ways to explain how the market works. Economic theory never rests, as there are always new games to be played on the field.

From 1990 to 2008 Guidelines have kept the old limit price paradigm as a guide to intervention in an industry. This would be considered as triumph of classical market structural models over the new game models. There are two questions in the air: firstly, how these theoretical proposals come to be included in the American competition system; secondly, if economic theory is able to offer a tool for judges and courts which demonstrates accurately that a firm or industry behaved badly and caused injury to other companies or to customers; in judicial jargon, conclusive evidence which justifieds the intervention in product strategy of the firm.

Chapter 6 concludes with the controversy around the Guidelines themselves, because to respect the rules and keep the antitrust behaviour of the companies within the guidelines could generate inefficiencies in the market and losses in the customers' surplus.

I include tables of this research because they facilitate at a glance the relevant literature about barriers to entry, predecessor papers and line of economic thought. At the same time the tables show the main barrier analysed in each paper and how it was confirmed in terms of period, industries and countries. Sometimes the articles concluded that this barrier could not be demonstrated. There is also information relevant to firms which are enrolled in a trial; they can find the way to demonstrate that their behaviour was acceptable according to jurisprudence, not because a lot of cases are included in this research but because this research allows the following of a logical path.

There are different ways to read this book, the main theme is barriers to entry but I keep in mind that some extra topics should be included. It is quite difficult to write a book about how firms erect entry barriers while forgetting elements that are important in every market. Collusion understanding as the agreement among incumbents to share market works by agreement in prices, every firm maintains the same price to customers, the goal is earning extra-profits because the accorded price is higher than the competition price. Agreements to control output, for example OPEC, every firm respect the quota in order to hold on the price of the output. Also, collusion should be considered in the way that a company manipulates the regulations into its market, while the others as followers enjoy an umbrella of privileges.

If you're an academic professor you can find the way to trace an economic idea, barriers to entry and collaterals, from its birth to present. The main authors who included new successful proposals within the traditional model are included in this book, therefore it is possible to follow the path in the text of the book and summarized in the tables, and sometimes the proposals are included in the Merger Guidelines, and begin to be used as characteristics of a market, the most important prize that an economic idea can obtain is to be used in real life because it explains how markets work.

If you're student this book is worthwhile because you will be able to very quickly see if competition and antitrust suits your preferences. It is not necessary to waste a lot of time checking books and papers. Perhaps you can find an article which opens a door to future research that would be discovered by young minds strong enough to support successive studies.

If you are working as a CEO in any kind of company, this book offers the opportunity to know when behaviour (or a course of action that you are considering) is punishable, or which is the way to demonstrate that a new product project is legitimate strategy and must be analyzed far of antitrust legal system. Also you can find out how the industry, you are involved in at present, was investigated and when; surely an interesting article concludes with an interesting and worthwhile piece of advice.

1 IMPERFECT COMPETITION IN ECONOMIC THEORY BEFORE 1956

The Sherman Law has been in force in United States since 1890, and President Wilson signed the Federal Trade Commission into law in 1914.[1] Both are the origin of controversy over the intervention of the government in the traditional *laissez faire* prevailing in America's industrial development. This chapter intends to achieve a big goal: to illustrate the debate between the academics who believe in the benevolence of the free market against academics who believe in the market power exercised by a big company. As they fight to survive nowadays, we are faced with one of the most important debates in the field of economic theory. Most of this book is about how academia has been able to develop worthwhile economic tools for the courts since 1956; the Guidelines should be considered as the legal framework within the courts' decisions can be taken based on economic theory. In this chapter we intend to discuss only the origins of the issue, marked from 1890, the date of the Sherman Law, until 1956 – the date when what could be considered the first economic book full of economic tools – *Barriers to Competition* emerged. Bain's book is a deliberate attempt to control trusts in the United States, through economic framework and empirically-supported arguments. Academics who believed in the exercise of market power by trust found in Bain's book the scientific support they needed. The bad behaviour of a firm within an industry, mainly against rivals within a market it considers its own, began to be taken into account in economic theory as a result of the book's publication. The main consequence was the publication of the 1968 Guidelines, which limited the capacity of trust's performance, followed by the 1984, 1992 and 2000 Guidelines. Economic science must wait until the 1980s when game theory became a tool to demonstrate the behaviour of companies.

We begin this chapter with a survey about the main topics in theory of the firm during the 1940s, both in England and in United States. The first objective should be to get approximation of the predominant economic thought at this time, we can then include the American economic thought in the theory of imperfect competition and its main economic tools to support these imperfections: the barriers to entry. The main reason for the present analysis could be detected is that the majority of the arguments find their origins in the 1930s and 40s; when the limit price framework was developed as well as the barriers to entry theory.

This section includes a revision of the behaviorism school and its promoters, Herbert Simon, Richard Cyert and James March. The inclusion of behaviour premises in the theory of the firm as well in Industrial Organization analysis could consider Joe Bain's as its main contributor and followed by the Structure-Conduct-Performance paradigm, in the field of economics theory.

The second section of this chapter refers to the lines developed by academics to demonstrate the non-workable competition in the main American markets. The starting point could be John Bates Clark's report of 1902, where he mentioned the convenience of some kind of market control. The second book of John Bates and John Maurice Clark published in 1912 is another example of the raised interest in reducing the market power of the big companies in order to maintain customer welfare. The controversy between Joe Bain and George Stigler about workable competition is included in this section, yet it is only the starting point of the Harvard School and the Chicago School debate. At that stage they exchanged ideas, which were published in the most relevant scientific magazines. It was an intellectual debate between them; no one else was included at this time, despite the lasting battle lines developed several years later. The main argument about how markets work, making Chicago and Harvard confront each other, still survives nowadays. It is dealt with in Chapter 4 of this book, this long fight centred around the convenience of state market intervention, which aren't exactly regulation issues but yet still is about pursuing non-workable competition or unfair business.

The third section tries to achieve the earlier theoretical support of the main barriers to entry as excess of capacity and advertising. We keep in mind the possibility of finding earlier references about barriers to entry at some point in the future.

1.1. - Perfect Competition and Imperfect Competition: Including the firm in Marginalism Analysis.

In Cournot's[2] model, and according to his theory of oligopoly, when the excess of price over marginal cost approached zero as the number of like producers became large.

Let the revenue of the firm be: $qi \cdot p$ and MC: marginal cost
The equation for maximum profits for one firm would be

$$p \cdot qi \cdot (dp/dq) = MC$$

The sum of such n equations would be

$$n \cdot p + q \cdot (dp/dq) = n \cdot MC$$

For $n \cdot qi = q$ the least equation may be written:
$$p = MC - p/n \cdot E$$
Where E is the elasticity of market demand.

Cournot paid no attention to conditions of entry and so his definition of competition also held for industries with numerous firms even though no more firms could enter. Then the three necessary conditions of perfect competition are:

1. Large numbers of participants on both sides of the market,
2. Complete absence of limitations upon self-seeking behaviour and
3. Complete divisibility of the commodities traded.

Under these assumptions competition should be restricted to meaning the absence of monopoly power in a market, and a perfect market is one in which the traders have full knowledge of all offer and bid prices. Perfect competition is defined by the condition that the rate of return of each resource be equal in all uses, Stigler established that: 'Industrial competition requires 1. - that there be market within each industry, 2.- the owners of resources be informed of the returns obtainable in each industry and 3.- there be free to enter or leave any industry'.[3]

In the *Cournot* model, firms simultaneously choose quantities, and the price is set at the market-clearing level by a fictitious auctioneer. In the *Bertrand*[4] model, firms simultaneously choose prices, and then must produce to meet demand after the price choices become known. In each model, firms choose their best responses to the anticipated play of their opponents. In the *Stackelberg*[5] model, one firm behaves as leader while the other is the follower; the leader moves first, and chooses an output which is observed by the follower before the follower makes its own choice. Technically, 'The Stackelberg equilibrium is not an alternative equilibrium for the Cournot game, but rather a shorthand way of describing equilibrium of an alternative extensive form'.[6] The Cournot and Bertrand models are all static games, in which firms make their choices once and for all. The economic theory indebted to Nash his theorem, in game theory Nash-theorem is: every finite n-player normal form game has mixed strategy equilibrium.

From the beginning of the twentieth century, it became increasingly obvious that a new model of imperfect competition was needed which would include the firm as an endogenous variable. The old model built by Cournot and developed by Leon Walras and Alfred Marshall was under siege from a variety of new proposals. Each new proposal included important modifications of the original model, until, finally, a new analytical framework emerged known as the imperfect competition model. Economists both British and American published new approaches to the traditional supply and demand equations: Edward Chamberlin from Harvard University, Arthur Pigou, Joan Robinson, John Hicks and Kenneth Boulding from different British Universities; Frank Knight, George Stigler and Ronald Coase from Chicago University; Fritz Machlup from Johns Hopkins University in Baltimore. Edith Penrose discussed the industrial theory developed by Marshall because she built a theoretical model to demonstrate that while a firm is growing the market structure on its industry changes simultaneously.

Making a tight summary of the vision of Marshall defended in his *Principles of Economics,* 1890, about the company we saw the thinking that led him to design a model in a certain way. Marshall develops the idea that a company follows the normal cycle of life is born, grows and when managers are unable to make it grow, dies. Therefore, in this industry will be new generations of managers who will continue the cycle. This reasoning leads him to believe that the history of an industry is more than just the history of the companies that compose it and that therefore it is interesting to study the total industrial output. The behaviour of each particular company will depend, consequently, on the industry group that it belongs to and its age within the industry. The resulting theoretical model is a model of a theory of industry, where equilibrium is characterized by a more or less constant number of aggregate outputs and a fixed number of firms. The advantage of such models is that it is possible to prove the theory with empirical data. The framework is restrictive but it allows to economic science began to explain the real world.

The behaviour of firms within the market in which they operate is a subject which has often been dealt with in economic theory. There is a sense in which imperfect competition can be seen as part of the different strategies undertaken by firms to exclude a competitor from a market. We assume that when a new producer takes the decision not to enter a given market, those firms already set up within the market see their profits decrease since they have to relinquish part of their market share to the newcomer. Then, when firms already operating within a market set up barriers to entry, for example, they agree to share out the market amongst themselves or obtain sets of regulations which prevent new competitors entering the market, what they are really doing is guaranteeing rents not profits. Rents are inefficient from the point of view of production theory, apart from for appropriating consumer surpluses: the consumer is obliged to pay more for a product, which he would have been able to buy more cheaply if the market works in perfect competition: because perfect competition means, among others requirements, free entry. Price theory deals with this problem.

In chronological order, then, we will begin with Frank Knight's major book, *Risk, Uncertainty and Profit*, published in 1921; here Knight expressed his support for Marshall's partial equilibrium analysis, based on equations taken from mechanics in Physics, and his model is essentially Marshallian. Despite his view of John Bates Clark as master, he doesn't hide his admiration to Marshall, mainly when Marshall became theoretically flexible, he said: 'But Marshall himself has adopted a cautious, almost anti-theoretical attitude toward fundamentals, he refuses to lay down and follow rigidly defined hypothesis, but he insists on sticking as closely as possible to concrete reality and discussing representative conditions as opposed to limiting tendencies'.[7] The method of economics is simple, Knight pointed out that we have quite a few possibilities to discuss, and describing effects or results under given conditions, he wrote: 'Every movement in the world is and can be clearly seen to be a progress toward an equilibrium'.[8] From inside of predominant economic theory in the twenties, he expresses his nonconformity with Marshallian price theory with the next words:

> But in actual society, cost and value only "tend" to equality; it is only by an occasional accident that they are precisely equal in fact; they are usually separated by a margin of "profit" positive or negative. Hence the problem of profit is one way to looking at the problem of the contrast between perfect competition and actual competition.[9]

The first steps to transforming the theory of Marshall in a modern theory of the firm were given by two economists at the School of Cambridge, funded by Alfred Marshall himself. In 1920, Arthur Pigou,[10] in his book entitled *Economics of Welfare*, he analysed the effect of industrial profits rising, falling and remaining steady. While Piero Sraffa[11] in 1926, in his article entitled 'The Laws of Returns under Competitive Conditions', noted that most firms operate under such conditions that demand does not allow them to exhaust their capacity, in other words, have to face fixed costs and unused capacity. This item comes into serious conflict with the static model of industry that Marshall had designed, as any company that faces a market price and yield subject to increasing profits are at their incentives to increase production without limit.

The third step was proposed by Chamberlin from Harvard University. It assumed that firms in an industry characterized by the same cost curves, where each business also faces the same demand, when the number of firms is sufficiently small, Chamberlin said: 'Especially since the demand curve is known only in a vague and uncertain way'.[12] Technically each company in the industry will face a decreasing demand curve, therefore, to a monopoly in the direction of Marshall. Since a decreasing demand curve means that consumers are indifferent to the supplies of others companies in the same industry. Using a framework without any type of agreement (not tacit included) the interdependence among competitors must be neglected, as the influence to each other should be; it make sense to consider an infinite number of sellers with movements instantaneous in this case: 'The prices of all move together, and from this it follows at once that the equilibrium price will be the monopoly one'.[13] By way of a footnote, Chamberlin included the special case of the existence of a price leader in the industry; he pointed out that: 'The price leader, knowing that the others will follow him, has as much control as the group acting in unison'.[14] This proposal is the origin of the Stigler's umbrella into his oligopoly theory, at the same time that Stigler critiqued the core of Chamberlin's apparatus, he said: 'It will be observed that the theory of monopolistic competition now contains no conditions of equilibrium, only a definition of equilibrium'.[15]

Chamberlin's model is analysed several years after it was published, Drew Fudenberg and Jean Tirole said that games provide a framework able to formalize some of Chamberlin's intuitions; the myopic behaviour of firms resultant of the Cournot or Bertrand models could be solved because the theory of repeated games allows 'cooperation' to reach an equilibrium. Fudenberg and Tirole wrote: 'But it does not eliminate the 'uncooperative' static equilibria, and indeed can create new equilibria which are worse for all players than if the game had been played only once'.[16]

Around the same time, in Cambridge, Joan Robinson published *The Economy of Imperfect Competition* (1933), where she set out a series of criticisms of the Marshallian partial equilibrium model. She tried to close the equations to the real world, in order to reach her goal she said that whether the supply and demand conditions remain constant during a sufficiently long time, it is possible to find the most rentable production value of the industry. That means, on a Marginalist model with costs and incomes, it should be possible to find an equilibrium which allows for analysing the increase of sales with increased or decreased profits. Thus Robinson criticized the old equilibrium model of the microeconomic while using mechanical equations imported from Physics. In other words, Robinson defends it: 'Would be more appropriate to dwell on the analysis of monopoly and perfect competition treat as a special case'.[17]

Political reflection that leads to the model of Robinson was that the traditional models, the benefits tend to flow towards the capital at the expense of labour. Thus opened the doors of models with imperfections (we must not forget that this imbalance is that Schumpeter used over thirty years to defend his 'chronic imbalance'). We only see the remainder of costs for companies. Joan Robinson and Edward Chamberlin managed to show that large firms face fixed costs arising from their investment in specialized equipment to differentiate their products from those of other companies and working with excess of capacity. The model Robinson-Chamberlin questioned that markets tend towards perfect competition. The sales are limited by price, product differentiation, fixed costs and advertising outlays. Paradoxically, Robinson's model has no entry barriers to new suppliers within a market; just the product differentiation is the cause of the removal of rivals in the market

In successive editions of *The Theory of Monopolistic Competition*, Chamberlin included his personal opinion about the Robinson model, he wrote:

We may begin with the view that 'restriction of entry' is incompatible with perfect competition, and hence necessarily indicates monopoly or 'imperfection'. Ms Robinson has dealt with this matter at length, and I can only record my agreement with her conclusion that restriction of entry into an industry is quite compatible with perfect (and with pure) competition, provided only that conditions within the industry are such as to make the demand curve for the output of an individual firm perfectly elastic.[18]

From Oxford University, in 1934, Roy Harrod wrote a survey about the doctrines of imperfect competition, he criticized the inductive method used at this moment, mainly because the goal was to build a theoretical framework into which market imperfections could easily be fitted. One of his arguments was that: 'Some competitors have any special advantages in production, and this supposition is not necessarily inconsistent with perfect competition'.[19] He refuted the hypothesis of imperfect competition theory about a new competitor capturing a market; his point of view was that newcomers can be excluded, even within an industry which is operating with profits, while the entrant is reaching the optimum scale of production. He said: 'In conditions of imperfect competition, long period equilibrium is consistent with lay-outs of less than the optimum size and their exploitation below their optimum capacity',[20] in this case the price will be above the competitive level. Paolo Sylos Labini took this argument to point out that when entrepreneurs noticeably raise prices they are making their markets vulnerable, because the curve of demand in the long run is less sloping than in short run.

At the same time, in 1934, from Cambridge University, Abba Lerner was developing a new way to measure market power; his proposal should be considered new and fascinating; mainly we have to keep in mind the time in which it was created. Lerner proposed: 'One could construct some kind of index of the degree of monopoly, such as the inverse of the number of sellers, which would give values ranging from unity in the case of this kind of 'complete' monopoly to zero in the case of an infinite number of sellers'.[21] The second step could be to know the divergence between the industrial price and the marginal *social*[22] cost. The problem occurred because using this theoretical approach we are not able to distinguish monopolistic gains which come from rents of scarce property that the monopoly owns, from another source of individual income. The relevance of this article is the conclusion; in order to respect the original idea of Lerner I include the whole paragraph:

> What is relevant for general analysis is not the sum of individual degrees of monopoly but their *deviations*. The standard deviations as suggested above may perhaps be used one day to give an estimate of the divergence of society from the social optimum of production relative to a given distribution of income.[23]

In 1935, Frank Knight, from Chicago University, published *The Ethics of Competition and Other Essays*,[24] where he appears to have changed his mind about the validity of the Walras/Marshall paradigm. In the chapter entitled 'production cost and price in the short and long run', he said that it is necessary to specify the basic principles of the economic theory and relate them directly to social politic.

Addressing Robinson-Chamberlin to analyse the costs decreasing, Knight asks if the reduction of costs in an industry is possible thanks to the excess capacity of key elements of industrial equipment (using the rail industry as an empirical demonstration). But theoretically, if one works with industry excess capacity is supposed to enjoy a journey along the curve of average costs to establish the final selling price of the product, in other words, the equilibrium price does not match the minimum average cost curve at the exact point where it joins with the curve of long-term marginal costs in the industry. Technically it is breaking the conditions of equilibrium in a market, but equations can be proposed tha t lead to an equilibrium. At the time the excess capacity could be used by companies already operating in an industry to reduce the final price of the product by increasing the amount of product shipped to the market response is a price reduction; being the sense using to support capacity installed as a barrier to entry.

Also from Chicago University, in 1937, Ronald Coase[25] had published 'The Nature of the Firm', in which the size of the firm could be explained through a function of transaction cost. His main contributions were: 'The most obvious cost of "organising" production through the price mechanism is that of discovering what the relevant prices are',[26] he noted that running with traditional price mechanisms means costs, because the relevant question is: 'Why the allocation of resources is not done directly by the price mechanism'.[27] Nowadays, this article is a must-reference in the field of the theory of the firm, not only because its contribution to the economic knowledge as the theory of transaction cost, but also because Coase proposed the change of the costs functions, and consequently, a change in the analysis of price, which means that he was critical of the old nineteenth-century equations. This article was acknowledged by the scientific community several years after it was published and widely cited.

In 1939 John Hicks published *Value and Capital: an Inquiry into some Fundamental Principles of Economic Theory*. This book supports the idea that perfect competition conditions are the basis on which to built economic laws. He wrote:

> We first examine what conditions are necessary in order that given equilibrium system should be stable: then we make an assumption of regularity, that positions in the neighbourhood of the equilibrium position will be stable also, and thence we deduce rules about the way in which the price-system will react to changes in tastes and resources.[28]

The main inconvenience of this way of obtaining equilibrium can be found in the fact that prices must remain constant over time, however 'For practical purposes, the ideal condition of equilibrium over time can be interpreted quite loosely'.[29] At the same time, Hicks worked with the behaviour rules of the firm within its own market, these rules were drawn by Joan Robinson.

The survival problem, for Hicks, was the firm's dimension, because while the firm is growing, there is an increase of difficulty in direction and control. This problem would be solved by Coase, two years before; Coase based his argument on transaction costs, which means, among other things, on the companies' difficulties in growing because of the increase of transaction costs due to direction and control. Hicks attempted to make the Marshallian model more dynamic through the substitution of static prices by discounting prices, by demanding to have increase the risk included in the model, or perhaps, to include intuition, however, both are moves further away from the mechanical laws.

In 1942 Kenneth Boulding[30] published 'The Theory of the Firm in the Last Ten Years'; for the moment the theory of the firm belonged to Joan Robinson and Richard Chamberlin, because he believed that both books marked the explicit recognition of the theory of the firm as an integral division of economic analysis. The former working in Cambridge, England; and the latter working in Cambridge, Massachusetts, while Boulding pointed out that the theory of the firm should be considered as a division of economic analysis, and in that case the General equilibrium theory needs to give a place to the company. Boulding argued about Marshallian theory that: 'The weakness of this theory was that it completely neglected the time element in enterprise, and consequently worked with a concept of the firm so far from reality that it cannot be considered more than a rough first approximation'.[31] In this way the entrepreneur maximizes rates of investment returns instead of maximizing profits.

Our final author is Fritz Machlup,[32] who worked at Johns Hopkins University. Machlup published in 1946 a key article in The American Economic Review entitled 'Marginal Analysis and Empirical Research' The core of his analysis was a study of entrepreneurial behaviour in the real world, where he emphasizes the difference between these patterns of behaviour and the assumptions maintained in orthodox economic theory. His basic idea comes across the following quotation:

> Business men do not always calculate before they make decisions, and they do not always decide before they act. For they think that they know their business well enough without having to make repeated calculations, and their actions are frequently routine. ... Yet his reasoning or his routine behavior is most conveniently analyzed in terms of marginal revenue'.[33]

At this time, Machlup coined the widely-disseminated expression *cutting the throat of the competitor*[34] turned by Stigler in 1968 to *the theory of oligopoly is solved by murder*.[35]

Some years later, in 1967, Machlup rethought the assessing of routine with tools of marginalism because noncompetitive cases were developed naively. The topic is mainly theoretical, using his words:

> To show that the theoretical variables need not be estimated and the theoretical equations need not be solved through actual calculation by the actors in the real world whose idealized types are supposed to perform these difficult operations in the models constructed for the explanation of recorded observations.[36]

In 1946 Machlup was deputy director of a Researching Group which used empirical models to study how firms grew. The group included Edith Penrose who was later to solve Hicks's problem of how exactly firms grow; the result was a book entitled *The Theory of the Growth of the Firm,* (1959).

According to Penrose,[37] the conventional theory does not use any variable to explain any equation endogenous growth companies. Therefore, growth is the only way to adjust the size of the balance of the company in its industry. She therefore proposed a growth model in which the company is an administrative organization, which can always bring new resources to expand to any size and then set the limit to this growth with a 'variable time' for training. Penrose measured the training process only if the senior can effectively perform the functions of planning and directing the various activities required for sustainable growth, one of which was the *work of recruiting*. Adjust of the size of a company into its industry is one argument using by 'Chicago School' in order to discuss 'industrial concentration and economies of scale' as barrier to entry.

1.1.1.- The Behaviourism School, the Origins of Joe Bain's thought and the Separation between Economic Theory and the Theory of the Firm.

According to George Stigler, the main contribution of Joe Bain to economic theory was the inclusion of behaviour in the analysis of markets. We think it would be convenient to include some references to the behaviourism school, because this school came to be quite relevant as a school of economic thought.

The use of behaviour as an economic idea was put in black and white by Edward Chamberlin in 1927; he wrote that firms play chess when they decide prices and outputs. Edward Mason, working with Joe Bain during the 1930s, included *behaviour* in the analysis of companies, at this moment it was only *conduct* that was the second name of the paradigm developed by them. The theoretical formalization must wait until 1944 when John von Neumann and Oskar Morgenstern developed the way to use mathematical games in economic theory. In 1947, Joe Bain included behaviour in *Literature and Price Policy and*

Related Topics, 1933–1947,[38] this book is only a student's handbook. Not until the 1980s were games widely applied by the economists.

It was interesting to point out that at the end of the century behaviourism doesn't reach its goal, the lack of theoretical framework and its limited influence in policy because of difficulties in predicting circumstances in anomalous behaviour have been driving this peculiar school of economic thought out of the premier league of influence.

Early in the twentieth century, behaviour was considered interesting in economic theory. In 1939 Hall and Hitch wrote a pioneer article about firms' actions against potential competitors. Under the lens of price theory and using the concept of aggressive price policies, developed by Cassels two year before; the cornerstone of research should be to assume that the price is *unstable* and dependent of reaction of competitors, including both installed and potential, in conclusion they said: 'There is a strong tendency among business men to fix price directly at a level which they regard as their "full cost"'.[39]

The rules of thumb should be considered a worthwhile proxy to a model of rationality behaviour, and this route was followed by several scholars from different origins, Fritz Machlup, William Baumol, Joan Woodward, Richard Caves and Garrel Pottinger are some examples. In the 1960s, Herbert Simon, Joe Bain, Richard Cyert and James March created and developed the Behaviourism School and at the end of this decade; Oliver Williamson developed a model of business behaviour that focuses on the self-interested behaviour of corporate managers. Behaviour, however, is precisely Williamson's comfort zone and he works with mathematical tools. Obviously for the 'Chicago School' the analysis of behaviour will be less important; perhaps it may touch on the oligopolistic theory, however in the eighties, game theory became visible as a theoretical instrument which put strategic behaviour together with neoclassic theoretical tools. The firm is an old issue between theoretical scholars, and sometimes someone takes up this hot potato. The main concern used to be how to put the firm in the theoretical economic model, whether this question is of interest and furthermore whether it is feasible to make a fruitful hypothesis of the firm's behaviour.

We could continue using models with limited production and endogenously established, but where firms should have no internal working, like a Marshallian model. This, however, isn't the case. From the 1940s until now, scholars have been trying to find the mechanisms of behaviour of firms in relation to others in the market, and managerial behaviour inside the firm. Following are some examples such as Machlup, who wrote at the beginning of this controversy, Baumol from The Chicago School and Woodward from The Harvard School. A criticism of Marshall's model was made by Fritz Machlup in 1967; he said that the model of the firm in the traditional price theory is not accurately designed to explain the real behaviour of companies, only to explain changes in prices; then connection with real firms is just theoretical, he was eloquent on this topic: 'Any likeness between the theoretical construct of the firm and the empirical firm is purely coincidental'.[40]

The behaviourism school became relevant in the sixties when some scholars developed a new idea about the behaviour of the firms within their own industries. Herbert Simon, Joe Bain, Richard Cyert and James March were the first behaviourists. Over the foundations laid by Simon and Bain, in the early 1960s. James March with Richard Cyert began to analyse the behaviour of the firm, in their own words:

> It is fruitful to develop an understanding of the process of decisions making within the firm. 1. - How does the allocation of resources within the firm's budget relate to organizational goals. 2. - How do objectives change over time. 3. - What happens to information, and so on.[41]

This proposal should provide a good approach to behaviour of the firms selling in non-competitive markets. In a framework where firms working on perfect markets and having unique behaviour pursue equilibrium, marginalism offers the better theoretical model. The main contribution of this model was that these firms have some freedom to develop decisions, strategies or rules that become part of the decision-making system within the firm.

For Industrial Organization, firm behaviour may be at least as much the result of conscious choice as it is a forgone conclusion from industry structure. In 1963 the Behaviourism School was closed to the Harvard School and the Carnegie Mellon Group, under Richard Cyert's leadership. This school began to draft a theory of behaviour; the proposal was to try to develop a methodological alternative with more theories of organizational goals and because time is always a main question, Behaviourist theory works in the short-term. Cyert and March wrote, in their book entitled *A Behavioural Theory of the Firm,*

> For the organizational goals, for a certain class of decisions over a relatively long period of time, we can specify the major classes of coalition members. As a result, we will be able to develop models of organizational decision making (for the short run) that pay only limited attention to the process by which the coalition is changed, but any such simplification involves some clear risks when we generalize to long run dynamics.[42]

Due to the fight against marginalism having a huge theoretical importance, it would be better to reproduce their words. The basis of Cyert discussion was:

> In neoclassical theories of the firm, organizations identify, choose, and implement optimal alternatives. In behavioural theories, organizations simplify the decision problem in a number of ways. They set targets and look for alternatives that satisfy

those targets, rather than try to find the best imaginable solution. They allocate attention by monitoring performance with respect to target.[43]

In Neoclassical theory the importance of plan predictions is obscured by the
assumption that the predictions are always correct. Cyert ended the book with
the conclusion that modern theories of the firm assume that rational action in
a firm is subject to limited rationality and also to conflicts of interest between
lobbies, but under maximization targets, the proposal of behavioural theories of
organizations have been built on somewhat less rationalized versions of the same
ideas. The topic of the long-term should be reflected through a special mechanism of adaptation to changes of goals within the industrial structure.

In the origins of this theoretical issue, William Baumol in 'Reasonable Rules
for Rate Regulation: Plausible Policies for an Imperfect World' (1964) said the
following about the behaviour of firms:

> As a result managers have developed behavioural rules for making decisions. Behav-
> ioural rules (rules of thumb) are modes of behaviour that the firm (or individual)
> develops as a guide for making decisions in a complex environment with uncertainty
> and incomplete information.[44]

But, the point is how the firms behave within their industry, the possibilities are
to compete or to collude, or change strategy depending on the environment.

The first trial to develop a theory of behaviour was made at Harvard University by Joan Woodward in 1965. Her book entitled *Industrial Organization,
Theory and Practice*, reprinted in 1980, set forth her theoretical approach over
the next point:

> An understanding of the limits to the rationalities individuals and groups becomes
> even more important if it is acknowledged that organizations are collections of
> groups of people with different interests, stratified along a number of important, but
> not necessarily congruent dimensions such as function, level, and occupational refer-
> ence group.[45]

This proposal was to understand how the mechanisms by the organizational process and outcomes work, because of how these groups of people are held together
and pursue their own interests. Woodward kept in mind that different interest
groups have access and a range of power resources, such as information, skill,
expertise and ability to offer rewards and sanctions. She draws up the anatomy
of organization of the firm but, like Fayol or Ford, it is only for management. She
used dates 'day to day' to understand the planning, production, marketing, etc.
The most significant point to keep in mind was that her theoretical proposition
was different because changes in organization and behaviour happened as she
had predicted they would occur.

In the same vein, during the 1960s and the 1970s, Oliver Williamson developed a model of business behaviour which focuses on the self-interested behaviour of corporate managers. In 'A Dynamic Theory of Interfirm Behaviour' (1965), working with Almarin Phillips, he argued that a unified framework that combines organizational with economic variables is needed, and they proposed a general set of relationships designed to achieve this end. The model was, as a performance variable, an index of the level of achievement of the firms in the industry and as endogenous variables they propose that one of them should be a variable adhering to a group goals variable and an interfirm communication variable; under the condition that the values that these variables take on are not independent but are mutually determined as part of a simultaneous system. The econometrical issue of this model was a model built as described above:

> Ordinarily this will be a profits measure, and obviously it will depend, among other things, on the condition of competition that prevails in the industry. Such a variable is essential to transmit the influence of changes in the condition of environment that occupied an essential role in the description of interfirm behaviour.[46]

In the line of the rules of thumb as the right way to explain the firm, in 1979, Richard Cyert and Garrel Pottinger wrote 'Toward a Better Micro Economic Theory'. They affirm that:

> The firm develops these rules of thumb as guides for making decisions in a complex environment with uncertainty and incomplete information. The aim of the behavioural approach to the theory of the firm is to make business judgment susceptible of rational, theoretical treatment by analyzing what is essential to the process of judgment in terms of sets of behavioural rules.[47]

Richard Caves, from Harvard University, in his article entitled 'Industrial organization, corporate strategy and structure' (1980) said that: 'Decisions rules are learned and the ways in which such rules are modified in the face of feedback from the environment. This approach takes the view that the firm is an adaptive mechanism that can learn from its environment'.[48]

Williamson's 1983 model was mathematically much more exact. In his article entitled 'Antitrust enforcement: Where it has been; Where it is going' he said that it seems useful to point them out:

> The study of strategic behaviour has been clarified in the following significant respects:
> (a) Severe structural preconditions in both concentration and entry barrier respects need to be satisfied before an incentive to behave strategically can be claimed to exist;
> (b) Attention to investment and asset characteristics is needed in assessing the condition of entry – specifically, nontrivial irreversible investments, of a transaction- specific kinds have especially strong deterrent effects;

(c) History matters in assessing rivalry – both with respect to the leadership advantage enjoyed by a sitting monopolist as well as in the incidence and evaluation of comparative costs; and

(d) Reputation effects are important in assessing the rationality of predatory behaviour.[49]

Only one difficulty survives in Williamson's model in 1983, which still hasn't found the theoretical solution for a model of oligopolistic behaviour. The main point was the old controversial issue between the Harvard and Chicago Schools, namely barriers to entry, because some barriers survive through time and these are not necessarily economic ones. In this case it is difficult to satisfy the conditions of equilibrium. Williamson said that: 'Recent models in the entry barrier tradition have avoided this problem by explicitly casting the analysis in a sitting monopolist-duopoly framework.'[50] This issue only can be solved for the dominant firm in an industry but not for the followers, because it is necessary to include a lot of preconditions to find an oligopolistic equilibrium.

Some years later, most theoretical scholars agree that game theory and conflict strategy should be a worthwhile theoretical framework in order to explain the old topic of behaviour of the firm. Indeed, at the beginning of the twenty-first century the science of economics has game theory as a proxy for the behaviour of the firm. The framework of game theory is critiqued with a different argument, however, it is the paradigm in force. In 2003 William Baumol wrote defending game theory stating that economic growth of the capitalist economies must be explained by the behaviour of firms, and in the process of innovation which happen into the set of routine business decisions it should be possible to bring innovation closer to the core of micro-theory. In his own words:

> Game theory certainly contributed a powerful and revolutionary set of mathematical instruments, offering economists a route for escape from exclusive dependence upon the physicists' formal tools. The new approach is a flexible way to deal with a variety of special issues and situations in oligopoly markets. Add to that the demonstrated relationship of the theory to mathematical programming, duality theory, and other analytic developments of the twentieth century, and it is clear that the field of oligopoly analysis has undergone a major and useful upheaval.[51]

Criticism of game theories and dynamics come mainly from Pankat Ghemawat and Dennis Carlton. In 2002 Pankat Ghemawat wrote 'Competition and Business Strategy in Historical Perspective' pointing out that Industrial Organization started to turn to game theory in the late 1970s as a way of studying competitor dynamics. However, this theoretical model requires high assumptions:

> The formalism of game theory is accompanied by several significant limitations, the sensitivity of the predictions of game theory models to details, the limited number of

variables considered in any one model, and assumptions of rationality that are often heroic, to name just a few.[52]

Dennis Carlton who in 2004 published 'Why barriers to entry are barriers to understanding', wrote: 'The source of any successful strategic behaviour must ultimately be traceable to an asymmetry among firms',[53] and this is the field of game theory and contestability literature. The main question become how will uncertainty affect the option value of entering?

1.2. Sherman Law, Federal Trade Commission and the Debate about Trust Control

Since 1890 the Sherman Law has governed workable competition in the United States. From its implementation, the Sherman Law has had several critics; the argument was the inevitable target of reducing monopolies or agreements among companies, could cause firms with high fixed costs to be ruined or go bankrupt. The majority of them are rooted in the freedom of business and the American dream. Defences of the Sherman Law centred on customer welfare and plays on fear of big corporations, which at this moment are growing to hitherto unknown levels. John Bates Clark with John Maurice Clark, Donald Wallace, Edward Mason and Donald Turner are the main defenders of the Sherman Law.

This is the argument and the empirical test used by John Bates Clark[54] and John Maurice Clark[55] in their book *Control of Trust* (1912). The point was if the civil law had economic law on its side. Both were alarmed at the increasing power gained by trusts, the reduction of prices of raw materials, rising influence in workers' wages, and the ever-growing selling price of their products. Clark and Clark wanted there to be some means of control over trust behaviour, they said:

> If a combination of producers raises its price beyond a *certain limit*, it encounters the old check, which comes, not by any act of the government, but from the new mills which spring into existence and bring the prices down.[56]

Monopolies are unfavourable to the welfare of labourers, as well as to that of consumers, despite the firms' claims to the contrary. Competition is the only way that independent producers can find a way to enter within an industry and reduce prices.

Their proposal was: 'It will afford the best method of putting a limit on the raising of prices'.[57] We can argue for years about this proposal, while the prices are rising in an industry, new incumbents become interested in entering the market, in order to get a piece of the pie. At the same time, customers welfare is diminishing; but the price may show an increasing demand for this product or, conversely, the price indicates an exercise of power by a big company. Clark and realized this task, writing, 'If we can get the right diagnosis of the disease, we shall not go fatally wrong in the treatment, and there are only two diagnoses form which to choose'.[58] Abolishing the big corporations was not an option, so with regard to what should be done, they said:

> We cannot afford to be blindly guided by the theory of law, which holds that a corporation is an 'artificial legal person' if this leads us to forget or to ignore the plain fact of business, that a corporation is a real association of real persons, the stockholders.[59]

This is the beginning of the division between Lawyers' and economists' points of view on business, on how to change the company from an invisible object to a specific individual who invests his savings in business.

At the end of the book they leave to the government a role in preventing agreements on prices, restrictions on trade and another nonworkable competition, leaving free competition understood as *live and let live*. In conclusion they wrote: 'The law are already being developed that will help to strengthen competition against its new dangers, and we may welcome the opportunity to have some part in that development'.[60] Not in vain, both Clark must be considered as the brains that developed the next economic thought about imperfect competition and the government action.

The same year that Clark and Clark published their book, the Federal Trade Commission[61] started its role in consumer defence. The welfare of customers – as opposed to market power – came to be considered the measure of companies in the markets, because fair price of products due to competition indicates an increase in customer welfare and reduction of market price control by companies. In 1920 Pigou researched social welfare and private welfare, following the same line of thought as Clark and Clark, and being aware of their work, Pigou pointed out that: 'The effects upon economic welfare produced by any economic cause are likely to be modified by the non economic conditions, which, in one form or another, are always present, but which economic science is not adapted to investigate'.[62] He supported the theory in the fact of the existence of agreements among companies, or using his words, restricted entry, and therefore the allocation of resources changes, in footnote he wrote: 'If entry to the industry is not restricted, more resources will flow into it than would so flow under simple competition'.[63] How many losses could be measured by the misallocation of resources? The answer is:

> The dividend, therefore, will be reduced below what it would have been under as system of restricted entry, by the difference between the productivity of that quantity of resources which it pays to set to work in the monopolized industry and the productivity of that quantity for which the receipts of the industry would suffice to provide normal earnings.[64]

Clark and Pigou's arguments about the allocation of resources and the power of big companies, use the argument that it is social welfare that has become the way to defend social earnings against private ones.

The American Supreme Court is the institution that supports the competition system, helped by several departments and agencies. Traditionally competition was considered as a legal question; how to establish a fair price, and torts and other legal issues were discussed by lawyers in courts. In 1925 an economist, Harlan Fiske Stone, was needed for the Supreme Court, in order to work on an antitrust decision, while in 1926 Myron Watkins wrote a critical survey about the Federal Trade Commission. His article included different kinds of arguments, from the jurisprudential role to the capacity of American public to distinguish between Swiss watches in general and Genevan watches in particular. The economic point of view becomes relevant to juries between companies; while the criticism from the judiciary system appears because the economics enters the field of business competition at an early stage.

Earlier, we discussed the evolution of the economic thought in order to explain how the economy as science has developed tools to accurately write reports or surveys to FTC, juries or the Supreme Court. We keep in mind that it is the beginning of a very long path, unfortunately not always agreeing with law professionals.

In 1936, from Harvard University, Donald Wallace wrote a pioneer article about monopolistic competition and public policy, and following the path of Clark and Pigou, he tried to connect monopoly and economic welfare. His argument began with the following words: 'Where substantial monopolistic elements are operative, competition does not automatically produce the ideal quantitative market relations contemplated by the theory upon which public policy has been based. That theory implied a very limited amount of government control economic activity'.[65] He pointed out that when the incumbents of an industry are few, under maximizing profit conditions, each seller estimates supply and demand slope curve in the same way, then the quantitative relationship among sellers tends to be quite different to predictions on competitive theory, he argued that: 'If entry to the field is effectively barred, underinvestment and monopoly profits may result without any agreement'.[66] Under this assumption, when the companies which look for profits and growth, achieve power over the market, should be expected a change in the timing of decisions, from the short-term to the long-term and the rigidity of monopoly prices increases the severity of economic cycle. He proposed an in-depth study of barriers to free entry. The theoretical arguments defended along the paper had a unique goal to get a public policy programme that fitted with reality and which paid attention to the fact that:

Public policy seems to have overlooked such important barriers to free entry as control of scarce resources of raw materials, lack of pure competition among investment bankers, and the impressive formidability of size and length of purse supplemented by industrial and financial affiliations.[67]

Edward Mason could be considered the pioneer in the use of behaviour theory in social sciences such as economics, he is also one of the founders of the Harvard School with Joe Bain. In 1937 Mason wrote 'Monopoly in Law and Economics' in the wake of Clark, over the different ways of viewing companies. He said: 'Lawyers and economists are therefore rapidly ceasing to talk the same language'.[68] Mason's argument is quite difficult to contradict, he wrote:

The economists' emphasis on free entry into the industry as characteristic of competition and restriction of entry as the *differentia specifica* of monopoly was in complete harmony with the judicial predilection. Restraints of trade can exist without anything that the courts would be willing to call control of the market. And, control of the market, in the economic sense, can exist independently of any practice which the law would call a restraint of trade.[69]

That seems to be one good reason to give an opportunity to economists in the judicial arena. Traditionally, American courts have found monopolistic practices in conspiracies to expel competitor rather than control of the market. At this moment economic theory related to the behaviour of prices and outputs, the relationship between prices and costs, the market share among incumbents, price discrimination, and so on; all of these are proof of market control and economically successful tools never used by lawyers before. In short, price and output control and restriction of trade should be the pillar over which to construct a doctrine of reasonableness in the interest of the contracting parties. Mason established four points which included in next cite:

1) The courts, the injury to numerous private interests, and consequently to the public interest, from predatory attacks on established business enterprises.
2) Monopoly, contrary to the public interest required the selection of test capable of distinguishing competitive from monopoly situations.
3) Control of the market, dependent upon restriction of entry and other types of restriction of competition through predatory practices and harassing tactics than at present.
4) Private interest, more likely to be directly affected adversely by predatory practices or attempts at exclusion form the market than by control of prices.[70]

The conclusion of this argument is not judicial ignorance but a legislation that is old and far from reality. The point is not to destroy every monopoly, the idea is to respect the scope and scale of production with a desirable business practices, and 'It is, in any case, the only way in which economics can contribute directly to the shaping of public policy'.[71] Most industrial organization studies were conceived by Edward Mason at Harvard during the 1930s and extended by numerous scholars such as Joe Bain or John Maurice Clark.

Three years later, in 1940, John Maurice Clark wrote, 'Toward a Concept of Workable Competition', perhaps the first article which had a bigger influence in the American legal system of antitrust than in the study of law and economics. Transcendence of workable competition's definition, next to consecution and empirical demonstration of markets' imperfections gave rise to the 1968 Guidelines. Later developments made by Joe Bain in the fifties and Frederic Scherer in the sixties followed the line drawn by this article. The first definition made by Clark was:

> Workable competition to mean a rivalry in selling goods in which each selling unit normally seeks maximum net revenue under conditions such that the price or prices each seller can charge are effectively limited by the free option of the buyer to buy from a rival seller or sellers of what we think of as the same product, necessitating an effort by each seller to equal or exceed the attractiveness of the others' offering to a sufficient number of buyers to accomplish the end in view.[72]

Clark believed in tactic agreements among installed firms in an industry, he also said that the market is plenty of irregularities, secrets, discriminatory pricing, and so on. Because of that, the possibility of any form of oligopoly and cutthroat price war has to be considered more than probable. He catalogued ten conditioning factors worth noting, apart from diverse variants or gradations, the list is reproduced below:

1. - The standardized or un-standardized character of the product.
2. - The number and size-distribution of producers.
3. - The general method of price-making.
4. - Method of selling.
5. - The character and means of market information.
6. - The geographical distribution of production and consumption.
7. - The degree of current control of output.
8. - Variation of cost with varying size of plant or enterprise.
9. - Variation of cost with short-run fluctuations of output.
10. - Flexibility of productive capacity.[73]

Clark tried to include these factors respecting traditional price theory and he is on top of the implications short run and long run in the economic theory; he said: 'Workable competition is that there shall not be too gross discrepancies between the action of short-run pressures and long-run tendencies'.[74] The main issue to solve was the use of capacity installed in an industry, while it is conditioned to demand fluctuations, the margin to reach equilibrium at the same time in short and in long run will be reduced. The excess of capacity installed increased the marginal cost, as well as average cost, the fair price calculated using the minimum of average cost and limited to marginal cost could create bottlenecks on industrial expansion and because of that, perfect competition requires operation at full capacity. In conclusion he proposed a few tentative propositions:

1) The immediate effect on net warnings.
2) The effect with some account taken of the probable early reactions of others.
3) Long-run effects, chiefly reflected in effects on volume of sales.
4) Intangibles including effects on good-will and on the satisfaction or dissatisfaction of customers.[75]

1.2.1.- The Controversy about Workable Competition

Since 1940 Clark's article has developed among economic theorists into a controversy about what workable competition means. Joe Bain and George Stigler[76] could be considered as the main representative authors of this controversy, which survived for a long time.

Stigler in 1942 wrote *The Theory of Competitive Price* and he exposed the conditions of perfect competition, using his words:

1. - Each economic unit is so small relative to the market that it exerts no perceptible influence on the prices of the things it buys and sells.
2. - All markets are free from special institutional restraints, or more positively, prices and the mobility of resources are not restricted.
3. - All economic unit possess complete knowledge.[77]

These conditions respect the old Marshall model, but Stigler used a new production function; this new function allows a firm to obtain the monopoly within its own industry, mainly through new input combinations or because it was a pioneer in an industry. The point of Stigler's contribution is to smoke out the tendency to impede entry of new competitors within an industry under the guise of regular firms' behaviour. Stigler pointed out that some unfair trade practices have been a tribute to American ingenuity, and he said that Federal Trade Commission admits that some of them survives and they could be considered as barriers to trade:

Localized price cutting, bribery and coercion of customers, bribery and coercion of sources of supplies; fake infringement suits, creation of dissent among employees, spreading rumours that competing products are inferior, and sabotage.[78]

Also, the control of entry by incumbents, have been made using:

1. - Geographical barriers (tax powers, highway control, health and sanitation powers, suppress out-of-state competition) (state legislation about the use of 75% of local butter as raw material in Alabama).
2. - Discrimination between types of organizations (anti-chain store legislation) and
3. - Licensing of new competitors. (Crafts).[79]

He included suppression of substitutes, prevention of price competition, restriction of output and miscellaneous policies. The conclusion of these frictions in markets is that the determination of cartel price is much more difficult than competitive markets. The relevant point has to be found in the fact that:

> If a cartel does not change its price when demand falls because it fears that as subsequent increase would lead to an antitrust prosecution, the prospective loss in revenue or increase in cost because of such a prosecution is included in the calculations of the cartel.[80]

Since then, Stigler develops his economic thought in close connection with law, and thinking about the pecuniary consequences of juries against companies.

That year, Joe Bain wrote 'Market Classifications in Modern Price Theory' as a title that indicated that he made a complete classification of markets into the unique objective of theorizing price determinants, because the Robinsonian price theory lack empirical content. In 1943 Bain wrote the core of this economic thought: the use of market prices in order to redistribute income; competition being the only way to reach such big objective. He pointed out that chronic excess capacity should be seriously examined because it changes the allocation of factors among uses. He said that the only way to know the industrial market behaviour is price and 'The character of the relationship between market structure and pricing result is as yet not fully enough understood that dependable norms can be drawn in terms of market structure'.[81] This is the starting point of his connections with Edward Mason's thought and with the intent to touch political influence in competitive issues. Following the Pigou line connecting prices with welfare, Bain wrote: 'The ratio of price to average cost is thus of primary significance to the level of employment, since it affects both the distribution of income between wages and profits and the prices of and yields on investment goods'.[82] This strong assumption let him to support that:

> The government might try to modify the structure of markets (including collusive agreements) sufficiently that the unregulated pursuit of gain would automatically result in normative prices. Second, it might leave market structure alone and simply administer a price other than that chosen by the enterprise, through direct regulation, manipulative taxation, government competition, or other means.[83]

It is not difficult to argue that his thought came to be the origin of Guidelines at the end of the sixties, but one is obliged to point out that he always protected private property with a strict correction of bad behaviour of firms by the political authorities. It is in this book precisely where he wrote one of the most criticized ideas about prices, promoting disputes for decades:

> It would seem desirable that the ratio of price to the average of currently incurred (non-sunk) costs should be relatively stable over the cycle ... This is not a norm, how-

ever, of the price rigidity per se, but of relative stability at a level so low as to allow only normative net profits in the long run.[84]

The determination of price using cost (average, marginal, sunken and so on) has been the core of Structure Conduct Performance Paradigm, and a big field of battle in economic science, but no less than the discussion about the survival of profits in the long run; both sink their roots in the Bainian's thought. Some years later Bain tried to solve the problem of long run profits, and he suggest the way to connect it with market structure, he said: 'Four principal dimensions, degree of monopolistic output restrictions, profits, selling costs, and the level, relative to the ideal, of the long-term average costs of producing given industry output'.[85] As these four variables behave as we are explaining the long run profits.

During the 1940s, Bain built the theory of limit price, following the reasoning shown above and the behaviour of companies in their industry, under the lens of oligopoly theory Bain wrote in 1948:

> If they are subject to an effective threat of entry, so that new firms would enter at the price OP, but can exclude entry at a lower 'limit' price, they may do this if the long-run profits promised to them by the later policy are greater.[86]

Technically, if one company detects a rival, the natural course of action should be to lower the price in the market: a low price means low profits for the new entrant and perhaps to rethink decision; which means, incidentally, that profits in the long-term have to survive otherwise the incumbents could have problems. As this theory had to include what exactly a barrier to entry means, Bain made one of the lesser-known definitions of entry barrier, he wrote:

> A *barrier to entry* of some height instead typically permits established firms to raise price above the minimum cost level without inducting an automatic correction through entry and potentially to raise it high enough to permit them to operate profitably with unit costs which are not the lowest attainable for the going industry output.[87]

Putting together the theory about market structure developed in 1943 and conduct built into an oligopoly model where firms behave in a natural way, expelling rivals, only performance is left in order to have a whole analytical framework. Even at this time the weakness of limit price theory shows, in the case that the market structure was made accurately, even with a precise model for conduct, scientifically there is no way to confirm performance.

Edward Mason in 1949 studied in deep the problem of performance; he classified five standards of acceptable business performance as:

1. - Cost in relation to size of plant can, in most industries, be well enough estimated to form a judgment on the minimum scale required for efficiency.
2. - Distribution.

3. - Cyclical variations in sales and by high overhead cost, to cut-throat competition which in periods of depression destroys efficient business organizations.
4. - One of the market conditions required for workable competition is the absence of collusion or agreement among the firms and
5. - Innovations.[88]

He built a test of workable competition which tried to establish market power and with it help judges' decisions; he was in touch with real world, it is quite clear because Mason realized that market share of a firm in its market is relevant to antitrust but does not directly mean that this firm have market control, the questions about performance exceed the answers. In antitrust issues Mason wrote:

> Extremely difficult to devise tests that can be administered by a court of law:
> 1. - Progressiveness: are the firms in the industry actively and effectively engaged in product and process innovation?
> 2. - Cost-price relationship: are reductions in cost, whether due to falling wages or material prices, technical improvements, discovery of new sources of supply, passed on promptly to buyers in the form of price reductions?
> 3. - Capacity-output relationships: is investment excessive in relation to output?
> 4. - The level of profits: are profits continually and substantially higher than in other industries exhibiting similar trends in sales, costs, innovations, etc?
> 5. - Selling expenditures: is competitive effort chiefly indicated by selling expenditures rather than by service and product improvements and price reductions?[89]

The inclusion of this unanswered question in the Structure-Conduct-Performance analytical framework shows the interest in doing the right thing, the target is competition and the way has to be made.

Joe Bain and George Stigler in 1949 wrote in sum four articles in the *American Economic Review* and one in the *Journal of Political Economy* opening wedge to the oligopoly theory, including behaviour, both wrote with admiration about to each other. Bain, on the side of the SCP paradigm, stood up for limit price, he said: 'If the established sellers set a 'limit' price which turns out to be too high to exclude entry, of course, their error may result in an effectively irreversible change in the structure of the industry'.[90] Then, the oligopoly equilibrium has to reach into strategic models. Stigler, on the side of Chicago School, worked in entry models, 'If the rate of entry is a function of price and profits, the merger can reduce or retard entry by a lower price policy; in effect it buys a longer period of monopoly at the price of a lower rate of monopoly profits',[91] survive come to be the only test to demonstrate that a firm is able to manage its own prices. Both agreed about limitations of the competition system in force at this moment in EEUU, Stigler put salt on the wound, and Stigler wrote: 'It is possible to change the trend of industrial organization by the lackadaisical enforcement of an antitrust law'[92] the answer of Bain to the entry models' Stigler was, as should be expected, natural behaviour of firms:

> My hypothesis in general is that under conditions of very or moderately difficult entry, reasonable long-run efficiency in scale and capacity should develop, whereas under easy entry (if this is found in oligopoly) the prospect is much less certain and substantial inefficiency may result.[93]

Following a second hypothesis about the relationship between condition of entry and price, profits, degree of monopolistic output restriction; accepting that he only had tested concentration with profit rate, he honestly wrote that relation between condition of entry and price and profits is not clear. Stigler's answer was irrefutable: 'I suggest that when attention is turned to this question (how long will they enjoy this position and what are the conditions of entry) oligopoly behaviour loses much of its arbitrariness and oligopoly price much of its indeterminacy'.[94] In my personal opinion this discussion has to be considered the starting point of successive developments in oligopoly theory, it is an inflection point, at least for three lines of economic thought, microeconomics, industrial organization and behaviourism.

In *Papers and Proceedings* of the International Economic Association in 1954 relevant economists wrote about competition and regulation, Joan Robinson, Kurt Rothschild and Edward Chamberlin. Chamberlin didn't stay out of this controversy during the fifties;, he wrote about measuring degree of monopoly and competition and proposed Mr Lerner's index as a good measure of 'social optimum'.[95] John Maurice Clark wrote a premonitory sentence for competition theory and guidelines including in an article entitled 'Competition and the Objectives of Government Policy': 'Unfortunately, what is public available consists of the briefs and arguments of lawyers prosecuting and defending cases'.[96] In the same vein, Stigler wrote that the American system to solve competition issues was corrective; he was interested in concentration or degree of monopoly, and made considerations to set rules as:

> Every firm with less than five to ten per cent of an industry's output (after merger) may engage in the merger ... Every merger by a firm which possesses one-fifth or more of an industry's output after the merger shall be presumed to violate the statute. In the situation that lie between these limits, the merger should be investigated by the enforcement agencies if the aggregate annual sales of the merging firms will exceed some absolute level – say five million dollars- after merger.[97]

Even one of the prominent representative of the Chicago School proposed limits to mergers. Mason could not be quiet and he claimed in a study of competition that it is convenient to limit the degree of market power but 'The critical questions are how much market power and how obtained or maintained?'[98]

In the same line of thought, Howard Hines, working for the National Science Foundation,[99] wrote about effectiveness of entry and his conclusions including the existence of lobbying and infiltration of regulatory bodies by business officials, as the use of techniques for gaining political influence by companies, he wrote: 'Unfortunately, however, the whole question of the social and political results of "big business" has been more characterized by rhetoric than by research'.[100]

The last papers cited above show the imperative of having tools capable of demonstrating market power exercised by big companies within their markets, and could be considered as prelude of barriers to competition, because this is precisely the target followed by Joe Bain, to offer economic tools, to lawyers and judges, which could be used as proof in a court.

1.3. The Origins of Barriers to Entry

The sole objective of this section is to grant some relevance to the authors who considered some barriers to entry in their analysis of competition prior to the publication of *Barriers to Competition* in a particular way or a way separate from general theory. During the 40s and 50s the theory of competition had a lot of contributions which improved the framework, not exactly to help courts as target, much more as an intellectual exercise to demonstrate how markets work. The generalization of theories or proposals got bigger academic awards than the real application, that explain why the particularities did not get the same consideration. We could find seeds of barriers to entry in Chamberlin; the use of capacity and advertising are quite important in the analysis of imperfect competition.

1.3.1. Excess of Capacity as a Barrier to Entry

The use of capacity to expel competitors into an industry is the oldest barrier to entry; the idea was introduced by Edward Chamberlin into his thesis of 1927, but not in this way. Professor Chamberlin said that excess of capacity 'wastes of competition'[101] tied with the John Maurice Clark idea about that excess of capacity must be considered as characteristic of industry and connected with peaks of demand. At this time the capacity installed in an industry was considered only as the means of satisfying clients every time; companies have to invest in capacity in order to anticipate future demands. Until the 50s, the capacity installed in an industry, as the sum of the capacity of all firms or industrial plants was not used as strategic a decision. It is necessary to assume that the industry behave as a oligopoly and to include a leader in the industry, who should be able to increase output and go down equilibrium price and then expel new entrants because the new price is too low to earn money entering the industry. While economists analysed decreasing costs they considered that it was possibly due to the excess of capacity installed in an industry (at this time, they have an empirical demonstration, by Clark, on railway industry). That means, if an industry works with excess of capacity it assumes that it can move through the average costs curve to get the price in a benchmark. In other words, the equilibrium price on the long run is not getting in the minimum of the average costs curve where the connection with the marginal costs curve happens. Technically it is a breaking point in the Marshallian equilibrium conditions; nonetheless it should be possible to propose new equations capable of reaching the equilibrium.

Cassels defines excess of capacity as: 'The difference between the output that the productive agent in question is capable of producing and the output it is actually called on to produce'.[102] The only way to use the excess of capacity to expel competitors is to lower prices, but in Chamberlin's sense, when demand is elastic the price policies (or wars) of companies are likely non-aggressive. In this case we must to distinguish excess capacity of overinvestment because second one is close to monopolistic competition with aggressive price policies where excess of capacity could be considered as involuntary fixed cost.

In the same vein, and arguing about the use of installed capacity, Nicolas Kaldor wrote that: 'The heart of the whole matter ... is the relation of price to marginal cost'[103] for the whole industry or for each company, if we are able to discover each marginal cost of each differentiated product of each company, then: 'The degree of market imperfection depends on the numbers of firms in any given section of the competitive field'.[104] It seems that the use of capacity isn't first-class tool for expelling competitors. Therefore, Kaldor established that the degree of freedom of entry depends on the strength of institutional privileges.

1.3.2. Advertising as a Barrier to Entry

Chamberlin reconciles monopolistic and competitive forces, by introducing a modelling paradigm that emphasizes advertising; the way to do this is through expanding demand and as required selling costs. The main effect of advertising is its ability to change prices due to the elasticity effect; technically: 'If advertising makes the firm's demand less elastic, as advertising might when it creates wants and encourages brand loyalty',[105] and this is precisely the way it works as a barrier to entry because when advertising creates brand loyalty, followed by: 'Established firms are then able to charge high prices and earn significant profits without facing entry',[106] and the advertising generate a deterrence of entry in an industry.

Dorothea Braithwaite wrote in 1928 'The economic effects of advertising', this article should be considered as the starting point of these issues, firstly because she defined accurately what advertising means and secondly due to the fact that she connected advertising with economic welfare. She pointed out that consumers are induced to pay a price for the commodity high enough to cover advertisement costs plus production cost; also the power of advertising to change demand for products; she answered herself on the evidence of competition by advertisement and competition by price. The conclusion reached to explain how markets work deserves special consideration, it was written early and it showed an irrefutable weakness of perfect competition theory, she said:

> Under conditions of perfect competition producers would gain nothing by spending money on advertisement, for those conditions assume two things. 1. - The demand curve is fixed and cannot be altered directly by producers and 2.- Since producers can sell all that they can produce at the market price, none of them could produce (at a given moment) more at that price than they are already doing.[107]

When prices rise because of advertising, economic welfare is at risk. As Kyle Bagwell noted several years after: 'Advertising increases consumer surplus only if it is accompanied by a strict reduction in price'.[108]

Nicholas Kaldor proposed, in 1950, a measure of monopoly power, the relevant contribution of his article was the inclusion of cost of advertising (or selling cost). About the measure of monopoly power using prices and cost in next way: $p-c/p$ being: 'p is price which covers the costs of product of potential entrant and c is cost of the representative firm. P-c is the amount by which the selling price of the representative firm can exceed its own costs'[109] connected with advertising expenditures he said that: 'No generalisation seems possible as to how far p can be raised by the expenditure of selling cost and how much of the difference $p-c$ will tend to be taken up by these outlays'[110] reaching the same conclusion as Chamberlin, the economic analysis of advertising is not enough to get an accurate understanding. Connected with welfare Kaldor draws a distinction between direct and indirect effects of advertising in social welfare as follows: 'The direct effect of advertising is associated with it role in the provision of price and product-quality information to consumers, while the indirect effects of advertising include any consequent scale economies in production and distribution'[111] in the same line of thought, Joe Bain's analysis included advertising as a preference for reputation and considers that it erected an entry barrier in front of new products from rivals. This should be analysed in the same way as product differentiation.

Conclusion

This first chapter refers to the origins of antitrust and early economic contributions. Edward Chamberlin's thought should be considered as the path followed by researchers in noncompetitive markets, the references of Chamberlin's model set the standard, and academia tried to improve on his framework.

In order to be more technical, we began by explaining the three different way to reach equilibrium in an oligopoly model, Cournot, Bertrand and Stackelberg. Once we set framework out to analysis, it seems convenient to write about the intention of improving this theoretical model. The point is to include the behaviour of firms in markets, how firms survive, how they grow, how they sell and at which price they do so. From Frank Knight in the 20s to Edith Penrose in the 50s, a lot of academic production was made; the majority of these contributions are seeds of later development which concluded as independent economic schools of thought, such as institutionalism, behaviourism or business administration.

Academic relevance was reached by the behaviourist school, because this line of thought is connected to psychology and tools of social behaviour; unfortunately the significance of the Carnegie-Mellon School, the name usually associated with behaviourism, has been limited. Generalizations on business behaviour are not an easy goal, actually in the classrooms of business schools around the world, case studies should be used to teach how good business should be conducted. Proposals built by academics during the sixties and seventies, as rules of thumb, are successful in a narrow leeway. The publication of *Competitive Strategy* by Michael Porter in 1980 classified different kinds of strategies and put the stress on the fact that survival depends on first making this strategy real. The Behaviourism school deserves consideration because it develops a way to explain competition.

John Bates Clark could be considered the pioneer of antitrust as an economic issue. It is true that antitrust has been a legal topic for years, but Clarks, father and son, realized that the behaviour of big companies was destroying customer welfare due to the rise of prices of products and customers being unable to bargain on price. While prices are increasing and demand doesn't change the tendency, something is wrong in this market. The point is, however, the capacity of the Clarks and Mason to reach methods of decision and include a debate about this topic in American politician life. Two consequences of attempting to change the rules are: the economists developed workable competition models following their path and a great controversy over how non-competitive markets should be corrected without infringing upon business freedom, the symbol of the United States. The political implementation of these notions to wait till 1968 when the Guidelines put all these ideas into practice.

Concerning barriers to competition as an important part of competition, we have included the origins in the early economic thought in the twentieth century. Under the lens of economic thought finding the first time that a concept or idea was used by economist, seems fanciful. Mainly, because when you are looking for economic seeds and they are only in the one unique book, *The Theory of Monopolistic Competition*.

2 BARRIERS TO ENTRY: THE LATE 1950s AND THE 1960s

Introduction

In the last chapter we mentioned economic scholars' main difficulties in building a framework to demonstrate how imperfect competition works. In the present chapter we shall present the birth of the economic idea known as 'barriers to entry' and discuss how this new proposal is capable of demonstrating that markets usually don't work in a perfect competitive way. This chapter is about the Bain-Sylos-Modigliani theoretical model, and the empirical demonstration of their theories during the 1960s. We will begin with a brief biography of both, following with a description of the contribution of each to the formal model. The next section refers to the difference between the theory in the real world and how they included personal contributions. The chapter concludes with an argument about cross-section data and its limits in demonstrating the existence of barriers to entry. At the same time, the concept and the theoretical economic framework got a good reception in the American antitrust policy which inspired the creation of merger Guidelines in 1968.

The economic theory offers two definitions of barriers to entry, one was written by Joe Bain and the other one was written twelve years later by George Stigler. Bain wrote in 1956:

> Let us understand the term 'condition of entry' to an industry to mean something equivalent to the 'state of potential competition' from possible new sellers. Let us view it moreover as evaluated roughly by the advantages of established sellers in an industry over potential entrant sellers, these advantages being reflected in the extent to which established sellers can persistently raise their prices above a competitive level without attracting new firms to enter the industry. As such, the 'condition of entry' is then primarily a structural condition, determining in any industry the intra-industry adjustments which will and will not induce entry ... If we understand the condition of entry in this way, its possible importance as a determinant of competitive behavior is clear.[1]

However and paradoxically, the definition that everybody remembers was created by George Stigler: 'Barriers to entry as a cost of producing which must be borne by a firm which seeks to enter an industry but is not borne by firms already in the industry'.[2] Barriers work in two different ways, firstly, for example, when a firm that lobbies for a government-imposed restriction on new entry, such as taxi-licences, in these cases the firm is protecting itself and other incumbents against new competitors. Secondly, when a firm, in a strategic decision, opens a price war, in this case the firm injures its rivals in its own market, while also injuring new entrants.

The point was to fit a new hypothesis into the classical price theory. Because when accepting that price is a good indicator of market competition, it should also show the bad behaviour of firms in their own market. An unusually high price for any product seems a signal that something is not working in a market, the direct correspondence could be, that one part of the market (supply) is capable of raising the price, and the other parts, its competitors and consumers, are not able to bargain. Bain defined 'competitive level of prices' as 'the minimum attainable average cost of production, distribution, and selling for the good in question, such cost being measured to include a normal interest return on investment in the enterprise'.[3]

I should now like to move on to a more detailed study of the Bain-Sylos imperfect competition model. It is worth bearing in mind that any contribution designed to modify Marshall's Theory must inevitably be cast within a general (or partial) equilibrium framework. Economic theory prevalent at the time assumed the natural tendency of markets toward equilibrium; which imply that in the long run, entrepreneur's profits will disappear. The explanation of this assumption is that since firms within a sector produce and sell similar products, they will compete amongst each other for clients, and profit margins will inevitably fall.

Joe Bain and Paolo Sylos Labini at the end of the 1950s formalized an economic model which defined how a price can be suspiciously high compared with the marginal cost of the product. Price theory allows for finding disequilibrium's price into the average costs curve in the long run. This so-called limit price should be estimated for each industrial sector, and calculated as enough to prevent new entrants in the industry. At the same time, when limit price is higher than the competitive price of the market, customers suffer because they have to pay more money for the same product in comparison to the price obtained if the firms were to compete with each other.

The main protagonists of this chapter are Joe Bain, Paolo Sylos Labini and Franco Modigliani. Allow me to introduce them each with a short biography. Joe Bain (1912–91) did his undergraduate work at UCLA and his graduate work at Harvard, obtaining a PhD in 1940. He was appointed lecturer in economics at the University of California, Berkeley in 1939 and remained on this faculty until his retirement in 1975. Nonetheless he is considered the founder of the Harvard School of economic thought. He wrote *Barriers to New Com-*

petition (1956) offering a determinate solution to the oligopoly problem and figuring out the relationship between industry-structure-behaviour-performance. Another classic work of Bain's is entitled *Industrial Organization* (1959), in which he formalized using mathematical tools the analysis he had previously drafted. During the 60s he worked with Richard Caves and Julius Margolis in the book entitled *Northern California's Water Industry: The Comparative Efficiency of Public Enterprise in Developing a Scarce Natural Resource* (1966). Their colleagues said that Bain had a remarkable ability to pick research areas with long-lasting, escalating policy significance.

Franco Modigliani (1918–2003) was the 1984 winner of the Nobel prize. Although his main contribution to economic science is not connected with the limit price theory; he wrote 'New Developments on the Oligopoly Front' in 1958. Modigliani's contribution consists of a small reform of equations in order to sharpen consequences on price according to the response of the incumbents in industry.

Paolo Sylos Labini (1920–2005). Sylos was professor at the University of Bologna, Italy. He wrote *Oligopolio e progresso tecnico* in 1956, the English edition entitled *Oligopoly and Technical Progress* (1962). This book is considered a cornerstone in the theory of market organization. Sylos Labini's interest in the relationship between theory and history had been raised by intellectual exchanges with teachers such as Schumpeter and Joan Robinson, during his studies at Harvard and Cambridge. Sylos paid attention to reform policy as a tool to guide structural and institutional change following the classical British tradition of political economy.

It is usual to find the limit price theory named by together these three authors.

2.1. A New Framework for Explaining how Firms Behave.

Joe Bain worked on an economic model that was able to explain different market structures: he analysed production concentration, technological advantages, etc. He named this set of variables *barriers to new competition*. Following his market structure, Bain began to work into a new economic paradigm known as Structure-Conduct-Results or Harvard School. Bain knew the convenience of demonstrating his proposal in a theoretical model. The best way to obtain results would be to assess those barriers to entry and, at the same time, demonstrate how the companies which are able to almost get one barrier to entry achieve an advantage which allows the company exercise power in the market. The limit price theory, built by Paolo Sylos Labini, shows that nonetheless traditional price theory allows for demonstrating the existence of barriers to entry as a worthwhile model. Two year later Franco Modigliani published his article

'New Developments on the Oligopoly Front' which fits into the mathematical apparatus designed by Bain and Sylos.

Paolo Sylos Labini assumed the possibility that the incumbents into an industry could to impede new entrants. He built an equilibrium model with average and marginal cost in the long run, similar to the Marshallian theoretical model. He established an equilibrium price set up over the minimum of average costs curve in the long run. This benchmark is the price in which deterrence entry works. In other words, while incumbents keep an agreement on this limit price, through collusion, all of them reach over-returns, because there is no competition of prices between firms. Otherwise, if the incumbents collude on a price that is over the limit price, a new entrant would be attracted to those profits. Whenever this situation happens, the competition of prices between firms return in order to get new customers and the model reaches equilibrium at the point where the minimum of average costs curve connects with the marginal costs curve in the long run.

The model of Joe Bain, Paolo Sylos Labini and Franco Modigliani works into the prices theory described above, using the theoretical Marshallian framework of production function and costs function. Their proposal applies mathematical tools to explain the economic analysis. Bain, Sylos and Modigliani a few years later, did not criticize the basic assumptions of the mechanical rules that come from physics in order to calculate the equilibrium of markets.

The contribution of Paolo Sylos Labini was to accept the traditional framework while including a new proposal regarding supply and demand curves, as well as the average and marginal costs curve. Sylos defended the possibility of obtaining a market equilibrium with a quite a few anomalies; that some markets work in an imperfect competition because one firm, or a few of them, are able to keep the industry's price within the direction of their own benefit.

The new proposals of Bain-Sylos-Modigliani opened a new door to analysing firms' abusive behaviour, which can be exercised only by the incumbent firms, and was called 'exercise of market power'. At that time, it was at first considered of interest so as to assess through synthetic variables such as the level of industry concentration of the main firms. Asymmetry in cost was the second issue which received attention, and the only way of assessing it was the scale economies in production. Some years later, this kind of measurement was questioned because it included both strategic behaviour in themselves. Econometrics is not able to distinguish which part of a variable is an exercise of market power and which part is a strategic behaviour to raise clients. Furthermore, one theoretical problem survives, the measurement barriers to entry that only work in the short run. A firm can manipulate its own price over the equilibrium price in the short run. The marginal framework assumes that in the long run the equilibrium is reached because friction markets tend to disappear. In this case it is convenient to accept that the analysis of behaviour of the firms on the short run is of interest.

2.2. Joe Bain, Paolo Sylos-Labini and Franco Modigliani model.

In 1956 Joe Bain published *Barriers of New Competition, Their Character and Consequences in Manufacturing Industries,* and even today this book is controversial. The beginning of Bain's research was how firms behave within their own industry. The best way to understand the idea is to read his own words:

> The investigation was made because of two beliefs: (1) that most analyses of how business competition works and what makes it work have given little emphasis to the force of the potential or threatened competition of possible new competitors, placing a disproportionate emphasis on competition among firms already established in any industry; (2) that so far as economists have recognized the possible importance of this 'condition of entry', they have no very good idea of how important it actually is.[4]

A few pages later Bain defined exactly what he had in mind when thinking of entry conditions, as a state of potential competition from possible new sellers. Bain thought of the advantages of established firms within the industry over its rivals and concluded that the only way to demonstrate that the incumbents exercise market power got by this advantages should be reflected in a persistently raise of industry prices above the competitive level, but the maximum value of raise is a price which seems unattractive to new companies. This price is known as limit price.

Technically Bain's static, non-stochastic limit price π^0 is high for low entry barriers, then drops to $\pi^0 = \pi^f$ (with $\delta\pi^f /\delta B > 0$ for non blockaded entry) for higher barriers. While the second unobserved variable is the entry forestalling level of profits, π^f, as a function of entry costs (barriers) and growth,
This is:

$$\pi^f = h(B, G_t)$$

where:

B is a vector of entry barriers

G_t is growth in t.

As the limit price theory is developed, some assumptions are modified, for example, Gaskins' dynamic limit pricing where π^0 starts high and is either

a) Monotonically decreasing in barrier, or

b) Monotonically decreasing in barriers to π^0 fall to π^f and

c) Then $\pi^0 = \pi^f$ for higher (non-blockaded) barriers.[5]

In order to develop his idea Joe Bain follows three steps. The first step is to clarify barriers to entry in order to facilitate successful evaluation: The first barrier is called economies of large scale as barriers of entry, and had three subtitles:

1. The entrant may enter at a small enough scale so that his entry will tend to have no perceptible effect on the prices or outputs of established firms.
2. The entrant may enter at larger scales thus necessarily influencing either prices or outputs in the industry.
3. With entry at or near the minimum optimal scale established firms may restrict output enough to allow the entrant a significant market share with unchanged prices.

The second barrier, known as 'product differentiation', is of at least the same general order of importance as an impediment to entry as are economies of large-scale production and distribution. The last barrier is called 'absolute cost advantages of established firms'. In the terminology of price theory, the long run average cost or scale curve would then lie at a higher level for the entrant than for the established firm.

The second step was to develop a successful way of measuring the conditions of entry; they may be conveniently evaluated in the following terms for price theory, meaning the relevant gap between market price and minimal cost at which entry may be forestalled.

For the typical circumstances giving rise to an *absolute cost advantage* to established firms, the measure will be:

- control of production techniques by established firms,
- imperfections in the markets for hired factors of production,
- significant limitations of the supplies of productive factors in specific markets,
- money-market conditions imposing higher interest rates upon potential entrants than upon established firms.

For the typical circumstances giving rise to a *product differentiation advantage* to established firms, the successful variables are:

- the accumulative preference of buyers for established brand names and company reputations,
- control of superior product designs by established firms through patents,
- ownership or contractual control by established firms of favored distributive outlets.

Economies of large scale as barrier to entry works because the entrant enters at a small enough scale that his entry will tend to have no perceptible effect on the prices or outputs of established firms. But if the new entrant enters at a large scale it necessarily influences both prices and output in the industry. In a model with entry near the minimum optimal scale, established firms may reduce their total output enough to allow new entrant a market share, even at unchanged prices.

The way to assess economies of scale should be to find the relationship between the scale of production in a plant or firm and the unit cost of production and distribution. The excess of concentration in an industry, in the sense that illustrates a firm's size, is evidently needed for the lowest possible production and distribution costs. The theoretical origins are to be found in the old model of Cournot's oligopoly; where equilibrium is obtained through the sharing of production between firms, since when one firm shifts a product, the other has to follow suit, and since both operate in the same market, the competitor sees market prices fall, technically as low as the Bain-Sylos-Modigliani limit price.

The Sylos Labini contribution was that in a Cournot's oligopoly with a high concentration of production in a few numbers of firms, the limit price should be calculated as follows:

x= amount of production.

v= average cost of production

q' = percentage which covered the fix cost named **K**

q'' = Cost necessarily to get a net profit named **g**

$$P = v + q'v + q''v$$

If $q = q' + q''$ Then $p = v + qv$

Where $q'v = \dfrac{K}{x}$ and $q''v = g$

If we assumed that a net margin doesn't exist (g) the profit is zero, in other words

$qv = K/Xn + g$ then the amount which determines the price is:

$Xm > Xn > Xo$

Xm.- Maxim amount

Xn.- Normal amount

Xo .- Amount without profits

When the marginal cost m is equal to the direct cost:

$p = m + qm$ if $m = p - \dfrac{p}{\eta}$ and η is demand elasticity

But if a firm tries to enter in the market, it must adopt the known technology and can't increase its output over the maxim limit. Until this limit, the direct cost is constant and equal to the marginal cost, while the average cost is decreasing.

The possibility that new entrants enter the market is determinate, in the long run, on if they aim to obtain a profit equal to a minimum, this minimum we call S and we define S as:

$$S = \frac{px - K - vx}{k + vx}$$

If *Sm* is the profit minimum then minimum price should be *Pm*, defined below:

$$Pm = \left(\frac{K}{x} + v\right)(1 + Sm)$$

Any exclusion price is less than the minimum price in the short run and the elimination price *Pe* is any price less than *v*. In the long run the equilibrium price will be estimated by extension of market that means total sales, elasticity of demand, distribution of sales among companies and prices of production factors; in other words, production, incomes and costs of the oligopoly industry where firms of different size coexist.

Concerning the limit price proposed by Bain and Sylos, Modigliani assumed that entrants behave in a way defined as the incumbent adopt the policy most unfavourable to them, maintaining output while reducing price. Under this assumption the smallest entry-blocking industry output *Xo* is

$$Xo = Xe - x = Xe \frac{1 - x}{Xe} = Xe \left(1 - \frac{1}{S}\right)$$

Modigliani wrote:

> Even if the pre-entry price is above the lowest achievable cost, the additional output he proposes to sell may drive the price below cost, making the entry unprofitable... Unfortunately for the theorist, the exact anticipated effect of the entry on price is not independent of the (anticipated) reaction of existing producers. The more they are willing to contract their output in response to the entry the smaller will be the fall in price; in the limiting case the price may even be completely unaffected. Both authors have wisely refused to be stopped by this difficulty.[6]

In order to resolve this difficulty Modigliani defined S. Within a competitive market where the equilibrium price is Pc= K, and which corresponds to the minimum of average cost, S is the size of the market measured as a ratio of the competitive output to the optimum scale. This ratio S should be defined for each industry. The entry preventing output X_0 is set out in the following equations:

Lets define equilibrium output in a competitive market as $X_c = D(K) = D(P_c)$

Also it is possible to establish an output which adjusts to $X_0 = X_c(1 - 1/S)$. Where S and its equality have been defined above.

Modigliani wrote about the above output as follows:

> Suppose in fact that aggregate output was smaller, it would then be profitable for a firm of scale (**X**) to enter. Indeed, the post-entry output would then still be smaller than X_c, and hence the post-entry price would be larger than P_c which is in turn equal to the entrant's average cost. X_0 would make entry unattractive. The critical P_0 corresponding to X_0 can be read from the demand curve or found by solving for $\hat{P}$ the equation $X_0 = D(P)$. the relation between P_0 and the competitive equilibrium price P_c can be started in terms of elasticity of demand in the neighborhood of P_c; if we denote this elasticity by η, we have $P_0 \cong P_c(1 + 1/\eta S)$.[7]

In the long run, within an oligopolistic situation, Modigliani assumed that: 'With its precarious internal equilibrium, there is much to be gained form simple and widely understood rules of thumb, which minimize the danger of behavior intended to be peaceful and cooperative being misunderstood as predatory or retaliatory.'[8]

It's worthwhile bearing in mind that Edwards anticipated some of Sylos and Bain's conclusions in 1955, by way of a footnote. Referring to the use of the excess of capacity as barrier to entry, Edwards wrote: 'Excess of capacity in the sense of substantial unexploited economies of scale will not normally obtain.'[9] He differentiated a planned of imposed excess of capacity and an imposed one due to lack of demand. Thus contradicting Harrod's traditional theory which worked with excess capacity going only in one direction, it is likely that Joe Bain never read this article, but Modigliani did, and he found the proposal interesting.

The formal model changes few assumptions from the classical economic theory of prices. Nobody doubts the innovation of the analysis introduced by Bain in order to improve the knowledge of market imperfections. Mainly because it was the first time that an economist described regular behaviour of the firms and proposed how demonstrate it. In short, as Gilbert noted:

> The essential assumptions of the Bain-Sylos.-Modigliani limit pricing model are:
> 1. - There are two periods: pre-entry (t=0) and post-entry (t=1). Entry may occur only in period 1.
> 2. - There is a single established firm or a coordinated cartel, the incumbent (i) and a single potential entrant (e)

3. - Consumers are indifferent between purchases from the incumbent or the entrant and have no costs of switching suppliers.

4. - Demand does not change over time

5. - In period t=0 the incumbent can commit to an output level xi which it must maintain at all future period. (It implies that the incumbent can act as a Stackelberg leader in output).[10]

In the opinion of Gilbert:

> Joe Bain (1956) made the first systematic attempt to uncover a correlation between measures of market concentration, the conditions of entry, and monopoly profits. Bain identified a positive correlation between profits and both concentration and estimates of the height of barriers to entry, which he categorized as scale economies, absolute cost advantages, and product differentiation. In the absence of substantial barriers to entry, the correlation between profits and market concentration was weak, an observation which lends some support to the contestable market hypothesis.[11]

2.3. Into the Way to Confirm the Existence of Barriers to Entry.

Bain made a classification of barriers to new competition, as shown in the title of his book. This classification included economies of scale, brand identity and capital requirements, as well as access to distribution, access to necessary inputs, switching costs, proprietary learning curves, proprietary product differences, government policy, expected retaliation and so forth. The second step was to demonstrate how barriers work; Bain's objective was to describe a mechanism of behaviour of firms in their own market. In the 1960s the study of market power was the core of this line of research, and of course this was the third step in Bain's theoretical model. Barriers of entry affect the behaviour of the firm in the following way 'the extent to which, in the long run, established firms can elevate their selling prices above the minimal average costs of production and distribution ... without inducing potential entrant to enter the industry'.[12]

During this period, the majority of articles about barriers to entry tried to demonstrate empirically Bain's proposals. Like him, authors classified different kinds of barriers within the industry that they were interested in. Furthermore, Bain built a worthwhile theoretical framework in order to test his own assumptions. The main authors of the 60s were Kahn, Williamson, Mann, Comanor and Wilson, Mueller and Tilton, who were working mainly on political and business issues; they found in Bain's barriers an interesting way of testing the behaviour of the firms within their industry. Bain offered them an excellent tool, with data from different industries. Using this tool it should be possible to detect the nature of the real activities of firms against their competitors. It is worthwhile to know what each of the previously mentioned authors said and the data they used in order to reach their goals, which industries confirmed their proposals, and where they found methodological problems in their research. Following a chronological order of publication, then, these studies are described below.

In 1958, Andreano and Warner wrote about Bain's proposals, in their article entitled 'Professor Bain and Barriers to New Competition' they said 'Bain has presented the profession with a number of useful concepts which are already finding their way into popular technical usage'.[13] They took scale requirements (minimum plant size necessary for lowest unit cost) as a percentage of market capacity. Absolute capital disadvantages are analysed as capital requirements for a single optimal plant 'copper, gypsum and steel probably have the largest barrier of this type'.[14] The conclusions they drew from their model were that automobiles, cigarettes, copper, fountain pens (quality grade), liquor, tractors and typewriters are industries with very high entry barriers; on the other hand farm machinery (large and complex), petroleum refining, shoes (high-priced men's and specialties), soap and steel maintaining substantial entry barriers, and finally canned fruit and vegetables, cement, farm machinery, flour, low-priced fountain pens, gypsum products, meatpacking, metal containers, rayon, shoes (women's and low-priced men's), tires and tubes all presented moderate to low entry barriers.

Arthur Kahn H. in 1959 wrote 'Discriminatory Pricing as a Barrier to Entry: The Spark Plug Litigation'. This article seems to be written by an expert or a referee. It reads like a report for a trial, probably because one firm took the other to court. This article does not include any references to Joe Bain; nevertheless it uses denomination of barriers to entry in the same sense. The issue was to confirm discriminatory pricing as a barrier to entry and the author resolved the problem by mean of a specific *Case study*. Ford and Chrysler litigated against Champion Spark Plug Company and General Motors and Electric Auto-Lite because of price discrimination. If Ford and Chrysler entered but limited themselves to the production of plugs to meet only their own needs: 'Their would be little incentive for them to cut prices to the consumer since even their own market for replacement plugs would be virtually assured without the need for such a reduction'.[15] While the President of Champion testified: 'The manufacturer is not interested in having me supply him with just equipment plugs, and I am not interested in just selling him equipment plugs'.[16] The Commission's ruling amounts to official non-recognition of the fact, which decision permits 'tying of the original use and replacement-use plugs, a result otherwise illegal under section 3 of the Clayton Act and perhaps even under the Sherman Act'.[17] As an additional argument Kahn wrote that in the long run this decision will make producers of spark plugs more competitive because five producers are better than three, and this should eliminate some functionless monopoly profits on replacement plugs.

Initial references to Bain's work in the sixties were made by Oliver Williamson in 1963 and Michael Mann in 1966, both articles made sense to barriers
to entry. Williamson worked on selling expenses and Mann worked on seller
concentration and rates of return. The first article uses the limit price theory of
Bain and Modigliani, and was the occasion for Williamson to say 'that utilizing
resources at the level where the marginal value product is equal to the marginal
cost, the barrier is great, or effectively blockaded entry'.[18] However, we must bear
in mind that Williamson works under the assumption that established firms only
attempt to erect a barrier to entry against products which would be regarded as
equivalent. The point is how sloped are the isoquants and when it will be less,
because the answer should be formed in the characteristics of the product.

Oliver Williamson wrote 'Selling Expense as a Barrier to Entry' (1963), in
which he developed a theoretical model, based on older proposals made by A.
Demsetz, K. Boulding and F. Hahn a few years before. Within Williamson's
model, selling expense appears as a high 'barrier to entry' much more than a
blockade to entry in an industry. Some years later, in 1968, Williamson built
a *naïve* model, using his words, about the trade-off results of a merger. His target was to find a meeting point between economy and law, in order to help the
Federal Trade Commission. The main conclusion of this paper is not especially
optimistic, 'Once economies are admitted as a defence, the tools for assessing
these effects can be expected progressively to be refined'.[19]

Leonard Weiss, in 1963, attempted to account for the means of changes in
industrial concentration; he used the analyses of concentration based on *the law
of proportionate effect* which assume that the chance of any given proportional
change in firm-size is equal for all firms. Therefore, whether the variance of the
logarithms of firm-size or the dispersion of relative firms grows the concentration is more likely to increase. Weiss contrast his hypothesis in 134 four digit
American industries, with information dated from 1947–54 for the National
Resource Committee. His conclusion was an illustrative 'dilemma for public
policy'.[20]

On the other hand, Michael Mann,[21] in 1966, maintained that seller concentration is a barrier to entry. The cornerstone of this research was to demonstrate
the existence of seller concentration within the main industrial activities in the
USA, such as the Sulphur industry in Alberta, Canadian nickel, the Pharmaceutical industry in EEUU, the Aluminium industry 1945–58, Biscuit makers,
Glass container industries, Baking, the Midwestern coal industry and brewers.
The majority of the industries cited above were independently and thoroughly
analysed by researchers who worked in Universities and other Centers of Investigation.

Advertising and competition walk together since 1964, following the path
of Nicholas Kaldor when he published his article about the role of advertising

in 1950. Lester Telser[22] took the baton of Kaldor in 1964 and built a theoretical model with the starting point of considering advertising as a means of product differentiation. The equation has been made taking the following characteristics; advertising may give information, may signal quality, allow identifying sellers, it is a part of a product because in psychosomatic disorders the advertising propriety remedy may be more effective than the same product; altogether advertising offers entertainment. Once the equation has been defined, it is possible to describe advertising as a source of monopoly. Telser contrasts his hypothesis for forty-four three-digit American industries, mainly in beverage, food, clothes, drugs, perfumes, petroleum refining, communications, motor, jewelry industries, using data from 1947 to 1958. He confirmed firstly, that the price of advertising products is usually higher than non-advertising commodities, this situation should be considered monopoly profits. Secondly, taking deliberation advertising with industrial concentration or seller's concentration, the relationship between them is positive. Thirdly, advertising is a source of monopoly because the more heavily advertised class should also contain the products with the more stable market shares. The conclusion of this paper was that 'advertising is a barrier to entry depends on the nature of the returns to advertising, which cannot be analysed without clearly understanding the advertising mechanism'.[23]

Three years later, Michael Mann, J. Henning and J Meehan published an empirical investigation in order to confirm the conclusions of Telser, using the framework of Weiss. Data used to contest the hypothesis was the same cross-section data used by Telser, and their conclusions were in parallel, the efforts of advertising are ruled to get monopoly profits. The next sentence shows the intensity of conclusion: 'sales promotion efforts must receive high priority from any general policy which seeks to establish competitive markets'.[24]

At the same time, in 1967, William Comanor[25] and Thomas Wilson[26] worked on advertising as a determinant issue in order to understand market structure and performance, 'we shall examine the relationships which are likely to exist between product differentiation, advertising and entry barriers'.[27] They made multivariate regression equations which explain the inter-industry variation in profit rates as a function of different combinations of seller concentration, the rate of growth of demand, economies of scale in production in relation to the size of the market, absolute capital requirements for a plant of minimum efficient scale and advertising. They used forty-one American industries, starting with soft drinks, cereals, carpets, hats, books, drugs, motor vehicles and finishing with jewellery. With data obtained from the Internal Revenue Service Source Book of Statistics of Income, the Census of Manufactures and other sources, the period analysed was 1954–7. The general conclusion of the paper was 'Policies dealing with these matters would be an important component in a general policy designed to promote competition'.[28]

Dennis Mueller[29] and John Tilton[30] published their research entitled 'Research and Development Cost as a Barrier to Entry' in 1969. They take Bain's barrier, known as economies of scale in production and Schumpeter's hypothesis which accepts that the entrepreneur whose firm possesses some market power would lead in undertaking innovations, because he is sufficiently free from concerns of survival whereas the competitors have to devote energy, time and money to introduce innovations into their product process. With a vast amount of information referring to American companies, such as Xerox Corporation, firms working in the Petroleum industry, Steel, Big Steel, Oxygen Steel, Pharmaceutical, Electronic Capital Goods, Viscose and others, they demonstrated that R&D works like a barrier to entry because they measured it according to the economies of scale; the major variable used to measure the barrier was the accumulation of patents and know-how on the part of incumbent firms.

The sixties came to an end with several research projects which were able to confirm that barriers to entry exist as a behaviour pattern of the firms into the main industries in USA and the Federal Trade Commission follows closely the evolution of firms which behave illegally.

2.4. The Consequences in Political Economy: 1968 Merger Guidelines

Bain's proposals got a good reception from policy makers in the sixties. The Federal Trade Commission, founded in 1912, used these ideas in order to implement changes in the American market competitiveness. The main goal of the FTC was to protect American consumers. The point is, knowing that FTC only had an indicator of trust into a market, the final product price. If FTC marked the rules of competitiveness and courts tried to solve trust issues.

In the United States the legislation relatives to competition is evolved into the Clayton Act, Section 7, which contends that a merger is prohibited if its effect may be substantially to lessen competition, or to tend towards creating a monopoly. In 1968 merger guidelines were developed by Donald Turner, American Assistant Attorney General, as rules for fair competition between firms. The main organs in conjunction were the Department of Justice, particularly the Antitrust Division and the Federal Trade Commission. The main target of the guidelines was to offer to the courts a regulatory body to prevent mergers, market concentration, and horizontal and vertical integration as well. The theoretical framework considered to be worthwhile was the Structure-Conduct-Performance, mainly with regard to measures of market concentration, economies of scale, barriers to entry and advertising. The main limitation of these guidelines was that they only took into account concentration and how it could be measured. As it is shown in the selected ideas of merger Guidelines included below, only the conglomerate mergers section offers a tool for Judges, close to reasonable proof in judicial terminology, a percentage of total industry production in one, two of the four largest firms of the industry.

In order to understand the guidelines' spirit, they is reproduced, in part, below, with regard to the relevant issues, and the meanings included in the 1968 merger Guidelines:[31]

The Department's antitrust policy understands that a concentrated market structure, where a few firms account for a large share of the sales, tends to discourage vigorous price competition by the firms in the market and to encourage others kinds of conduct, such as use of inefficient methods of production or excessive promotional expenditures, of an economically undesirable nature. A market is defined both in terms of its product dimension (line of commerce) and its geographic dimension (section of the country). The market is ordinarily measured primarily by the dollar value of the sales or other transactions for the most recent twelve-month period for which the necessary figures for the merging firms and their competitor are generally available.

With respect to *mergers between direct competitors*, the Department's enforcement activity under Section 7 of the Clayton Act has the following interrelated purposes:

a) Preventing elimination as an independent business entity of any company likely to have been a substantial competitive influence in a market.
b) Preventing any company or small group of companies form obtaining a position of dominance in a market.
c) Preventing significant increases concentration in a market.
d) Preserving significant possibilities for eventual deconcetration in a concentrated market.

The Department accords primary significance to the size of the market share held by both the acquiring and the acquired firms. The larger the market share held by the acquired firms, the more likely it is that the firm has been a substantial competitive influence in the market or that concentration in the market will be significantly increased.

With respect to *vertical mergers*, the Department's enforcement activity under Section 7 of the Clayton Act, as in the merger field generally, is intended to prevent changes in market structure that are likely to lead over the course of time to significant anticompetitive consequences. In general, the Department believes that such consequences can be expected to occur whenever a particular vertical acquisition, or series of acquisitions, by one or more of the firms in a supplying or purchasing market, tends significantly to raise barriers to entry in either market or to disadvantage existing non-integrated or partly-integrated firms in either market in ways unrelated to economic efficiency.

It is, of course, difficult to identify with precision all circumstances in which vertical mergers are likely to have adverse effects on market structure. The Department believes that the most important aims of its enforcement policy on vertical mergers can be satisfactorily stated by guidelines framed primarily in terms of the market shares of the merging firms and the conditions of entry which already exists in the relevant markets. These factors will ordinarily serve to identify most of the situations in which any of the various possible adverse effects of vertical mergers may occur and be of substantial competitive significance.

Consequently, the Department will not accept as a justification for an acquisition normally subject to challenge under its vertical merger standards the claim that the merger will produce economies, because, among other reasons, 1) where substantial economies of vertical integration are potentially available to a firm, they can normally be realized through internal expansion into the supplying or purchasing market, and 2) where barriers to prevent entry into the supplying or purchasing market by internal expansion, the Department's adherence to the vertical merger standards will in any event usually result in no challenge being made to the acquisition of a firm or firms of sufficient size to overcome or adequately minimize the barriers to entry.

Department's enforcement activity regarding *conglomerate mergers* is to prevent changes in market structure that appear likely over the course of time to cause a substantial lessening of the competition that would otherwise exist or to create a tendency toward monopoly. First type: mergers involving potential entrants, the Department will ordinarily challenge any merger between one of most likely entrants into the market and any firm with 25 per cent or more of the market, two largest firms which shares of the two amount 50 per cent or more, four largest firms in a market in which the shares of the eight largest firms amount 75 per cent or more. Second type: mergers creating danger of reciprocal buying, the Department considers that a significant danger of reciprocal buying is present whenever approximately 15 per cent or more of the total purchases in a market in which one of the merging firms sells are accounted for by firms which also make substantial sales in markets where the other merging firm is both a substantial buyer and a more substantial buyer than all or most of the competitors of the selling firm.

At the end, the Department will ordinarily investigate the possibility of anticompetitive consequences, and may in particular circumstances bring suit, where an acquisition of a leading firms in a relatively concentrated or rapidly concentrating market may serve to entrench or increase the market power of that firm or raise barriers to entry in that market.

The consequence is that courts had only a price as sign of trust, and according to common law, a reasonable price is one fair to both the participants in the oligopoly and to the public. The court must rule that any efficiency merger is illegal because it threatens less efficient rivals or that this kind of merger threatens consumer welfare. This relatively interventionist philosophy was based on the view that scale economies were not important in many markets, that barriers to entry are often high and can be manipulated by dominant incumbent firms, and that supracompetitive monopolistic pricing is relatively prevalent. The main consequence of this kind of antitrust enforcement was that courts could protect anticompetitive conduct by appropriate rule-making.

Oliver Williamson reflected on guidelines in an article published in 2007, he said that Guidelines are the intellectual heritage of Structure-Conduct-Performance school, and the theory of the firms which support the guidelines is that of the firms as a production function, no words about management, within price theory prevailing during the 60s and this where the self-limits lie. In conclusion he noted that 'the 1968 Guidelines scarcely invite an economics defence, the Guidelines nevertheless viewed economies favourably'.[32]

On the other side, as Robert Bork said:

> The Supreme Court, encumbered by an incoherent economic theory of injury to competition through injury to competitors, the mystery of market definition, and the impossibility of reconciling rationally the contradictory values of consumer and small business welfare, may have turned the problem over to the Antitrust Division and may now be contenting itself with ratifying the decisions of the government.[33]

Technically, the only way to demonstrate the existence of barriers to entry was to demonstrate the existence of a non-competitive high price in a market, which is a signal of 'market power' which reflects at the same time a direct correspondence with market concentration. Market concentration is one way of the core firms performing in their market, to improve profits through the price control. Once it gets into this chain, it is possible to establish the correct legislative rules in order to change this bad behavior. The theory of a nonprice competition, opposite to Marshallian theory, opened a new door; the first consequence was that, in 1963, the Supreme Court recognized this analytical distinction in *White Motor Co.* v. *United States.*

The second technical problem refers to collected data capable of confirming empirically the theoretical developments. During the 60s widespread use of cross-section data led the Industrial Organization to sticky conclusions, throughout the 70s new analysts, paid by firms began to demonstrate incorrect conclusions that fit into the lens of Bain theoretical model. In a footnote of William Kovacic, the Chairman of the Federal Trade Commission in 2008, 'from a modern perspective, cross-sectional studies of this kind are inevitably limited by the quality of the data on market structure, which relates to the theory problem of accurately delineating the market's boundaries, much less measuring market shares and entry conditions'.[34]

Conclusions

The conclusion of this chapter is related to the birth of a new economic paradigm. In 1956 a new economic concept known as barriers to entry was born. This concept and its antecedents have deserved consideration at least until 2008, some times in favour and other times against. The long lives of the proposals plus the literature produced by both conflicting economic sides is more than what economic ideas have empirically implemented. This chapter exposes the theoretical framework noted by Sylos-Labini-Modigliani at the end of the 50s and the literature which had its source in their proposals until the end of the 60s; finishing with the political implementation of this economic improvement.

The limit price theory or the Structure-Conduct-Performance paradigm varies in time according to the variety of people who speak and wrote about it, nevertheless it has consequently improved the noncompetitive economy paradigm whereas it offers an answer that is of little use to a lawyer's requirements. At this moment one economic model is able to help courts in its hard work to decide if a firm has behaved badly within the market. The model offers a framework which can help courts because it gives them a new proof of the activities of the firms. The ideal position for a new economic idea is to become a precedent of law. Particularly if a model was built where economists academic are thinking of helping judges, attorneys and lawyers. As far as I know, only two cases went through the courts to the economic literature, the Standard-oil case and the Champion Spark Plug, both have contradictory final conclusions. The former concludes that the company is not using predatory price cutting, while in the latter Champion lost the case against Ford and Chrysler and the judge allows them to produce plugs in order to improve the competence market.

On the other hand, during the 50s barriers to entry began their path as an economic idea; as usual the new idea must be confirmed by empirical demonstration. Several academic reviews published articles about this topic. As the Table 2.1 shows seven articles confirm barriers to entry (one o more depends of the choice framework) and four articles are catalogued as theoretical because they improve or disconfirm the framework proposed by Bain-Sylos Labini.

In Table 2.1, we have classified, in chronological order, the articles about barriers to entry analyzed in this first chapter. The columns respond of year of publication, author of the article, barrier or barriers analysed, predecessors' authors in order to give to the reader a view about the economic thought line following by the author, even his framework choice. The next column contains information about the empirical confirmation of the theory, as main industries which data was used, and when information is available I include period of analysis and Country. The last column contains the author's main conclusion.

3 THE HARVARD AND CHICAGO SCHOOLS: TWO WAYS OF STUDYING BARRIERS TO ENTRY

Introduction

In the previous chapter we introduced a new economic idea or at least a new piece of terminology, as barriers to entry had not been spoken about as such before. Criticism of these ideas emerged from the ideas' diffusion in the 60s. George Stigler criticized the original Bain concept of barriers to entry while nonetheless including other barriers in their book, *The Organization of Industry* (1968).

Barriers to entry as economic idea is full of curiosities, Bain was the founder of Harvard School but worked his whole life at Berkeley University, California. George Stigler was a professor at Columbia University when he became associated with the Chicago School, at the same time that the Report of the Attorney General's National Committee to Study the Antitrust Law (1955) was published. Bain named barriers to new competition but the familiar definition is Stigler's.

We make a distinction between the Harvard and Chicago schools, while keeping in mind that some issues are common to other schools, and some authors are hard at work trying to place them in a specific school. The Harvard School draws up models with practical application for non-abstract business issues; the main theoretical tool is econometrics, its analysis is as well known as the Structure-Conduct-Performance paradigm, and is referred to as the Bain-Sylos Labini-Modigliani limit price. On the other hand, the Chicago School drafts mathematical models into theoretical neoclassical economics where the markets work freely.

It is important to emphasize that both schools have the same goal; defending competition between firms in the industry. Agricultural firms and service firms have not been of interest to researchers before the 90s; however, some conclusions may be useful for them. There is another caveat regarding market demand, the Harvard School accepts that it's possible to manipulate customers.

In this chapter we try to revise one of the most fruitful debates raised during the twentieth century. My target is not to analyse this conflict in depth. This research refers only to barriers to entry and I wish to remain solely within that field. The main actors of these debates were, on one side, the Federal Trade Commission, the Boston Group and the Harvard School, the goal of all was to protect customer welfare and to prevent *market power* held by existing companies from creating barriers to entry. On the other side, the Chicago School's goal was to preserve the free market, contending that when markets work freely, barriers to entry cannot survive in the long run. During two decades the fight was fierce, the battlefield was the courts where firms fought each other or the government; this happened every time one firm reported the bad behaviour of the another. Neither side would finish such a battle unharmed.

3.1. Joe Bain and the Harvard School

Most Industrial Organization studies were conceived by Edward Mason at Harvard during the 1930s, and then extended by numerous scholars. The research programme outlined by Mason sought to learn about imperfectly competitive markets by deduction from careful studies of particular examples. These studies made relatively little use of formal economic theory or of econometric techniques. The point was that while lawyers identified *abusive practices* the economists are seen as the *market power*.

At the end of the 1940s, Joe Bain began to work on the exertion of market power by firms in their own industry and agreements to maintain them. Bain considered it a necessity to learn the industry structure in order to know the conduct and achieve a proposal of performance for firms, most of the time firms pursued the status quo. He respected the scientific framework of the theory of price and the analysis of general equilibrium; he was well acquainted with George Stigler's work and vice-versa. The basic assumption introduced by Bain and changing the neoclassical assumption was that the unit cost goes down when the firm grows. This was the first step toward his theory of the relationship between industrial concentration and extraordinary profit for the firm (understanding as not connected with its own production). However the price theory made incorrect predictions for the behaviour and the performance of the firm within oligopolistic industries. Bain developed a model of how to measure and analyse a large group of industrial variables and barriers to entry in the industry known as Structure-Conduct-Performance. Altogether, Bain built a theoretical price, called limit price, which is used as indicator of non-workable market; this price is the limit at which potential rivals would have no interest in entering a market, because limit price is too low to guarantee profits, while limit price maintains extra profits for incumbents in the industry.

On *Barriers to New Competition, Their Character and Consequences in Manufacturing Industries* (1956) Joe Bain started:

> The more typically American school, however, reflects the popular antimonopoly or 'antitrust' bias of this country, and is consistent in general with a policy position that high concentration is not necessary for efficiency and that much of American industry is substantially more concentrated than necessary. This orientation is evidently in some cases alloyed with a kind of Simons-Knight tradition stemming from the University of Chicago, which (1) admires competition for various reasons, and (2) seeks for facts, or an interpretation of facts, that will support the thesis that atomistic competition is compatible with efficiency in the American economy. A further ingredient of the alloy is of course the views of the institutionalist or quasi-institutionalist interpreters of the American merger movement and of market conduct in American industry.[1]

Scholars of the Harvard School continue working along this line, drawing up models for market structures in different industries, barriers of entry, kinds of competitiveness, degrees of concentration, horizontal integration, vertical integration, delivery market and so on. After this analysis the second step is to understand the behaviour of firms, whether these are competitive, predatory or monopolistic. The last step consists of establishing conditions of performance. The Harvard School hired researchers like Oliver Williamson, Frederic Scherer, Michael Porter and Richard Caves.

The Methodological approach in the Harvard School should be, briefly, to determine the basic conditions of supply (raw materials, technology, and business attitudes) and demand (price elasticity, rate of growth, substitutes, marketing type, and purchase method). As well as more information to establish the market structure in the industry could be for instance, number of sellers and buyers, product differentiation, barriers to entry, cost structure, vertical integration. Once these data are collected, the next step consists of suggesting the conduct of the firm in its market, such as pricing behaviour, product strategy, research and innovation or legal tactics. At the end of the research it should show the performance of an enterprise, its production and allocative efficiency, progress, full employment and equity. The regulatory system could detect bad conduct on the part of the firm under these assumptions, and in this case should act to correct it.

At the beginning of his academic career Oliver Williamson wrote his PhD thesis entitled *The Economics of Discretionary Behavior Managerial Objectives in a Theory of the Firm* (1967). Here he noted that:

> Obviously the causality runs from concentration and entry barriers to profits rather than the reverse. Thus, by focusing on the market structure, the model directs attention to the ultimate determinants of discretionary behavior (competition in the product market) rather than the apparent determinant (the profit rate). Although these market variables might not perform as well as the profit rate among the smaller

firms in the industry, it does not seem inappropriate to use them for studying the behavior of the two largest firms where the relationship between market structure and behavior is probably reasonably direct.[2]

In *Industrial Market Structure and Economic Performance* (1970) Frederic Scherer included behaviourism to the old price theory and established differences between microeconomic analysis and Industrial Organization as follows:

> How does industrial organization analysis differ from pure theory? In fact, there is a fair amount of overlap, but there are also significant differences in goals and methodology. What distinguishes the scientific economic analysis from other people who think, talk, and write about economic topics, according to Schumpeter, is a command over three main techniques; history, statistics, and theory. Theory being defined as a box of tools or a set of models which permits one to deal analytically with broad classes of cases by focusing on certain properties or aspects they have in common.....the industrial organization economist must have a command over all three techniques to make the most of his trade. We must be at home in pure microeconomic theory or forge rigorous predictive links between fundamental assumptions and their behavioral consequences.[3]

3.1.1. Main Limitations of the Structure-Conduct-Performance Paradigm

Determining how a market structure works is a huge target, especially determining whether the conclusions are decisive enough to reprove an agent of the market. Firms' main goal is to earn more money, to improve profits and to appropriate clients of rivals in the market; where there is room for fair competition. When the tort is among competitors, courts have the legal authority to punish this behaviour yet this does not happen when the offended is the customer, who has to do something to defend himself. Policy markers have to borne this responsibility, but even they need to provide robust arguments in order to change the rules of thumb in an industry. The Harvard tradition tried to offer a scientific model able to demonstrate that the rules of free market don't work as well as would be expected. And this is the core of weakness of limit price theory, trying to suggest that its model is worthwhile for generalization between industries or firms.

Most attacks of the theoretical model of the Harvard tradition came from Chicago, Richard Posner in a symposium of antitrust law and economics held that the Industrial Organization:

> Tended to be untheoretical, descriptive, institutional and even metaphorical. Casual observation of business behavior, colorful characterizations (such as the term 'barriers to entry'), eclectic forays into sociology and psychology, descriptive statistics, and

verification by plausibility took the place of the carful definitions and parsimonious logical structure of economic theory.[4]

As expected, the results of this way to making economics created a contradictory economic theory. After these words, the theoretical war between these two schools of thought was visible.

Scholars of Harvard have been admitting their weakness, as is show in the following quotes. Michael Porter said that the main limitations of S-C-P paradigm was that the limit price model assumes that all firms in an industry are identical, in every way except size; which means that a firm makes choices based on economic objectives. The Bain-Sylos model is very close to the Marshallian model and keeps the same methodological inconvenience which is according to Porter: 'A general theory of oligopoly eluded (and still elude) IO researchers, and established modes of oligopoly were built on grossly unrealistic assumptions such as mechanical reactions functions, identical cost and demand functions among competitors, and the like'.[5] However, the main limitation of the Harvard School was statistical tools and the small amount of data. In 1987, Bresnahan and Schmalensee wrote, 'While few followed Bain's lead immediately, the journals began to fill with cross-section work in the 1960s as computation costs fell and government-supplied data became more widely available'.[6] Really, one of the first consequences of Bain's proposals was a raising interest in collect data; both schools of thought benefited from this issue:

> The careful collection of new evidence was always central to the case study tradition in both its 'Harvard School' and 'Chicago School' variants. But data collection is not a terribly activity, and as traditional case studies fell from fashion, so did the construction of new data sets.[7]

Other relevant criticism of the Harvard arguments to regulate markets was the consequences of these regulations, perhaps respectful incumbents with the law; they made problems because of it. During the period Structure-Conduct-Interventionist, some policy decisions had ill effects; Rubinfeld rescued the case Procter & Gamble in order to illustrate a bad consequence of tied economies of scale with extra-profits.

> Economies of scale are illustrative. That they can create a barrier to entry was emphasized under Bain's point of view, whereas the clear benefits that scale economics provide were given little recognition. For example, in 1967 The Supreme Court argued that 'possible economies cannot be used as defense to illegality' (Federal Trade Commission vs. Procter & Gamble Co.)[8]

Nowadays, and through the lens of globalization it is possible to defend that market power and high concentration could result from efficiency. This point will be argued in this book in Chapters 6 and 7.

In the same vein, Lawrence White said that two important decisions showed the change in direction. In *Continental T.V. Inc.* v. *G.T.E. Sylvania Inc, 433 U.S. 36* (1977), the court declared that territorial restraints should be examined under a rule of reason, rather than being automatically condemned as per se illegal under the rule of Schwinn (dated in 1967 in the trial *United States* v. *Arnold Schwinn & Co, 388 U.S. 365*) just ten years earlier (which upheld Sylvania's practice of requiring its dealer to sell only from specified locations, a practice that amounts to vertical market division) and in *United States Steel Corp.* v. *Fortner Enterprises, Inc.* 429 U.S. 610 (1977) 'The court found that the absence of market power in the tying market meant that a tying arrangement was acceptable'.[9]

3.2. George Stigler and the Chicago School

The Chicago School was founded by Frank Knight and Jacob Viner during the 1920s. The traditional Chicago School, or neoclassical theory, used models of the competitive firm, which means markets function freely, price and technology are known by bargains, with both firms and customers, and owners effectively controlling the use of their assets. The firm behaves in a price system but not its management, which is to say if the system works well, the resources are allocated well. Only with imperfect information is the risk relevant in the theoretical model. In 1942 George Stigler published *Theory of Price*. The production theory came from of Frank Knight, who Stigler always recognized as most important teacher. Stigler argued that a system of business should be explained as a market where the owners of any kind of assets sell them to the businessmen in exchange for money.

Some years later, in 1968, George Stigler published *The Organization of Industry*.[10] This book maintains some barriers to entry and discusses others of Bain's barriers to new competition. Stigler describes the most common definition of barrier to entry in an industry as 'a cost of producing which must be borne by a firm which seeks to enter an industry but is not borne by firms already in the industry'.[11] He argued against Clark Senior's article about workable competition and said 'Perhaps the most traditional test of the absence of competition is a high rate of return on investment'[12] this proposal was rescued, almost forty years later, by Bruce Greenwald and Judd Kahn in *Competition Demystified*, as a good indicator of the existence of barriers to entry. Also barriers to entry means a cost advantage that an incumbent firm enjoys compared to entrants. With such an advantage, the incumbent firm can permanently raise its price above its costs and thereby earn a supracompetitive return. At the same time, Stigler wrote that the tendency to prevent new competitors entering the market is normal. The limit price proposed by Bain would not have been welcomed in the Stiglerian's theory of organization of industry, because a rival could appear when it likes, and incumbents have to maintain the price even if the new entrant waits seven years to take the decision to enter. It is worth assuming that industry demand is growing, and to assume that the same price over time does not expect changes in demand which are able to change output shares and prices.

After a thorough analysis of Bain's barriers to entry, he enumerated the following private (and in some cases illegal) techniques: control of needed resources, commercial disloyalty such as a reduction of price, bribery and coercion of clients, fomenting resentment among workers, originating rumours regarding the inferiority of competitive products and sabotage. Stigler didn't agree with Bain's theory about the barriers to entry in industry mainly because according to him there could be no permanent obstacles, only transitory ones. Stigler argues against the market structure proposed by Bain, because he considered it irrelevant. He said that the ability to agree price in an oligopoly market is independent of the size and number of oligopolists, 'the theory of oligopoly is solved by murder'[13] and no empirical evidence support the theory. The Chicago School has great confidence in the long-term effectiveness of the working of the market mechanism.

Under the influence of George Stigler and others identified with the *Chicago School*, increasing use was made of the tools of Marshallian price theory, but little explicit modeling of imperfect competition was done, and econometric techniques were not heavily employed. Since the 70s the activity of the Chicago School continues unabated, with recent work making heavy use of the developing tools of noncooperative game theory. During the 70s, the Chicago School became to be less fundamentalist and in this new way John McGee, one of the fathers of *predatory pricing* who in 1958 defended the Standard Oil Company as a good company and not acting to cut prices in industry, in 1980 he said 'would speculate that large firms can stay large, and prosper, merely by acting ugly'.[14]

The main article, as scientific repercussion, about predatory pricing was written by Phillip Areeda[15] and Donald Turner[16] in 1975. They argued the lack of economic analysis of predatory pricing, and the point out that 'Selling by unremunerative prices is not competing on the merits. There is, therefore, good reason for including a 'predatory pricing' antitrust offence within the proscription of monopolization or attempts to monopolize in section 2 of the Sherman Act'[17] but proving the predatory behaviour of firms seems extremely rare.

Courts in the United States used to define predatory pricing as when firms sell their product below cost. Areeda and Turner offered a new framework to understanding, with no doubts, how demonstrate predatory activities. Selling at a loss is a desperate tactic for a firm, but when this behaviour has the goal of deterring new competitors, it acts as a very high barrier to entry. A firm produces goods with fixed and variable costs and knowing that in economics the short run is considered the period which a firm cannot replace or increase its equipment while in the long run the firm can vary quantities of all inputs, and for that reason all costs are variable over the long run. Also, we assume that the firms attempt to maximize profits in the short run. Under these assumptions 'The firm that is selling at a short run profit maximizing price is clearly not a predator ... because a necessary but not sufficient condition of predation is the sacrifice of shot run profits'.[18]

In front of the limit price theory they pointed out that a monopolist can charge whatever price will maximize his profit, and the lower price would thus be the long run, profit maximizing price, it is usually called limit price 'contrasted with the higher, short run, profit maximizing price determined without reference to possible entry'.[19] Areeda and Turner concluded with an accurate sentence:

> In sum, without even considering the formidable administrative problems which supervising a monopolist's pricing polices would impose, we conclude that more or less permanently low prices are competition on the merits and not an abuse of power or exclusionary behavior for the purposes of section two of the Sherman-Act.[20]

From the time when the market price is equal to average cost, they assumed that this kind of competition is on the qualities; still in the case in which average cost is above the marginal cost, because this special situation will not happen unless the monopolists possess an excess of capacity. They made an exception, when the price is below the marginal cost but above average cost; the reason is only possible in the special case of demand excess, because the firm must be required producing at minimum average cost. If excess of demand is permanent, and pricing below marginal cost, with the consequence of high output level, the firm is deterring enter of rivals and some adverse effect over the market. Their conclusion doesn't let any place to doubts 'We conclude that prices at or above marginal cost, even though they are not profit maximizing, should not be considered predatory'.[21] Only a monopolistic price below marginal cost should be presumed in a predatory or deterring practice. The unique problem predictable should be to assessing the marginal cost of any firm; for any kind of product, in each factory. Areeda and Turner accepted use of a benchmark price calculated in a *reasonably anticipated* way.

The Chicago tradition insists on using a theory of prices renewed to resolve the efficient functioning of the market to achieve welfare-enhancing ends. Inside the framework on neoclassical price theory, and assuming the perfect competition model, Stigler and Demsetz work in a maximized profits model, without information costs, and with a lot of suppliers and customers bargaining in the market. The first attack on the Bain-Sylos Labini was that advertising serves to provide information to customers. The other attacks were that the efficiency of the firm will be related to the vertical integration, and then that size and scope of the firm are determined by its efficiency. For the Bain-Industrial Organization studies the behaviour of the firm will be to maintain and even expand its place in a monopolistic market.

In 1976 Richard Posner wrote *Antitrust Law: an Economic Perspective*, this book includes several articles previously published. The reintroduction of litigation cases in the analysis of competition could be considered a new way to demonstrate his premises, keeping in mind that, at this time, the traditional Harvard School used to confirm the hypothesis with cross-section data. The new approach analyses predatory price cutting under the lens of exclusionary business practices, such as tie-in agreements, vertical integration, reciprocal buying, exclusive dealing, price discrimination and group boycotts, all of them remembering Stigler's barriers to entry. His conclusion was: 'Of course, the most effective method of excluding a competitor is to have lower costs that make it possible to under price him without selling at a loss'.[22]

The most remarkable contribution made in this book is that of critics of lawyers and judges, and economics, incidentally, because in 1976 the use of economic tools was generalized, Posner wrote: 'Since lawyers and judges are more comfortable with conspiracy doctrine than price theory, the displacement of emphasis form the economic consequences to the fact of conspiring is natural. But it is inconsistent with an effective antitrust policy'.[23] The criticism cited above marked an inflexion point in the economic theory of competition, Posner changed the way of thinking, the existing conspiracy, now we must to prove without doubt, this means if we consider punishing a company because of its behaviour we have to gather evidence against it. The economic framework and the traditional rule of reason implemented by lawyers are only consequences of the theory; firms work in the real world and don't know anything about models, dummies or other theoretical tools. Posner included a list of evidences of collusive behaviour:

Evidences of collusive behaviour relevant to such a demonstration are the following:

1. - Fixed relative market share; but it has not always been recognized as a proof
2. - Price discrimination; it would be very difficult to draft a decree forbidding systematic price discrimination that did not constrain or inhibit legitimate pricing behaviour as well.
3. - Exchange of price information
4. - Regional price variations (like cement)
5. - Identical bids
6. - Price, output and capacities changes at the formation of a cartel; unfortunately determining when capacity is excess is normally very hard to do

7.   - Industry-wide resale price maintenance; nothing more than a symptom of a dealer's cartel
8.   - Declining market share of leaders
9.   - Amplitude and fluctuation of price changes; disastrous results
10. - Demand elasticity of market price; if demand is inelastic at the current market price that price is not the monopoly price
11. - Level and pattern of profits.[24]

Richard Posner presented a paper at the Conference on Antitrust Law and Economics held at the University of Pennsylvania in November 1978, which was directed by Oliver Williamson. Posner returns to the two different approaches to the problem, the Chicago and the Harvard approach seeing and underlying single issue: the behaviour of firms in their markets. The point of his article was that through the lens of price theory the simplification of proposals, in order to explain long-term equilibrium, transformed monopoly questions into *simple* but not *easy* questions. Economic models built under Marshallian premises were impeccable, but the limit of these powerful simplifications is that they are inapplicable in a real world. We therefore need a new theory capable of proving the existence of welfare costs in a monopoly situation.

Some kinds of noncompetitive behavior such as tie-ins, vertical integration, restricted distribution or predatory pricing were analysed by Posner in his 1979 article entitled 'The Chicago School of Antitrust analysis', 'tie-in' means requiring a buyer to buy a second product as the condition of buying the first (ink with mimeograph machines, for instance). According to the economic theory of Joan Robinson this is a simple case of price discrimination, in the long run the monopolist's output moves to the competitive level of production. Oliver Williamson noted that price discrimination involves extra transaction costs. Posner concluded 'that tie-ins should not be forbidden seems both correct and increasingly influential on academic opinion'.[25] Vertical integration understood as the behaviour pattern when a supplier A buys all the retail outlets which distribute his products and thus obliging supplier B, in order to compete, to open his own chain of retail outlets. The theoretical analysis of this problem is the equivalent of analysing how new entrants manage to gain access to an industry and pertains to existing legal prescription. Restricted distribution or the possibility to of reselling a product among his distributors includes advertising or product differentiation as a barrier to entry. The conclusion of Posner was that 'advertising and related promotional methods create monopoly power, at least in any sense relevant to antitrust policy, cannot be derived from the premises of economic theory'.[26]

Predatory pricing means selling below cost in order to increase the number of clients in two ways, firstly because your price is cheaper than competitors, and secondly, predatory pricing pushes a new entrant to neglect the decision to invest in the industry. This behaviour is traditionally analyzed as *strategic* and difficult to detect. Of course, this is a short-term strategic decision, while long-term equilibrium remains, predatory prices will disappear. The predatory pricing theory is still being studied and ties in with the analysis of economies of scale. Posner concluded his article about the different approaches to barriers to entry between Harvard and Chicago Schools with a dramatic sentence: 'Differences remain, but increasingly they are technical rather than ideological'.[27]

3.2.1. Main Limitations of Chicago School Paradigm

The attack on Chicago School proposals (Stigler more than Knight) appeared early, the distance between mathematical models and the real life of firms was the cornerstone of the criticism. Simultaneously with the empirical demonstration of the survival of extra profits in the long run when the firms are capable to create and maintain any kind of barrier to entry; this point breaks the natural point of equilibrium in the markets defended by the neoclassical school of economic thought.

During the 70s, at the start of the limit price theory developed in the Harvard School, Chicago yielded the *predatory pricing* as one of the theoretical approaches to bad behaviour of firms. Initially proposed by Fritz Machlup, this was appropriated for economic science in 1958 by John McGee. The best formulation of predation was made by Robert Bork and cited by McGee, in his own words:

> Predation may be defined, provisionally, as a firm's deliberate aggression against one or more rivals through the employment of business practices that would not be considered profit maximizing except for the expectation either that 1.- rivals will be driven from the market, leaving the predator with a market share sufficient to command monopoly profits, or 2.- rivals will be chastened sufficiently to abandon competitive behavior the predator finds inconvenient or threatening.[28]

The issue is the probability of the occurrence of predatory behaviour and the means available for detecting it.

However, John McGee wrote in 1980:

> Theoretical and empirical work has shown that efficiency explanations of industrial structure can no longer be ignored. Massive mergers have been outlawed, and the theoretical and empirical support for many traditional 'monopolizing' practices and 'entry barriers' badly undetermined. Under the circumstances, it is not surprising that a new generation, like older ones, would speculate that large firms can stay large, and prosper, merely by acting ugly.[29]

Arguments against predatory pricing are that business maximize profits not rents, and predatory prices are more costly to predator than to prey. It is not clear if predatory behaviour acts against existing competitors or potential competitors. Sometimes predators are a not credible threat. It is not easy to prove that predatory behaviour is taking place. McGee wrote: 'There are also good reasons to be cautious in developing rules against predatory conduct'.[30] Even Chicago's academia was not especially in favor of predatory pricing because they considered that this behaviour is rare.

One stronger criticism of the Chicago model comes from the core of methodological studies; the relevant evidence is that which is explained by or *fits into* the model, conversely, irrelevant evidence is that which cannot be reported by the model. That means the model itself determines relevance. Secondly, in a neoclassical market model it is not easy to distinguish between efficient and inefficient policies. Economic efficiency, the pursuit of which should be the exclusive goal of the antitrust laws, consists of two relevant parts: allocative efficiency and productive efficiency. A properly defined antitrust policy will attempt to maximize net efficiency gains, which is inconvenient for the Chicago School because: 'Within the market efficiency model, wealth distribution is not an 'economic' concern at all'.[31] As Hovenkamp maintains the identity of gainers and losers is irrelevant: 'If a policy produces bigger gains to businesses than it does losses to consumers, the Chicago School would approve the policy as efficient'.[32] Baxter made a dramatic review of Posner's book *Antitrust Law*, he said that he had non-mathematical skills transcending elemental geometry and because of that the prisoner's dilemma was not dealt by Posner, technically lawyers don't know anything about games, as a consequence they see the '"Antitrust problem" typically is too many trees and no forest'.[33] Under the assumption of Posner in 1976: welfare can be measured by constant dollars, in which case a transfer of dollar from a customer to a firm has no welfare implications; because a change is efficient in the Pareto sense if the gains experimented by the winners of the exchange is larger than the losses of the loser. Once again, looking back at the economic thought, this should be well located into the Utilitarianism theory.

Price theory perspective doesn't take into account the number of firms into a market, ensuring whether it is a decisive point, but it is relevant nonetheless. Different firms' strategies take into account the possibility of collusion, product differentiation and the available information as much as the high cost in obtaining it. These issues should be considered when building a model able to explain how markets work.

3.3. The Points of Disagreement

Three topics were the main areas of disagreement between the Harvard and Chicago Schools. The first one concern to the firms which work in a market are able to create and to hold barriers to entry then profits will survive in the long run. The second disagreement is over the analysis of barriers to entry; a bad theoretical model could have disastrous consequences if policymakers used it to regulate the market. The third and last disagreement relate to the two previous ones, and is over the possibility that empirical data confirms the robustness of the economic model.

3.3.1. Profits in the Long Run

A survival profit in the long run becomes very old very fast in economic literature. It is not particularly risky to hold that come from the Walrasian equilibrium theory. In this case, within a competitive market the new entrants erode the profits of incumbents, because both have to share clients, and in a price war entrants and incumbent prices fall until they reach the competitive price; this price is the equilibrium price within which the profits are close to zero; in other words, as a result of competitiveness profits tend to zero in the long run. Technically, that profit rates have a tendency to converge on a single, competitive level is fundamental to a normative evaluation of the competitiveness of a market economy. In the real world, it seems that several firms can earn a lot of money for decades; is this wrong?

In 1986, Dennis Mueller carried out his research to show that profits in some markets survived in the long run. In a clear Structure-Conduct-Performance framework, and using cross section data, Mueller built a econometric model, plenty of variables, that were capable of demonstrating that the persistence of market power results in long run profits. The analyzed period was 1950–72, and he used the 1,000 large companies (with information of the Federal Trade Commission) of which only 583 could be identified as larges in 1972. 'The results of this book indicate that firm characteristics such as market share and growth add significantly to our ability to explain long-run differences in company returns.'[34] The report of this book for the policymakers in USA was clear 'Most mergers that have occurred in this country in the last thirty-five years have probably taken place with the expectation that they would neither substantially lessen competition nor improve economic efficiency'.[35] One year later Ariel Pakes improved the econometric model, he proposed distinguishing between profit margin and rate of return of capital, but he said that the Mueller's estimate of the long-term average profit rate is an innovative estimate. Pakes wrote about the convenience of considering 'movements in factor prices and in demand that generate common movements in the profitability of the firms in an industry, does have behavioral implications'.[36]

In the same vein, Carl Davidson and Raymond Denckere built a model in which a long run competition in capacity maintains a short-term competition price. It was published in 1986. They made a Bertrand-Cournot theoretical model with equilibrium in capacities. The conclusion of the model was: 'when a firm is choosing a production quantity is that it is choosing a long-run cost curve appropriate for that level. In the short run, competition occurs through price, but price policy and accompanying output decisions are not independent'.[37]

The survival of long-term profits generated several articles, John Cubbin and Paul Geroski tried to demonstrate it in the United Kingdom, with data of 217 large UK firms, forty-eight three-digit industries, during 1951–77, the conclusion was that there is a persistence of profitability above average profits, and they wrote: 'market power may indeed be a shared asset, but some firms certainly seem to enjoy a good deal more of it a good deal longer than others'.[38] Geroski continued working on market dynamics in the S-C-P paradigm. In 1987 he wrote both articles with Robert Masson, the last of them together with Joseph Shaanan. In the first article they hypothesized barriers to entry as an equation where the independent variable π depends on: industry growth, minimum efficient scale, industry capital requirements, advertising intensity. They assumed that an optimal level of profits exists that describes the extent to which limit pricing is in the interest of incumbents, and which, of course, depends on the height of entry barriers, exactly into a S-C-P model. Their conclusion is accurately:

> The long run equilibrium level of actual profits is given by π_i. It depends only on the height of entry barriers, and is thus (by construction) independent of the level of concentration. Hence, any correlation observed between profits and concentration in this system reflects both the short and the long run profitability consequences of the potential for inducing entry.[39]

Both know the Contestable Markets framework built by Baumol, Panzar and Willig and published five years later, in a footnote they said that:

> The contestability argument asserts that the only features of market structure that will affect performance are entry barriers (other than scale) and that whether a market is monopolized or not is largely irrelevant. If, however, market concentration affects π_i, then that implies that monopoly effects exists in the long run.[40]

In short, barriers to entry survive in the long run because profits survive also.

In 1987 Geroski, Masson and Shaanan wrote an article in order to better explain the main conclusion of the article mentioned above, the relationship between market concentration and profits, they noted that whether market concentration $C(t)$ depends on long run equilibrium levels of concentration C^* and a speed of adjustment (named λ); and defined λ as a function of price cost margin, a vector of entry barriers, and the time necessary to construct a new plant. Then C^* depends of industrial growth. Cleary λ and C^* are not observable, but can be indirectly identified and estimated by equations and in the model, both can be considered as a nonlinear restriction to the function $C(t)$ or market concentration. One year later Paul Geroski and Alexis Jacquemin published an article about the persistence of profits in the European economic industry, with data come from France, United Kingdom and Germany in 134 large firms: fifty-one from the UK, twenty-eight from West Germany and fifty-five from France. The profits were measured as rates of return on total assets, before taxes; they concluded that: 'Specific assets and barriers to entry may enable firms to earn higher profits in the long run, such factors may also enable firms to enjoy purely transitory returns for longer periods of time'.[41]

At present no agreement has been reached on this subject. In 2002 Pankaj Ghemawat confirmed that things still haven't changed 'The structure of an industry would earn positive economic profits over long periods of time. Chicago School doubted the empirical importance of this possibility'.[42] In the same vein Schmidt writing about profit maximization in 1989 stated 'For the Chicago school profits that have not been eroded over a long time show a firm operates efficiently in the market'[43] while Harvard School representatives admit that high profits can persist over a longer period of time when the observed enterprise has cost advantages (or market power) in comparison to actual or potential competitors.

3.3.2. Theoretical Demonstration of the Existence of Barriers to Entry

The second point of disagreement is about the possibility of demonstrating the existence of barriers to entry and their role in the market competitiveness. This is the cornerstone of this book, I'm trying to illustrate if economic science has chance of having a theoretical model as robust as possible about barriers to entry and accepted by everyone, the Harvard school developed the limit price theory, with some weakness, as a theoretical framework useful in demonstrating collusion between firms and other not legally binding agreements because the equilibrium price in a market should show the bargaining among actors. If the price in which output is selling and buying is far from a competitive price, economists set an indicator out of this market that doesn't work in the limits of competitiveness. Meanwhile Chicago School never accepted this framework. Richard Posner wrote about it '"barriers to entry" given the lack of any clear theoretical basis for oligopoly theory, given Harberger's tiny estimate of the welfare costs of monopoly'.[44] There is another argument to disapprove barriers to entry; in a free market every friction tends to disappear in the long run, both profits; unless the barrier was created by any kind on political intervention. Next Demsetz's cite illustrate perfectly the disagreement on this point:

> For Bain and Ferguson, such negative slopes demand curves are identified as barrier to entry if price exceeds unit cost, but not otherwise. For Stigler, the limiting factor is

more properly viewed as demand than as one of cost advantages, so (probably) from his viewpoint no barrier is involved.[45]

Herbert Hovenkamp wrote long ago about the Harvard–Chicago conflict and he held that: 'The Chicago School has been quick to recognize the role of the State in the creation of entry barriers'.[46] Which means policymakers can and do make barriers to entry that do not disappear with competitiveness between firms within an industry. These barriers survive in the long run and give extra profits to the firms which also survive in the long run. A few years later Hovenkamp was quite polite, particularly when he argued that the Chicago view about barriers to entry was that the traditional definition penalized firms for being innovative and efficient: 'Particularly if high entry barriers was used as a justification for government intervention'.[47]

3.3.3. Data and the Contrast of Hypothesis

The last point of disagreement is the data which theoretical proposals confirm or disconfirm. This topic is like an ouroboros, in the beginning of limit price theory when scholars had a new theoretical model they needed to confirm their hypothesis, in this case, they asked the Federal Trade Commission about the possibility of gathering new information that came from the firms. The answer was a complete mailing cross-section data, better than the old historical series; Sherwin Rosen wrote about the relationship between theory and data that Stigler sketched in 1939:

> How a more flexible organization of production would better accommodate varia-
> tions in output and why this refinement of the standard model was needed to account
> for empirical time-series insensitivity of average productions cost ... and how an
> industry pricing practice can be explained as a subtle form of price discrimination.[48]

During the second half of the century more complicated data series have been gathered, since the 90s, panel data should be considered as an improvement in the information of companies available for researches.

Joe Bain changed the core of empirical research in industrial economics for statistical studies of industry cross-section data. Richard Schmalensee and Timothy Bresnahan in *The Empirical Renaissance in Industrial Economics* (1987) wrote about the statistical tools. They argued that empirical research in industrial economics should make more use of panel data. The methodological basis for considering panel data better than cross-section data was explained by Cheng Hsiao; in *Analysis of Panel Data* (2003) he said:

> If individual behaviors are similar conditional on certain variables, panel data provide
> the possibility of learning an individual's behavior by observing the behavior of oth-

ers, in addition to the information on that individual's behavior. Thus, a more accurate description of an individual's behavior can be obtained by pooling the data.[49]

Deepening the econometric question, Harvard tried to improve its model through better proof of new data, Bresnahan and Schamalensee wrote:

> Like the earlier 'Chicago-style' industry studies, recent efforts generally focus on particular aspects of conduct. But, in a departure from the earlier traditions, the tools of imperfect competition theory are now routinely used or construct explicit structural models, and the latest econometric techniques are used to estimate structural parameters and to test structural hypotheses.[50]

The point is that the relation between structural hypotheses and estimated coefficients is often unclear or controversial, Schmalensee wrote some years later:

> Panel data sets make it possible in principle to control for or to study cyclical and secular disequilibria and to analyze directly the long run differences among industries [while] most of the cross-section literature focuses on relations involving one or more of the following variables: profitability, concentration, and barriers to entry.[51]

And the assessment of buyer concentration is difficult to prove. The author is thinking in legal terms, not in vain is he an expert with several years of legal experience under his belt. Bresnahan wrote some years later about price–cost margins, and he noted that they are not directly observable, and that if perfect competition used this data, the correlation between market power and price cost margins should be questioned.

Again, panel data solved this issue, Cheng Hsiao wrote in 2003:

> The use of panel data also provides a means of resolving or reducing the magnitude of a key econometric problem that often arises in empirical studies, namely, the often heard assertion that the real reason one finds (or does not find) certain effects is the presence of omitted (mismeasured or unobserved) variables that are correlated with explanatory variables. By utilizing information on both the intertemporal dynamics and the individuality of the entities being investigated, one is better able to control in a more natural way for the effects of missing or unobserved variables.[52]

3.4. Harvard and Chicago School's influences

It is possible to argue that most of the ensuing studies about market structure, as applied to all kind of industries, follows the methodological proposals of the Harvard School and altogether they analyse some kinds of barriers to entry. Bain considered the need to understand the structure of industry in order to understand its behaviour. This will make it possible to formulate a theory of how firms operate since firms tend to maintain the status quo. The analysis of the firms which would fall within the Chicago School framework assumes that the firm behaves within a price system but not its management, which is to say that the system works well and resources are allocated efficiently. Only with imperfect information is risk relevant in this theoretical model. On these brief key proposals hinges the supervision of industrial markets during the second half of the twentieth century. If we assume that firms try to earn money at any price, it seems convenient to control their activities when this behaviour damages other companies or customers. But if we assume that markets work in *workable competitiveness* the better acceptable intervention should be respect the market rules.

If during the 60s and 70s, the Harvard School came to have a huge influence in the antitrust policy in the United States, as was shown in the past chapter, the Chicago School theory gained relevance during the Reagan era. The Supreme Court changed its final conclusions towards relaxing the markets control. Kovacic and Shapiro don't let doubts about the direction of the change, they wrote:

> The new Chicago School, 1973–1991, continued the earlier Chicago Tradition by abhorring comprehensive regulation of entry and prices ... many of Richard Nixon's appointees to the Supreme Court and the lower courts had comparatively narrow preferences for antitrust intervention ... during this period the Justice Department and the Federal Trade Commission brought numerous cases challenging dominant firm conduct, United States versus AT&T, Maryland versus United States. For the most part, the courts gave dominant firms considerable freedom in choose pricing, product development, and promotional strategies.[53]

Daniel Rubinfeld wrote 'Antitrust Policy' in the *International Encyclopedia of Social and Behavioral Sciences,* and deserves a special consideration in this paragraph, which tries to find a meeting point in this conflict, about the Influence of Chicago School during the 1970s, Rubinfeld said:

a) A belief that the allocative efficiencies associated with economies of scale and scope are of paramount importance.

b) A belief that most markets are competitive, even if they contain a relatively few number of firms. Accordingly, even if price competition is reduced, other nonprice forms of competition will fill the gap.

c) A view that monopolies will not last forever. Accordingly, the high profits earned by dominant monopolistic firms will attract new entry that in most cases will replace the monopolist or al least erode its position of dominance.

d) A view that most barriers to entry, except perhaps those created by government, are not nearly as significant as once thought.

e) A belief that monopolistic firms have no incentive to facilitate or leverage their monopoly power in vertically related markets (the 'single monopoly rent' theory).

f) A view that most business organizations maximize profits, firms that do not will not survive over time.

g) A belief that even when markets generate anticompetitive outcomes, government intervention, which is itself less than perfect, is appropriate only when it improves economic efficiency.[54]

In an article entitled 'Antitrust Enforcement: Where it has been; Where it is going' (1983) Oliver Williamson held that the reforms of antitrust enforcement in the 1970s had their origins in critiques of the 1960s. He wrote:

> These include (a) the insistence of the Chicago School that antitrust issues be studied through the lens of price theory; (b) related critiques of the entry barrier approach; (c) application of the partial-equilibrium welfare-economics model to an assessment of the trade-offs between market power and efficiency; and (d) a reformulation of the theory of the modern corporation whereby transaction-cost-economizing considerations were brought to the fore.[55]

In the same vein Kovacic and Shapiro wrote that it is clear that the courts, under the Chicago School influence, were trimming back antitrust doctrine. They wrote:

> Yet the same analytical tools that economists used to challenge interventionist antitrust doctrine of the 1950's and 1960's, by showing that certain practices often could increase efficiency and boost competitiveness, were simultaneously offering new methods for arguing that many business practices sometimes could harm competition.[56]

Conclusions

Industrial Organization as a branch of economics differs from microeconomics in that it attempts to build models which are as close as possible to the real world. At the beginning, orthodox economists failed to recognize the methodological advances which were being made in the subject. In time, the models used in both Industrial Organization and Microeconomics have come to resemble each other ever more closely, and today it would not be easy to distinguish which of the two approaches was being used in any given study of an industry.

One of the most stimulating methodological debates within Industrial Organization is that between the Harvard School and the Chicago School, largely because Chicago has always preferred models taken from Microeconomics. Joe Bain and George Stigler were the main protagonists in this debate, even though they were in agreement over many points as to how to build models which explain different industrial structures and the behaviour of firms.

After years of fighting, three issues have yet to be resolved, the survival of profits in the long run in an industry, the analysis of barriers to entry and the use of collected data in order to confirm the proposed hypothesis. The first issue refers to how to achieve equilibrium price in an economic theoretical model in the long run. If we assume a perfect competitive market then the free play of market strength tends to reduce the price to a level where companies' profits should be close to zero. Under the lens of the Harvard School, it is possible to demonstrate the survival of companies' profits during several years, long run. In other words, that means the economic science must reject this assumption, because it doesn't fit into the real world. Another key issue over which they disagreed is known as barriers to entry in an industry. That is to say, a hypothesis which seeks to explain how firms are already set up prevent a new firm from entering successfully into their market, thus reducing the market segment of the industry which had been conquered and maintained at great cost. In the competitive framework of the Chicago School almost every kind of friction in a market disappears in the long run. And barriers to entry will follow suit. The last issue in conflict is about information, mainly statistic data collected by state institutions. The point is what kind of information the firms want to share.

4 BARRIERS TO ENTRY IN THE 1970s

Introduction

This chapter refers to the economic literature about barriers to entry during the 1970s; no Guidelines were published at this time. The 1968 Guidelines were still enforced. The organization of this chapter is centred on the analyses of the four main barriers to entry, because the changes that occurred at this time were made in order to concentrate scientific efforts on demonstrating with more worthwhile theoretical approximations the existence of all four kinds of barrier. The present chapter covers new theoretical models that tried to disconfirm the Bain-Sylos Labini paradigm. Some, but not all, of these came from the University of Chicago. The old Bain framework began to be considered unsuccessful and new theoretical proposals were published. At the same time, several articles were published at Harvard University trying to prove the existence of barriers to entry.

During the 70s the analysis of barriers to entry changed, mainly because the different researchers chose only one of Bain's proposed routes. For instance and maintaining an order within the large number of articles this one route produced, it may be useful to pause before considering the following four barriers: the use of excess capacity in the production system, industrial concentration and its consequences for the share in profits, advertising and new models of entry.

These years presented a new battle between the Harvard School and the Chicago School. The winner was the Chicago School because during the 1980s neoclassical theory was predominant in the economic background. The Chicago School was beginning to demonstrate that the oligopoly theory developed by the Harvard School through the limit price was weak. The essence of this criticism was that limit price is a not equilibrium price and in the long run every market tends toward equilibrium. On the other side, American courts worked with the 1968 Guidelines, which respond to Harvard School concerns; first the Guidelines followed the ideas proposed by John Maurice Clark and Joe Bain. The noncompetitive markets and barriers to entry have been analysed in the limit price theory. From 1968 to the present day, courts and judges used several guidelines as a reference point to judge firms' behaviour within markets.

In this chapter, there are three relevant kinds of barrier to entry, excess of capacity, industrial concentration and advertising; each barrier exposed below includes articles written for and against it. Another section is included on entry models; these are separate because they should not be analysed in a barrier to entry framework but rather as a new theoretical proposal to explain the possibilities that a company has when trying to enter in a market. This model concluded with easy entry or its opposite, and it reflects the possibilities that a company has to become incumbent in any kind of market.

This is a period of constant intellectual debate, and one of the most fruitful times in the creation of hypotheses of work, proposals, models and so on. Wenders, Caves, Spence, and Kamien and Schwartz should be considered the most cited authors during the following decades. Keeping in mind that Michael Spence won the Nobel Prize for Economics in 2001 and that Kamien and Schwartz's 1975 article included a proposal about timing of rival entry was included in the 2000 Guidelines.

4.1. Excess Capacity as a Barrier to Entry

In the 70s the excess of capacity as a measure of barriers to entry was the most successful proposal. The amount of excess of capacity installed in an industry is easy to collect using statistics, because is just the difference between the real production of the industry and the maximum possible production. By following the old Cournot model; the new theoretical model named the pricing limit theory which was developed by Joe Bain, Paolo Sylos-Labini and Franco Modigliani during the 60s had used it to explain this barrier to entry. This new model demonstrated and predicted that while a new firm is trying to enter in an industry the incumbents increase their offers to inform a new rival that the market doesn't need new producers because they are able to supply the market. At the same time, when rivalry among firms grows the prices fall, in the Bain-Sylos model the limit price exists because the industry can reduce the price under threats to the new entrants.

Cournot's model, or the oligopoly model, is the one which describes how equilibrium is obtained by adjusting production between the incumbent and the entrant. Joe Bain called the use of capacity to expel new entrants into the barrier known as economies of large scale, where an established firm's behaviour in the face threats from rivals is described as an increase of output industry which reduces the price and discourages the entry of new firms. In 1957 Edward Chamberlin brought excess capacity into economic models, changing his assumptions of 1927, when he considered the excess of capacity as *wastes of competition*; but it wasn't until the early 70s when the development of one of its main consequences began: to have an opportunity to exclude a new competitor using excess of capacity in the production process. Maintaining excess capacity in a plant gives the chance to raise production in the short-term, the object being that competitors see market prices fall, technically until Bain-Sylos-Modigliani's limit price. Usually the competitor has calculated his investment project at the highest prices.

Since the 1970s, several authors such as Wenders, Gaskins, Pyatt, Kamien and Schwartz, Osborne and others have worked on disconfirming excess of capacity as a barrier to entry. Most of them can be included within the Chicago School framework. The point of their proposal was how much it costs to maintain excess capacity in the production process and the difficulty of controlling this cost in the long run. They discussed the centre of the limit price theory because within a limit price model, the oligopoly solution is reached by the movement of production of the industry towards equilibrium. Therefore, the total production of some of the industries analysed depends on the use of its production capacity. Whereas the scholars who follow Bain-Sylos-Modigliani's price limit theory, believe that excess capacity works as barrier to entry, while other researches don't agree, and affirm that to maintain an excess capacity is expensive for firms in every industry. We should at this point review all those authors on this subject, but not all of them have written exclusively and directly about the problem of excess capacity.

In more detail, the contributions of these authors were, John Wenders who in 1971 wrote 'Excess Capacity as a Barrier to Entry'. He discusses excess capacity as a barrier to entry, or as a way to intimidate potential entrants. His assumption is that excess capacity increases short-run costs in four different ways:

> a) The higher short-run costs involved in operating a plant designed for a smaller level of output, b) the higher costs caused by building a plant which sacrifices efficiency for flexibility, c) higher costs of carrying excess inventory: and/or d) the higher costs caused by increasing output rapidly when the entrant appears.[1]

However, in the long run the monopoly price loses its significance, and at the same time invalidates the Sylos Labini postulate, because excess inventory means sacrificed efficiency, and will only be valid if one were entering a very competitive industry. Paradoxically only in this case could the entrant expect to be ignored.

In the same vein, and based in an old theory that Osborne developed in 1964, Darius Gaskins worked on dynamic limit pricing, his article was published, in 1971, in *The Journal of Economic Theory* and entitled 'Dynamic Limit Pricing: Optimal Pricing under Threat of Entry'. He built a theoretical model which had the following conditions, as the dominant firm's discount rate increases it will sacrifice a portion of its long-run market share and rival firms will respond to price signals more rapidly than the dominant firm. Gaskins like Wenders came to the conclusion that:

The major substantive changes in the optimal pricing strategy resulting from growth of the product market are that the equilibrium price is raised above the limit price, and the dominant firms with no cost advantage no longer price themselves out of the market in the long-run.[2]

In 1972 Morton Kamien and Nancy Schwartz built a model entitled 'Uncertain Entry and Excess Capacity' on the basis of the model of 'the equilibrium of the firm' developed by Nicolas Kaldor in the middle of the 30s and expanded successively by Harrod, Hicks and Hahn; with modern models of limit pricing. They conclude that the firm attempts to retard entry by means other than pricing, however, they have set out: 'An alternative hypothesis to the sales maximization theory of Baumol to explain failure to maximize instantaneous profits'.[3] This is an issue which should be rescued later.

Graham Pyatt in 1971 also wrote about excess capacity as a barrier to entry. His model referred to Chamberlin, Hahn and Harrod's models. He supports the idea that a new entrant will make a successful entry if it can earn profits with a price-output combination which cannot be cut by the firm within its industry. In this case the incumbent firm accepts less than normal profit only in the hope of eliminating a new entrant. The conclusion of Pyatt was 'We have found that in many, but not in all situations, firms may maximize profits in the short-run even if they believe that this will lead to new entry'.[4]

The main attack on the Bain-Sylos-Modigliani limit pricing theory was made by D. Osborne in 1973; he developed a model in order to express his dissatisfaction with the limit price under the assumption of the irrationality within the theory. Osborne worked within Stackelberg's framework which means that model equilibrium must be reached by price negotiation; as opposed to Cournot's model when model equilibrium is reached by product sharing. In conclusion, Osborne wrote:

> The limit price, when it is different from the Stackelberg price and hence irrational according to the postulates, could nevertheless be a rational choice if the monopolist were uncertain about the number of potential entrants. His post-entry profits might then fall short of those at the block point, leading him to regret his choice. Thus the lower computed profit at the block point could be preferred to the apparently greater but uncertain profit at the Stackelberg point.[5]

At the same time, David Qualls was developing a model in order to assess barriers to entry, with a new and sophisticated methodology, and a large amount of data demonstrating his hypothesis. He tried to confirm or to disprove Bain-Mann's barriers to entry; his theory had a proposal based on the analysis of variance. Qualls concludes: 'The use of this technique merely reflects the virtual impossibility of quantitatively pinpointing an assessment of the specific height of the barrier to entry except with regard to broad class ranges'.[6] That means, barriers to entry exist, but it is very difficult to know how high they are. He used data from twenty industries for the periods 1936–40 and 1947–51, such as Automobiles, Cigarettes, Liquor, Typewriters, Fountain pens, Copper, Steel, Farm machinery, Petroleum, Soap, Shoes, Gypsum products, Metal containers, Canned fruits, Cement, Flour, Meat Packing, Rayon, Tires and Tubes. He used data from thirty industries for the period 1950–60, including the industries cited above plus nickel, sulphur, chewing gum, ethical drugs, flat glass, beer, baking, etc.

In the same vein, and based on Bain-Mann models and after taking into consideration Rhoades's disagreement with Mann, Dale Orr, in 1974 built an index of entry barriers and its application to the market structure performance relationship; he also found statistical problems, mainly when assessing barriers and concentration, because of multicollinearity, in the majority of cases the variance in profit rates across industries is left unexplained. This means that some conclusions should be interpreted with caution. He used data from the main Canadian industries, and his calculus was an index of overall barriers, with the following significant variables: capital required, advertising, R & D, risk and industrial concentration. He used data from the industries of smelting and refining, aircraft, breweries, petroleum, toilets, cement, iron, distilleries, cotton, tobacco batteries, pharmaceuticals, motors and so on.

Richard Caves, Javad Khalilzadeh-Shirazi and Michael Porter in 1975 tried to demonstrate the market power through the scale economics, not through the industrial concentration as it was usual. The main reason is that they improved the limit price theory, and that means to employ the cost curves better than the amount of product concentrated in a few number of firms. Technically they moved the analysis from the industry to the firm. Their proposal was that

> Bain's analysis of the sources of barriers to new competition suggests that scale econo-
> mies to the plant or firm allow sellers to elevate price somewhat above average cost
> without attracting new rivals. This paper proposes a new way to form these surrogate
> measures.[7]

One assumption of Bain's model was that incumbents in an industry decide to produce beyond minimum efficient scale; because production costs curves are J-shaped. If a new rival firm expects an established firm will hold their output constant, including price falls, the production limit at which new entrants decide to come in should be a suboptimal scale. Because the cost disadvantage of small units and the elasticity of demand interact to determine the most likely scale of entry. This new proposal gives a new variable worthy to contrast with data, an inverse measure of variations in average unit cost. They said 'The data permit an approximate comparison between the average plant sizes of multi-plant firms and of single-plant firms in numerous four-digit United States manufacturing industries'.[8] The data used comes from forty-two American industries and sixty

British industries to contrast their model; for the American industries the source was the Census Bureau's Enterprise Statistics. The Minimum Efficient Scale, which was the popular name of the variable, is co-linear with seller concentration, and perhaps proves a statistically insignificant determinant of profits, the authors had to refine the model: 'We need to know whether this insignificance occurs because concentration is really an endogenous variable controlled by other elements of market structure or because multicollinearity is built into the proxies for minimum efficient scale and other structural variables'.[9]

Arthur de Vany in 1975 developed a theoretical model to prove how firm excess of capacity used is. He applies his theory in the taxi market and in airlines. The target was to compare the price-getting in regulation with the price that should be obtained in a competitive market. The first case is equal to the price in a monopolistic-competition model. He demonstrates the existence of a price above the efficient level. The efficient level is calculated within a model of marginal cost curves and average cost curves while the monopolist established his efficient level according to his interest in raising price by cutting output (using less than capacity installed in his industry). In conclusion De Vany wrote that the lesser level of production is caused by the regulator's setting price. Looking at the airlines De Vany reached the same conclusions, but he warned about the necessary distinction between overcapitalization and excess of capacity. The main conclusion of these case studies should have considered which regulation could make the industries produce a non-optimal level of capacity, and at the same time underutilize capacity. Canadian scholars also tried to discover how the use of installed capacity in an industry works in their country. Dickson made the study for 146 Canadian industries from 1961 to 1966 and said: 'Scale efficiency is positively related to market size, concentration, exports, and steepness of the average cost curve and negatively related to effective rates of protection, transportation costs and the advertising-sales ratio'.[10]

At the end of the 70s Richard Caves, Michael Porter and Michael Spence rescued some of Bain's barriers and the limit price theory. While Chicago scholars were developing new arguments to remove the limit price theory, Friedman, Osborne, Orr and Posner; the answer from the Harvard School was strong and direct, 'the simplifications conceals more that it exposes'.[11] In 1977, Caves and Porter improved classical barriers to entry in order to get mobility barriers; under the limit pricing theory they developed a model as a framework for empirical analysis and research in the field of industrial organization. Mancur Olson gave them new support for their proposals, his theory of groups. They made a new catalogue of barriers to entry, and they included a new concept: exit barriers. Caves and Porter disproved the theories of Needham, Wenders, Gaskins and Baron. They used several empirical studies of different American industries, the major home appliance industry, US computer industry, petroleum industry and the aluminium Industry.

Michael Spence[12] developed a model which had entry threats and he compared this proposal with the limit price theory. His main addition to the Bain-Mann model was:

> The empirical research of Bain (1956) and Mann (1966) uses rates of return to measure the effects of entry barriers. While this is done partly because the relevant price-cost margins are difficult to measure, the analysis here suggests that rates of return may be the best index of the combined effect of structural barriers.[13]

In the same vein, Steven Salop wrote about strategic entry deterrence in 1979, his main conclusion was that in limit pricing models, the pre-entry price is effectively converted into capital by its role in forming the basis of the entrant's expectation of cost and elasticity. To convert to capital is something that makes sense with the Stiglitz proposal as it pointed out that all instruments of deterrence create intertemporal relationships in the profit function. The next step should be to discriminate between sunk cost and no sunk cost, because this is the key to open the door of capital as a barrier to entry identified as absolute cost advantage. In 1980, Curtis Eaton and Richard Lipsey worked on models where exit barriers are entry barriers. Using Caves and Porter, Schmalensee and Spence's theoretical proposal, they wrote a paper about the durability of capital as a barrier to entry. They based their proposal on the intertemporal commitment of specific capital to a market plus decreasing costs which creates an entry barrier.

In 1979 and 1980 Avinash Dixit worked on a model of duopoly suggesting a theory of entry barriers, under the Bain-Sylos-Modigliani model, with proposals of Gaskins and Wenders, resolving as in a Nash equilibrium, the cornerstone was without doubt the credibility of threats. His second paper about the role of investment in entry deterrence is a model under Spence's proposals from which the conclusion laid in the necessity to know whether one firm can change the rules in its own favour. Game theory began to be used as economic framework at the end of the 70s, and became the tool to resolve threat-entry models.

In fact, excess of capacity works as barrier to entry if rivals believe the threats launched by incumbents. In the case of capacity the point is what costs the old producers support and for how long. Only if one takes into account the storage of no sellers' products and the reduction of price during the fight is it possible to reckon how convenient it is to keep the market in front to share it. The limit price theory had serious theoretical problems to hold any industrial's price as a measure of a barrier to entry. At least, a barrier to entry denominates the utilization of excess of installed capacity in an industry in order to expel new entrants in the market could be reconsidered.

4.2. Industrial Concentration or Seller Concentration as a Barrier to Entry

Industrial concentration works as a barrier to entry because of its repercussions on profit concentration and in the randomness of agreement between incumbents to maintain established market share, shortly collusion. Furthermore, it is worth assuming that industrial concentration allows control of the price within the industry, and at the same time the entry of new competitors; at least, under the lens of limit price theory. Under the considerations written above, Industrial Concentration as barrier to entry fits into the limit price theory of Bain-Sylos-Modigliani. During the 70s, the main defence of this barrier comes from The Federal Trade Commission, mainly the Director of the Bureau of Economics, Michael Mann.

One of the first articles published opposing the Bain-Mann proposals of Industrial concentration were written by Stephen Rhoades. In 1970 and in 1972, Rhoades built a statistical model of regression in order to discuss the relationship between industry concentration and rate of return within an industry. He analysed twenty-three of the thirty manufacturing industries included in previous Mann's study. His conclusion was that further investigation is required before accepting or rejecting his own hypothesis. Michael Mann, who was Director of the Bureau of Economics at the Federal Trade Commission, and Stephen Rhoades, who was staff economist at the same Commission, began a controversy about an *outright statistical mistake* due to use of a dummy variable. That means, the correlation between industrial concentration and rates of return exist notwithstanding. The point was, and still is, to decide which is the best way of assessing both.

Frederic Scherer tried in 1970 to offer a new way of assessing pecuniary economies of scale. He used the simple case which large firms obtain price concession from suppliers, and his conclusions were:

> If differential bargaining power is the cause, income is merely redistributed from the supplier to the buyer. Still the ability to obtain such concessions can solidify a large firm's position in the market, and so pecuniary economies in procurement are, like other scale economies, a concentration increasing influence.[14]

Furthermore, big enterprises should enjoy a cost advantage in raising financial capital, usually they get lower interest rates, and other privileges in their loans. The conclusion is clear, if researchers have observable data in the real world, firm size distributions 'often correspond closely to those generated by stochastic process models'.[15] That means researchers have the option of demonstrating unfair competition in markets due to market power of big firms, using statistical tools.

The main consequence of the step forward in this field is the inclusion of *behaviour* in the traditional Industrial Organization models. The theory of Thomas Schelling written in his famous book entitled *The Strategy of Conflict* (1960) allows for Scherer to assume that when market concentration is high, the sellers' decisions about prices are dependent, and firms barely avoid recognizing their connections, the advantages are bigger than looking only after their self interest, understood as compete to each other and get more clients. Scherer wrote: 'As a result, we should expect oligopolistic industries to exhibit a tendency toward the maximization of collective profits, approximating the pricing behavior associated with pure monopoly'[16] Since Scherers's hypothesis some economic scholars assume that within an oligopoly, coordination among incumbents to agree costs and prices will occur. This is an old rule of economic theory, but now it is possible to solve the old problem that refers to how much responsibility in prices is due to the cost and how much is due to changes in demand. The conclusion of Scherer leaves no doubts to our mind:

> Coordination of pricing decisions is also aided when a trade association develops standard cost accounting systems for the benefit of its members. When pricing decisions are based upon some kind of full cost rule, we should expect as a corollary that prices will be more responsive to changes in cost than to changes in demand.[17]

Harold Demsetz in 1973 worked on the research programme in Competition and Public Policy at UCLA. Demsetz also discusses industrial concentration and market power. He began his paper recognizing that the power due to industrial concentration is necessary to the economic system, with these words: 'To destroy such power when it arises may very well remove the incentive to progress'.[18] He said that industrial concentration does not always mean monopoly power behaviour, the correlation is not direct, at any given collusive price, the amounts of monopoly profits will be proportional to output, also capital investment will be proportional to output, so we can expect the rate of return to be invariant with respect to size of firm. Demsetz demonstrated his conclusion empirically by calculus of industrial concentration and monopoly power for ninety-five three-digit American industries in 1963.

At the same time, David Baron demonstrated the opposite idea of Demsetz, using Cournot's model, and others like the Osborne, Sylos Labini, Modigliani, Bain, Mann, Kamien and Schwartz models, found a positive relationship between profitability and concentration and agreed with the behaviour of classical Cournot markets with regard to entry. Also Baron accepted, like Harrod, that: 'If entry is easy the established firm will price equal to average cost in order to prevent entry'.[19] Within the limit pricing theory, he said that: 'Risk aversion may act to lower the limit price and thus has an effect similar to barrier to entry'.[20]

In order to demonstrate the relationship between barriers to entry and profitability, Thomas Duchesneau built a regression model in 1974. He made a dummy variable representing entry conditions and tested the correlation with concentration ratio. The empirical data used thirty American industries from 1947 until 1967. His conclusion is clearly 'in conjunction with the Bain-Mann results'.[21] At the same time, and using data collected from 461 four-digit industries from 1961 to 1966, Charles Berry found that in industries where concentration is high, it is more likely that entry by small firms would reduce the market share, together with no factor which tends to reinforce concentration.

Sam Pelzman wrote in 1977 about gains and losses from industrial concentration. His model put the Bain and Stigler theories together. The point was to separate how much of the profits due to concentration fit in to cost effects and how much is due to price effects. The measure is connected with Minimum Efficient Scale of production, which was defined above, in excess of capacity as barrier to entry. Bain and Stigler thought that 2 per cent of national output is the minimum efficient scale for the steel industry. In spite of knowing that smaller firms had less than 20 per cent of national capacity in America steel industry in 1951. Pelzman developed this proposal in 165 four-digit Standard Industrial Classification manufacturing American industries from 1947–67 and his conclusion was: 'any extensive deconcetration program would risk imposing losses which are many times greater than the typical estimates of the benefits such a policy might have been thought to produce'.[22] The recommendations for policy makers, the way to destroy this barrier to entry is through forced reductions of concentration, does not seem to be very convenient.

Some years later Frederic Scherer built a theoretical model in order to explain the causes and consequences of growing industrial concentration. His first step was to analyse Pelzman's article on concentration written two years before. Scherer says that the links between concentration and unit cost changes supported by Pelzman were partly *spurious*. Bain-Stigler's barriers tradition has several mistakes, according to his point of view; the majority of them in the analysis of the measure of variables. The indices of two-digit industry groups, price deflators, technological change, unit cost in plant labour, materials, capital costs, etc. offer to Scherer, using data of Federal Trade Commission, some statistical solutions for these problems, mainly for those conclusions that have policy implications. For instance and on statistical evidence, it would seem to be interesting to keep in mind that: 'Once process technology is generally available, its rate of diffusion through the rest of the industry is likely to be accelerated with a more fragmented market structure, if existing statistical studies on this point are any guide'.[23]

During the 70s industrial concentration was analysed within the Bain-Sylos model and considered a barrier to entry. The biggest industries in America show production's concentration in the hands of four or five firms. But it isn't easy to separate industrial concentration aimed at earning more money through market power from the concentration due to necessary economies of scale, although both presuppose the survival of the company in its market, nonetheless.

4.3. Advertising as a Barrier to Entry

Nicholas Kaldor, in 1950, was the first economist to take advertising into account as an issue that should be considered because of its relationship with competition. Lester Telser in 1964, following this path theorized about barriers to entry and advertising. William Comanor and Thomas Wilson wrote in 1967 an original article about advertising and market structure, following the Bain-Sylos model they built a multivariate regression equations in order to explain the inter industry variation in profit rates using different variables, seller concentration, the rate of growth of demand, economies of scale in production in relation to the size of the market, absolute capital requirements for a plant of minimum efficient scale and advertising. This is the first time that advertising was used as data into an economic model. A lot of research flourished following this proposal.

To shed some light on advertising as barrier to entry it is convenient to have a basic knowledge about the writings and the results of certain research. The authors selected, for the 70s, who proved advertising as barrier to entry are Schmalensee, Vernon and Nourse, Siegfried and Weiss, Needham, Martin, Comanor and Wilson, and Demsetz.

It was Richard Schmalensee who explained how advertising works as a barrier to entry is the field in the 70s. He wrote a book entitled *On the Economics of Advertising* (1972) where he outlined the first step of advertising into the economic field. Two years later, and using mainly the models of Bain, Caves, Scherer and Orr, this author built his own model in order to explain how advertising erects a barrier to entry because of its ability to create loyalty to the products of existing firms having dynamic effects on demand. He said: 'It seems plausible to suppose that both loyalty and inertia can be adequately modelled by a demand structure characterized by distributed lags'.[24] Even with demand asymmetry which is not sufficient to produce barriers to entry this issue has been analysed in econometric studies of demand and it is usually described by means of some form of distributed lag mechanism in the models estimated. Schmalensee concluded that it may build worthwhile theoretical models, which advertising effects should be used by firms in order to deter entry of rivals in a market.

In 1973, John Vernon and Robert Nourse set up a statistical regression model with two dependent variables, the firm's net income plus interest expense, divided by total assets, averaged over the years 1964–8 and the firm's net income divided by shareholders' equity, averaged over the years 1963–8. The independent variables chosen were the estimated shares of the big four firms over the total sales in each four-digit industry; a dummy variable that the estimated shares of the four firms' total sales should be between fifty and zero. The weighted average of industry advertising to sales ratios, the overall advertising to sales ratio of the firm in those four-digit industries, the weighted average of percentage changes in industry sales in the firm's market, the firm's diversification and the firm's 1968 total assets. The conclusion of this article was that:

> Positive relationship between profit rates and advertising/sales ratios for large manufacturers of non-durable consumer products. We can report also only mild support for the hypothesis that capital requirements barriers to entry (measured by asset) are effective and equally weak support for a positive relationship between profit rates and concentration.[25]

This paper confirms the proposals of Schmalensee's 1972 work about advertising and barriers to entry, while contradicting Bain's earlier proposals concerning capital requirements as barrier to entry. Paradoxically, and when the analysis discriminates the kind of industries, they find that in consumer goods industries, firms attempt to create product differentiation through advertising, while in product goods industries they employed personal selling to achieve the same end.

In the same vein, John Siegfried and Leonard Weiss, in 1974, developed a theoretical model, in order to estimate *true* profits and rates of return for thirty-eight consumer good industries using ten large advertisers' information. They analysed the level of advertising, annual rate of depreciation and rate of growth of advertising expenditures; the period considered was 1958–63. They found a positive correlation between advertising and profits.

Douglas Needham continued the work which Schmalensee began. He worked within the Sylos postulate and in opposition to Osborne's conclusions. In 1976, he wrote about the non-price aspects of firms' behaviour, and he was interested in how advertising works as a barrier to entry. He didn't believe that advertising works automatically, but as a response to entry. He studied the behaviour of incumbent firms as to how much advertising spending must be made in order to ruin a new entrant. In this case, he wrote that the worthwhile framework should be built to include elasticity functions. The main point is to determine whether an observed positive correlation between profit rates and advertising intensity is attributable to advertising entry barriers, yet he couldn't find a good answer, because:

> One would therefore expect to find a closer correlation between the advertising intensity and profit rates of industries than between the advertising intensity and profit rates of individual firms in different industries, whatever the underlying causes of differences

in E$_d$ (Price-Elasticity of demand for the firm's product) and E$_a$ (Advertising-Elasticity of demand for the firm's product) between firms in different industries.[26]

Richard Schmalensee carried out his early research on advertising and barriers to entry. Since then, his framework has changed, adopting Salop and Willig's theoretical model, while including Caves and Porter's research. In 1978 he wrote about the behaviour of a new industry: it seems that price competition was avoided and rivalry focused on new brand introductions, which tends to deter entry and protect profits. Schmalensee applied this model to the breakfast cereal industry. Their assumptions were, first, in this industry the best available evidence suggests that the minimum efficient firm size in this market involved 3–5 per cent market share. Second, scale economies of this magnitude would not seem sufficient to explain the prolonged persistence of very high profits. Third, neither patents nor ownership of the sources of raw materials is important in this industry, and fourth, neither the absolute capital costs of efficient entry or cost nor any of the other factors would seem sufficient to explain the lack of entry into this market during the 1950–70 period. The solution to this dilemma is to create product differentiation. In this case, the barrier to entry turns from an old theoretical model to noncooperative games, such as a limit pricing theory to the new theoretical framework to be enforced in economics.

One year later, in 1979, Schmalensee published a new paper about antitrust policy, as far as I am aware, this was his first report to the Federal Trade Commission, one of many cases where Schmalensee has been required, one of the last being the Microsoft case in the 2000s. In his 1979 research he worked for the Federal Trade Commission on the case known as Realemon. Two corporations which produced lemon juice began a fight to control the Chicago area: Borden's Realemon Foods subdivision and Golden Crown. In 1971 Realemon's management had begun to consider: 'Golden Crown a force to be reckoned with',[27] consequently Realemon maintained different list prices, promotional allowances and discounts in different regions as well as different prices for different individual customers. Realemon made high sales and Golden Crown accused it of having unreasonably low prices. Schmalensee analysed this case under different hypotheses, predatory pricing with the conclusion that proof of this behaviour have been extremely rare. Even with the use of average variable cost as a proxy for short-run marginal cost it was not possible to maintain that Realemon sold lemon juice below its own average variable cost. Also, Schmalensee tried to confirm or disprove the facts by the theory of umbrella pricing. This theory assumes that the new entrant expected the maintainance of the price of industry by the incumbents, this hypothesis didn't work in this case. The only barrier to entry susceptible to theoretical demonstration was: 'Realemon's trademark was an important source of its power to exclude competition is apparently based on its historic price premium and on expert testimony characterizing it as a successful differentiated product'.[28] However, the empirical demonstration of any barrier to entry has to overcome the difficulty to fitting the facts of the case into a theoretical model; and by the way, this argument shows the weakness of the 1968 Guidelines enforced at this time.

At the same time, Stephen Martin published a paper entitled 'Advertising, Concentration and Profitability: The Simultaneity Problem', in which he comes to a similar conclusion to Schmalensee. Martin estimated a general profitability equation with variables to measure variations in the entry conditions in an industry, variations in the price elasticity of demand, etc. and a measure of profitability is the price–cost margin, and the capital-sales ratio appears to allow for a normal rate of return of capital. The conclusion was: 'We have outlined a model of industrial organization within which advertising intensity, seller concentration, and profitability are simultaneously determined'.[29]

Harold Demsetz revived the old proposal of Comanor and Wilson, about advertising and profits, next to the distinction in two possible sources of intangible capital coming from George Stigler. He found positive correlation between profit rates and advertising intensity and fails, and said that it was acceptable: 'to support the belief that advertising derive their value from the creation of barriers to entry'.[30] The period analysed was 1958–67 and he tested it empirically in seventy-seven American industries.

William Comanor and Thomas Wilson made a survey of 'The Effect of Advertising on Competition' in 1979. They both worked at the American Trade Commission; however in this paper they do not necessarily represent its views. They revised the literature of advertising as barriers to entry; in a sort of conclusion Comanor and Wilson wrote:

> The primary source of disagreement lies in the fact that the market power achieved due to advertising results from the willingness of consumers to purchase high priced highly advertised products when lower priced substitutes are available... The key issue is how consumer preferences for highly advertised products should influence the policy implications of the observed relationship between advertising and competition.[31]

This conclusion will need more research, we will return to this issue in the next chapter.

4.4. Entry: a New Theoretical Framework

Morton Kamien and Nancy Schwartz developed a new theoretical model with uncertain entry in 1975. They said that oligopoly theory has progressed along two lines. The first line, into old Cournot model tries to analyse firms' behaviour in order to defend their peice of the pie. The second line, into limit price theory, studied the firms' actions to preserve positive profits. Kamien and Schwartz presented a model within which the timing of rival entry is regarded as a random variable whose probability distribution is dependent on current industry price. They assumed that the potential rivals were attracted by the recent price rather recent profit and the speed of entry is one dimension of potential rivalry.

The first version of this idea enjoys a good reception in the scientific community, and this is one of most cited articles in Industrial Organizations theory. It was very brave proposal in which game theory was used for the first time in models of entry. Under this proposal a lot of papers flourished and the idea of timing was included in the 2000 Guidelines.

In this vein, in 1975, Paul Gorecki published an article about the determinants of entry in the United Kingdom manufacturing sector from 1958–63. He applied the old Bain-Sylos model in fifty-one British industries in order to confirm that economies of scales, product differentiation are barriers to entry because they are correlated with direct estimates. In 1978, Richard Levin worked out that technical change could become a barrier to entry. With the Kamien and Schwartz model of uncertain entry, he explores the influence of market structure, and with a textbook explanation, drawing on the work of Bain, Sylos Labini and Modigliani he invokes the concept of barrier to entry. His premise was: 'the existence of barriers to entry cannot explain the persistence of excess profits, because barriers to entry, even if effective in the short run, tend to be eroded in the face of market growth and the diffusion of knowledge'.[32] Under this assumption the main point at issue shifts to attempts to discover the mechanism for the reproduction of barriers to entry. This involves industrial innovation, and that means Industrial Organization has to abandon the old theoretical tool which supposes that all firms within the same industry are identical. This really is a new path in the analysis of barriers to entry, mainly due to relaxation of the neoclassical assumptions about firms' behaviour; meanwhile it should be possible to find optimal long-run equilibra.

De Bondt also used the Kamien and Schwartz model in order to develop a model of entry lag, and he obtained suggestive conclusions: 'Our analysis suggests that such behavior may be consistent with long-run profit maximization in industries where rivals need a time interval to make their entries effective'.[33] More theoretical models, where the price changes when a new firm gets to enter in an industry, are developed at the end of the seventies. These models allow us, when discovering new pre-entry and post-entry prices, to determine whether the entry really occurs or not. For instance, the model built by James Friedman[34] in 1977 into his article entitled 'On Entry Preventing Behaviour and Limit Price Models of Entry' suggested a model which entry preventing behaviour is possible. He built a game model: he turned Bain's limit price in a monopolistic industry entry to which is free. Under the assumption made above, the optimal price for a firm is inversely related to the size of its own capital stock; because the equilibrium under monopolistic behaviour in this market set up when firm is playing in, and he wants to know what profits he would have under such equilibrium. This proposal connects directly with strategic behaviour of the firm and can be considered one of the pioneers in this field.

Other research about entry models was published at this time, the core laid in strategy. There should be considered the seed over that Michael Porter built his strategy competition model, which will be analysed in the next chapter. In 1978, Howard Newman wrote about strategic groups, within the limit price theory or structure-conduct-performance framework. The first change proposed by Newman within the traditional limit price theory was to assume that industry's member firms differ not only in their market shares, but also in their individual goals, that means to include multiple strategic groups' analysis in the oligopoly theory. The oligopolies should be analysed into a model of rivalrous conduct, and made a deep research in the case of industries integrated vertically. Newman said that 'Our analysis of strategic groups suggests that this case of a competitive game with no goal congruence should be allotted parity with the prisoners' dilemma case as a possible non-trivial situation in oligopolistic markets'.[35] This article suggests that oligopoly' markets with heterogeneous strategic groups can change agreements on a common set of market goals and reduce some tacit agreements.

In the vein of strategy and entry deterrence model; at the end of the 70s, 1979, Michael Spence rescued the old von Stackelberg model, because strategic behaviour can be better analysed under the lens of this model. The market equilibrium in the Stackelberg model should be reached by changes in relative prices. The main point proposed by Spence is that entry is viewed as occurring sequentially and in response to the dissemination of information about the market's growth and its potential. Incidentally, this point means reviving the Edith Penrose proposal about how a firm grows. The von Stackelberg equilibrium is based upon the assumption of asymmetric behaviour by the firms; because of the incumbent firms in a market move first, the entrants should be to consider only the residual market opportunities. Michael Spence worked in the Federal Trade Commission as Steven Salop did, and both published different models of entry deterrence. Salop did so arguing about innocent entry barriers, such as scale economies or sunk costs. He built a model in which the deterrence instruments, such as capitalization rate, brand selection, innovation and advertising are altered. And the rules of post-entry interaction followed Nash-Cournot equilibrium. Joe Bain, at the time, had used the limit price as a signal for post-entry intentions. Salop in turn used advertising as a way to manipulate the signally process, and got the game equilibrium with a mixed strategy of randomizing prices (an entry-deterring noisy monopolist).

Paul Joskow and Alvin Klevorick in their article entitled 'A Framework for Analyzing Predatory Pricing Policy' said that predatory pricing: 'Describe[s] the adoption of a pricing policy that somehow restricts competition by driving out existing rivals or by excluding potential rivals from the market'.[36] They defined predatory behaviour as a special rule in business because the predator sacrifices short-run profits with expectation to earning long-run gains. This behaviour 'involves a reduction of price in the short run so as to drive competition firms out of the market or to discourage entry of new firms in an effort to gain larger profits via higher prices in the long run than would have been earned if the price reduction had not occurred'.[37] In order to help the fair market competition, economic science should offer a framework able to demonstrate this conduct in front of a court. These authors proposed to evaluate the effects on long-run market outcomes, and the structural characteristic could be considered capital requirements, brand preference, or condition of entry as technology among others. But they realized that they were unable to help antitrust policy.

Leonard Weiss in 1979 analysed the case of *United States* v. *IBM* in order to shed light on a sticky judgment. Weiss showed how the Structure-Conduct-Performance framework demonstrated that industrial concentration facilities collusion among incumbents, how barriers to entry should be considered and the price-cost margin of the leader firm raise. He argued against Bain-Sylos postulates whose cross-section data ignored important factors based on profit rates and price margins, where the possibility of error is large for both of them. He said under consumers testimony 'provides an indication of very strong brand loyalty on the part of IBM's customers and implies an extremely high product-differentiation barrier for potential new competitor',[38] that means IBM is a dominant firm protected by very high barriers to entry. At least, this case is an example to take into account, with Weiss' advice: 'The antitrust authorities could safely permit mergers that increased concentration short of the critical level. Within that range, increased concentration would gain economies of scale for us without the undesirable effect on price'.[39]

The end of 70s is the point when game theory began to offer a new framework to explain the non-competitive behavior of firms. Game theory provides new tools to improve limit pricing theory. The market is regarded as a supergame in which one established firm and one potential entrant are players. Both players know all the relevant demand and cost functions, and throughout the paper, noncooperative behaviour is assumed. As Kovacic and Shapiro wrote:

> Game-theoretic methods dominated industrial organization theory in the 1970's and 1980's. The flexibility of game theory allowed economic theorists to generate equilibrium predictions in settings involving a wide range of conduct, from R&D decisions to advertising to product positioning, as well as the classic problem of oligopolistic pricing.[40]

They accept the possibility that some kind of conduct could deter entry, for example, contracts. During the 1990s the analysis of contracts began to be a new and interesting field of research.

4.5. Consequences in Political Economy

During the 70s, the consequences of empirical and theoretical demonstration of the existence of barriers to entry were quite contradictory. There was not a new political regulation in order to change markets structure, but there was a predisposition of courts to correct a confirmed instance of bad behaviour within a market. Excess of capacity is directly connected with timing of production and the market size, no one firm can predict demand or the number of new clients in a year. Faced with this economic problem the rational behaviour of a firm is to keep an expense capacity in standby. A discontented client is not a faithful client, and firms cannot afford to have them. However, it is also true that an excess of capacity allows for incumbents to bring prices down when feel the threat of a rival, mainly if this rival is an outsider and is looking for new clients. Even in the case which allows to demonstrate the use of excess capacity to push a rival out, the legal regulation of this barrier to entry seems, almost, inadequate.

The industrial concentration is in touch with economies of scale. Therefore it is not possible to know in an accurate way, when and which degree of concentration allows for firm concentrates to enjoy market power in the market. As clients, all of us realized that we are powerless against a big firm, as economists should be required to demonstrate market power, in a reasonable doubt. Sometimes it is necessary for a firm to grow in order to have the possibility of offering a new commodity; otherwise the company would have to reject the fabrication of this new branch or product. In the worst case, with a restrictive regulation in competitiveness, the firm loses the market or opens the door to new firms which could erode its own clients list.

The relationship between advertising and barriers to entry is peculiar, at the outset; policymakers are not interested in regulating advertising. However, advertising as disloyal behaviour deserves consideration. Schmalensee and Telser confirmed that advertising could deter entry of new rivals in an industry, at the same time; it could improve extra profits due to brand loyalty which is not related with competitiveness. The question is does advertising regulation seem convenient? And what about advertising is a trick?

The new models of entry, with strategic analysis began during the 70s; they have only just blossomed in economic science. They were no accepted quickly, the live of these models was described by Joskow and Klevorick: 'How well these decision makers can apply the tools of economic theory to monopoly and monopolization cases has often troubled commentators who view economic efficiency as the goal of antitrust policy'.[41] The most influential article about predatory prices and market behaviour was written in 1975 by Areeda and Turner,[42] they proposed a test of predatory pricing with important political consequences; Baumol, Panzar and Willig noted out: 'That has been accepted by many courts (though not by all of them). They argue that no price can be predatory if it exceeds the corresponding (short-run) marginal cost'.[43]

As a summary of these political consequences of the improvements within in the field of economics, Hay and Kelley demonstrated in 1974 the existence of collusion in the American industry using forty-nine cases of industries with their respective court resolutions in the sixties. But they agreed about how unnecessary and unjustified Senator Hart's proposal of the Industrial Reorganization Act was. Also they criticized that in several cases the Antitrust Division had sought the dissolution of industry trade associations. Altering the structure of some industries did not necessarily create more competitive markets. On the other side is Shepherd who wrote in 1982 an article entitled 'Causes of Increased Competition in the U.S. Economy, 1939–1980'. Shepherd made a model of competition using ratios of the agriculture, manufacturing sector, mining, construction, transportation, trade, services, insurance and finance sectors in the United States during 1935--80, he notes: 'Antitrust pressure is needed to retain the new level of competition, restrictions against collusive behavior and horizontal mergers, free trade policies; deregulation has had sharp effects in a narrow set of sectors'.[44]

Conclusions

In the 1950s Joe Bain had classified the different barriers to entry, quantifying these barriers in a classification which went from important to insignificant, and George Stigler had added new barriers to the list. During the 1960s and 70s a lot of researchers using new empirical data either supported and reinforced or rejected some of the barriers to entry defended by Bain. More orthodox researches followed the same line by trying to improve the Cournot model of oligopolistic behaviour and the exclusion of competitors.

The use of excess capacity in an industry to avoid any new firm establishing itself, works through the mechanism of price modification or pre-entry price and post-entry price in an industry. We could also see that costs, principally storage costs, can turn out to be higher than any expected future profit; therefore we should also take into account the time the firm already established in the industry needs maintaining barriers to entry. Similarly, if the firm which wishes to enter any market believes that because of the threat of a low price it will not be able to cover production costs, this situation will give rise to a different theoretical model than if it does not believe in the threat. This dilemma had still not been resolved by the end of the 1970s. Present day models based on game theory are trying to solve the problems posed by these threat models.

The correlation between industrial concentration and extra profits continues to be an exhaustive stimulus to empirical research. A large number of publications devoted to a wide range of industries confirm the existence of additional profits which are not the result of competition but of the use of market power. Market power increases as production is concentrated in ever fewer firms. Thus in this situation it is easier to share out a market or agree and maintain prices if there are relatively few firms operating in an industry than when there are a larger number of firms, but the larger firms can impose their leadership over the smaller firms. More orthodox economists defend the position that extra profits will disappear as competition increases, and that concentration is usually the basis of further economic growth. According to this point of view any attempt to prevent concentration and control the size of firms through the intervention of public administration could result precisely in less efficient and less competitive firms in the country which attempts to implement these controls.

The economic thought which contends that publicity and advertising are barriers to entry in an industry, is accepted by most analysts of the firm's behaviour. In the 1970's the first research programmes began in an attempt to design operative models which include these new barriers to entry.

In table 4.1, there is classified, using a chronological order, the articles about barriers to entry analysed into this fourth chapter. We have separated the barriers to entry in three different kinds, excess of capacity, industrial concentration, advertising. Entry models deserve independent consideration. The columns correspond to the year of publication, author of the article, barrier or barriers analysed and when available the statistical variable used to confirm the hypothesis, predecessors' authors in order to give the reader a view about the economic thought-line followed by the author in question, including his framework of choice. The next column contains information about the empirical confirmation of the theory, as main industries which data was used, when information was available we include the period of analysis and its country of origin. We have inserted one more column with the author's main conclusion.

5 BARRIERS TO ENTRY IN THE 1980s

Introduction

The structure of Chapter 5 varies from the previous ones in this book. This is due to the 80s being a convulsive moment for the analysis of barriers to entry. First, owing to a survival of the old barriers, while some of them were analysed with the Bain-Sylos-Modigliani's model others were confirmed under the lens of a new paradigm: the game theory. Altogether, new advances were tested during this decade in the field of entry. In order to a better illustrate the Industrial Organization theory, it is convenient to introduce three main methodological branches: strategy competitive; contestable markets; and game theory. While barriers have been also divided in traditional branches; they are the same than in the last chapter: excess of capacity, industrial concentration and advertising. Entry models have an independent section as usual. The evolution of the analysis of barriers to entry will be analysed following a chronological order, which allows us to show, at the same time, the analytical change from limit price theory to game theory.

During the 80s two new branches in industrial organization emerged, perhaps following the old controversy between the Harvard and Chicago Schools. Contestable markets theory appears as a new economic framework to improve the market theory traditionally following the path of Chicago School. Strategic competitive is closer to the Structure-conduct-performance paradigm, or Harvard School. The controversy about barriers to entry continued, and the prevalence of long-run profits are the issue for discussion. The other point of disagreement relates to the use of statistical information, in particular the cross-section data; this subject shall not concern us any further for the time being.

The weakness of limit price theory can be clearly seen in this decade. Barriers to entry are not always the same, since firms are interested in different kinds of agreements to exclude competition. These will vary according to time and place. From an academic point of view it would be extremely interesting to understand how firms over time alter their behaviour towards competition. As a consequence of this adaptability it appears to be easy to set up barriers to entry and just as quickly make them disappear when competitors legally denounce them. One example of this behaviour is a barrier to entry which was not even questioned in the 1960s, the fixed percentage of production shared out amongst the five major firms in an industry. The theoretical argument in favour of this barrier maintained that the five firms exercised a kind of positive market power which enabled them to control and impose retail prices. There were even legal clauses which obliged firms not to grow, and keep to their market share on pain of punishment. Today opinion has shifted and we feel that the size of a firm is not a matter for an anti-trust regulator to decide, since any limit imposed on size would imply a limitation on the ability to compete in ever larger, more globalized markets.

The 80s began with two new methodological paradigms: contestable markets and competitive strategy. Competitive strategy as a theoretical framework was built by Michael Porter in 1980 following the old barriers to mobility having been developed by Richard Caves and Porter in 1977. Contestable markets saw light in 1982 and formed the paradigm proposed by William Baumol, John Panzar and Robert Willig. In 1987 Kenneth and Mary Louise Hatten wrote about strategic groups, barriers to entry and contestability. This is the first time that both new approaches and the Industrial Organization theory were combined. Hatten and Hatten worked on market's niches and on the blocked entry of a firm in a market due to strategic groups (through asymmetrical mobility barriers). Porter's strategic theory doesn't solve the issue accurately – they noted that contestability seems to lead to the best to the consecution of their target, the main reason should be because when markets are growing, structured market changes simultaneity. Contestable markets provide a framework which shows the efficiency or competitive advantage of incumbents, and then, the existence of niches in the market.

These two approaches, contestable markets and strategic behaviour, make up the main areas of research during the 90s. Inheriting the old Harvard–Chicago conflict, contestable market theory uses ideas about the Marshallian theoretical apparatus whereas strategic behaviour develops Bain's barriers to new competition. Once more the paths do not converge, one side still seeking to demonstrate an ever more precise model, the other still trying to make its schemes more realistic.

The paths developed by Bain, Richard Posner and Carl Christian von Weizsäcker, none of whom believed in the existence of barriers to entry, became relevant during the 80s. In order to demonstrate their proposal Posner analyzed barriers as tie-ins, vertical integration, restricted distribution or predatory pricing, while von Weizsäcker was interested in excess of capacity, the buildup of capital, economies of scale and goodwill. On the other side was Michael Spence, who believed in the existence of barriers to entry and tried to demonstrate their existence. Research workers built many theoretical models in an attempt to reach a widely accepted framework. Michael Spence is also the promoter of the use of game theory in order to move barriers to entry from a discussion of limit price theory to strategic decisions. Flaherty, Dixit, Eaton and Lipsey followed this new approach, while Schmalensee, Cubbin and Nagle continued to use price limit theory.

William Baumol opened up a new branch of research, contestable markets, whereas Michael Porter, working alone, although in touch with Richard Caves and Michael Spence, inaugurated another branch of strategic competetive research. The followers of this last proposal are Harrigan, Chappell, Waagstein, Marks and Park. During the 80s, Baumol and Schmalensee found a common point, the limits of economic theory to offer solutions able to raise the competitiveness. At the end of the 80s we might say there were two new trends of thought: we have discussed the first theoretical models, which analysed different barriers to entry one by one. The main authors in this line were Gilbert and Vives, Farrell, Aghion and Bolton, Gelfand and Spiller, Bagwell, Grossman and Horn. The other trend follows the line of sequential entry represented by the research of Eaton and Ware, Shapiro and Khemani, Smiley, Dunne and Roberts and Samuelson.

This decade is the point when game theory was considered the methodological approach used to solve issues in market and price theory. Games are used by Industrial Organization since at least 1977, the year in which Michael Spence published his model of threats to entry. Eaton and Lipsey, Gilbert, Milgrom and Roberts are the main authors on games, and they showed the main limitations of this method, especially when it is used to explain economic behaviour.

5.1. Main Methodological Proposals

5.1.1. Competitive Strategy: Michael Eugene Porter

In 1980 the analysis of barriers to entry seen as competitive strategies, as opposed to price theory, began to take shape. The most representative author of this school of thought was Michael Porter.[1] At this time he was working in the Harvard Business School, and in 1980 he published his book *Competitive Strategy: Techniques for Analyzing Industries and Competitors*, following in the path of Bain's framework of 1956, *Barriers to New Competition*. In Porter's model of determinants of the intensity of competition, he included threat of entry as one of these determinants, together with the intensity of rivalry among existing competitors, pressure from substitute products, bargaining power of buyers and bargaining power of suppliers. Threat of entry into an industry depends on the barriers to entry and the reaction from incumbents when an entrant is expected. The characterization of barriers to entry made by Porter has six major sources of barriers: economies of scale, product differentiation, capital requirements, switching costs, access of distribution channels and cost disadvantages independent of scale. Government policy takes place as a barrier to entry because of controls, licensing requirements and limits on access to raw materials. Porter recommended the exhaustive analysis of these barriers to entry together with exit barriers, and he offers a pack of recommendations which can be applied in diverse industries among countries and during a historical period.

Porter made a vast characterization of strategy and an accurate definition of every topic, following the old categories made by Bain and Hines in the 50s. In order to keep the exact sense of every barrier to entry it seems convenient to use his own words to explain how barriers work 'Economies of scale deter entry by forcing the entrant to come in at large scales and risk strong reaction from existing firms or come in at a small scale and accept a cost disadvantage, both undesirable options'.[2] 'Product differentiation creates a barrier to entry by forcing entrant to spend heavily to overcome existing customer loyalties'.[3] 'Capital requirements mainly if the capital is required for risky or unrecoverable up-front advertising or research and development ... Even if capital is available on the capital markets, entry represents a risky use of that capital which should be reflected in risk premiums charged the prospective entrant, these constitute advantages for going firms ... Switching costs[4] include employee retraining costs; cost of new ancillary equipment, cost and time in testing or qualifying a new source, and so on ... Access of distribution channels, a barrier to entry can be created by the new entrant's need to secure distribution for its product'.[5] 'Cost disadvantages independent of scale. The most critical advantages are factors such as know-how, access to raw materials, subsidies, learning or experience curve'.[6]

Following the Structure-Conduct-Performance framework, Michael Porter established a *limit-price* or *predatory price* capable excluding competitors from a market 'The threat of entry into an industry can be eliminated if incumbents firms choose or are forced by competition of price below this hypothetical entry deterring price'.[7] Porter defined, in a suggestive way, predatory price as the practice of a dominant firm selling at a loss to make competition more difficult for new firms who cannot suffer losses that a large dominant firm with extensive lines of credit or cash reserves can. It is illegal in most places; however it is difficult to prove. This definition does not have a pejorative sense, unlike to the predatory price theory dominant in the Chicago School, but is a different way to see how firms exclude competitors and how difficult is to demonstrate this kind of behaviour in court.

Porter and Caves, in the 70s, developed a proposal to improve the analysis of barrier to entry: exit barriers. Porter reproduced definition as follows:

> Exit barriers are economic, strategic, and emotional factors that keep companies competing in business even though they may be earning low or even negative returns on investment. The major sources of exit barriers are; specialized assets, fixed costs of exit (labor agreements, maintaining capabilities), strategic relationships (image, access of

financial markets) emotional barriers (loyalty of employees, pride) and government and social restrictions.[8]

Basically and briefly, the firms survive in a market if they are able to improve their position through a good strategy and take advantage of the weakness of their rivals. Regarding barriers to entry, Porter increased his list in later editions of *Competitive Strategy*, connected with capital requirement and government policy, for example, patents, which give a firm the sole legal right to produce a product for a given period of time. Patents are intended to encourage invention and technological progress by offering this financial incentive. In direct connection with economies of scale, there is new kind of barrier to entry which could be seen as the development of personal computers for example as it allows small companies to make use of database and communications technology that was once extremely expensive and thus only available to large corporations. The network effect is another case, because when a good or a service has a value that depends on the number of existing customers, competing players may have difficulties entering a market where a strong player has already captured a significant user base. Another example should be restrictive practices, such as air transport agreements that make it difficult for new airlines to obtain landing slots at some airports. The field of contracts as barrier to entry will be analysed at the end of this chapter, Porter noted exclusive agreements with key distributors or retailers can make it difficult for other manufacturers to enter the industry or exclusive agreements with key links in the supply chain can make it difficult for other manufacturers to enter the industry. At last, Porter considered the inelasticity of demand because the strategy of selling at a lower price in order to penetrate markets is ineffective with price-insensitive consumers.

Early in 1982, George Yip used data of fifty-nine entrants into thirty-one markets and defined a model close to Porter's proposals but only with a tripod of competitive strategy: market structure, business-level and corporate-level variables, his conclusion was 'The managerial factor of carrier risk is directly represented by the height of barriers and the entrant's ability to breach barriers'.[9] In the same vein, Briance Mascarenhas and David Aaker worked in mobility barriers; they made personal interviews with industrial officials of Oil drilling industry and used information of 142 firms for the period 1973–81. Their target was demonstrating the existence of the following barriers: brand name, loyal customer base, distribution channels, long-term contracts and managerial pride. They noted that the best option for strategists is to create barriers to entry in the group and reduce barriers to exit in order to keep out potential competitors from other groups. Their conclusion was: 'It seems clear that this asymmetry is important to understanding and influencing competition in the industry'.[10]

Following the path of Porter, Matthew Gelfand and Pablo Spiller[11] made a model, in 1987, with multiplicity of products and markets, which should make it difficult to hold a cartel and in which threats of increased output change production of the other firms. They used the banking system of Uruguay, before and after deregulation and considered legal entry barriers. Steven Lanning, at the same time, developed a theoretical model of trigger price and output verification strategies into a cartel. Mainly to explain how cheating works. Lanning assumed that the time until a firm detected cheating is an exponential distribution and the cheater affects the length of an episode by the degree of cheating. While the quota is considered a strategic variable because the optimal quota must incorporate a downward adjustment in responds to lower prices. His conclusion was: 'An implication for policy is also mixed. Increasing the costs of operating a cartel by imposing greater penalties may reduce the sustainability of some cartels and alter the optimal switching in a way that improves welfare'.[12]

This new proposal for research in the field of fair competition and especially in barriers to entry was condemned for having a court of followers. Some traditional barriers to entry survive as they were, but others are changed by strategic decisions. Has sin been turned into virtue? mainly when the firms manages the cutting edge and bad behaviour is very difficult to prove. From Porter until nowadays, researchers analyse deeply their proposals about competition in markets because a market is healthy when firms develop new sales strategy, and sometimes these strategies are among those which keep separate barriers to entry.

5.1.2. Contestable Markets: William Jack Baumol, John Panzar and Robert Willig

At the beginning of the 80s William Baumol, Robert Willig and John Panzar developed the framework for economic analysis known as *contestable market* to improve the theory of industry structure. Baumol and Willig wrote together about fixed cost and sunk cost as barrier to entry. In order to shed light on this issue, they defined fixed costs as those borne by firms even in the long run, which makes them production costs. Whereas sunk costs disappear in the long run. Sunk costs are those costs which that the firm has to lay out at the beginning but if the business works they are built into accounts as initial investment. Sunk costs become a barrier to entry when the business doesn't work because the investor risks his capital without the possibility of recovering his money. In this sense, the amount of capital that a firm has to risk in order to improve its market share, even in order to enter in the market, can be considered a significant data of the level of the barrier to entry. In conclusion, a contestable market demands two requisites: no artificial barriers to entry, and that fixed costs are not sunk costs.

William Baumol[13] and Robert Willig[14] wrote an article in 1981 entitled 'Fixed Costs, Sunk Costs, Entry Barriers and Sustainability of Monopoly' which was chapter 10 of their most important book, written jointly with John Panzar[15] and published in 1982 with the title of *Contestable Markets and the Theory of Industry Structure*. In 1982, Baumol wrote an article for the *American Economic Review* following the path of contestable markets. The target was to build a new theory of Industrial Structure. We have blended both articles and book, in order to make the comprehension of the whole proposal easier. Their analysis provides a generalization of the concept of a perfectly competitive market. Into a market oligopolist structure and identical behaviour they included free entry from their previous dependence on the conjectural variation of incumbents. In their words:

> A contestable market is one into which entry is absolutely free, and exit is absolutely costless. We use "freedom of entry" in Stigler's sense, not to mean that it is costless or easy, but that the entrant suffers no disadvantage in terms of production technique or perceived product quality relative to the incumbent and that potential entrant find it appropriate to evaluate the profitability of entry in terms of the incumbent firms' pre-entry prices.[16]

In a perfect contestable market, no cross subsidy is possible, that is, no predatory pricing can be used as a weapon of unfair competition. The average cost cannot be defined. Pricing behaviour and market structure should be determined simultaneously and endogenously with the analysis of the other variables more traditionally treated in the theory of the firm and the industry.

One weakness of limit price theory relates to economies of scale and the use of excess of capacity to expel rivals. Contestable markets solved this issued because of economies of scale in the production which the firm deliberately builds, sometimes including excess capacity in order to conveniently respond to the anticipated growth in sales volume. Altogether, when entry and exit are completely free, only efficient incumbent monopolists and oligopolists may in fact be able to prevent entry. On the industrial concentration as a barrier to entry Baumol noted that 'The minimum size of entry cost required to permit equilibrium will depend on the size of the deviation from zero profits under marginal cost pricing and Thijs ten Raa has given us rules for its determination',[17] he also said that the absence of entry in an industry and a high concentration index may be signs of virtue, not of vice. Under these assumptions they built a new economic model, because:

> This degree of freedom of entry forces the industry in equilibrium to adopt the structure that is efficient (in the sense of minimization of the cost of producing the industry's output vector) and it imposes a number of other surprising and desirable properties on any industry equilibrium.[18]

In order to determine what impediments to entry could exist in a theoretical industrial model, they reviewed the literature about barriers to entry and markets behaviour come from Bain, Caves and Porter, Spence, Stigler, von Weizsäcker or Dixit. They need to separate the different components of a market structure, in the beginning they defined entry barrier using two old definitions:

> The two leading candidate definitions of an entry barrier are those most clearly espoused by George Stigler and Christian von Weizsäcker, Stigler as "entry cost" and Weizsäcker as an impediment to the flow of resources into the industry, arising as a result of socially excessive protection of incumbent firms.[19]

Their target was looking for a sustainable price. Sustainability describes equilibrium vis-à-vis potential entrants who take as fixed the prices of incumbent. They defined this price as:

> A price output vector is said to be sustainable against entry if it satisfies two conditions: 1. - it permits incumbents to operate without loss and 2. - so long as incumbents remain in the market, no entrant can hope to produce without loss at or below those prices. The crucial point is that, in the absence of exogenous changes, if incumbents adopt prices sustainable against entry, then, in principle, they need never resort to strategic prices responses and countermove in order to prevent profitable entry opportunities.[20]

And they defined sustainability as a necessary condition for equilibrium under one of the following significant sets of circumstances. In the case of antitrust or regulatory policy which actually inhibits price changes by incumbents in response to entry, and on the other side within a theoretical Bertrand-Nash model on the part of potential entrants, in other words, they will assume that incumbents will not change prices in response to entry.

In order to separate fixed cost from sunk cost, Baumol argued that fixed costs assure the existence of a vector of sustainable prices (like a monopoly when firms try to enter the market). Fixed costs of sufficient magnitude will constitute an entry deterrent of sufficient magnitude to make sustainable prices possible. Nevertheless fixed costs don't have the welfare consequences attributed to barriers to entry. Entry barriers will lead to just the same sort of loss in welfare as a regulatory decision to permit supranormal profit. On the other hand, sunk costs are a barrier to entry (they're zero in the long run as presently defined), while fixed costs aren't reduced, even in the long run. This is the first time when fixed costs are analysed in separate analysis of sunk costs. In their words:

> The role of sunk costs in determining whether or not a market is contestable. Clearly, when entry requires the sinking of substantial costs, it will not be reversible because, by definition, the sunk costs are not recoverable. However, if efficient operation requires no sunken outlays, then entry can, by and large, be presumed to be reversible, and the market can be presumed to be contestable.[21]

Where fixed costs are not sunk and there are no artificial entry barriers, the market will be contestable, and so, where markets are contestable and sustainable prices exist, the course of the analysis is clear, the threat created by potential competition will determine the behaviour of firms and will tend to push them toward the adoption of sustainable prices, which was defined above.

In 1989 the first article to disconfirm the use of contestable market was published, the industry used to argue about the new paradigm was the airline industry in United States. Researchers of the Antitrust Division, Department of Justice, Washington and others, made an exhaustive analysis of this industry, assessing concentration, distribution of incumbents, sunk costs and a monopoly on nonstop air carriers on a pair of cities. They used data from 867 nonstop city pairs in regular flights and transfers. The conclusion was 'perfect contestability is rejected by the data'.[22] Also they noted that potential entrants are not significantly deterred by economies of scale and scope.

Baumol, Panzar and Willig develop a new framework to separate the regular activity of the firms from ugly competition in markets. The target was to offer to the courts an accurate way to demonstrate the existence of illegal behaviour of firms, then give the antitrust authorities support to change the bad practices of firms. Baumol, Panzar and Willig fit into the classical price theory defined by Stigler, and even though they support their model in a sustainable price.

5.1.3. The Game Theory Revolution

Game theory is the study of the ways in which *strategic interactions* among *rational players* produce *outcomes* with respect to the *preferences* (or *utilities*) of those players, none of which are necessarily intended by any of them.

The three elements of a game are first, the players, how many players are there, and does nature play a role? Second, a complete description of the strategies of each player, and third a description of the consequences (payoffs) for each player for every possible profile of strategy choices of all players.

The interaction of player's strategies results in an outcome that we call equilibrium. And in equilibrium, each player is playing the strategy that is a *best response* to the strategies of the other players, which is the strategy that yields the highest payoff given the strategies of the other players. That means in equilibrium, no one has an incentive to change his strategy given the strategy choice of all others. This means equilibrium is not the best possible outcome and in a situation where players always choose the same action, sometimes equilibrium will involve changing action choices (mixed strategy equilibrium).

There are different games, the traditional oligopoly game used is noncooperative because its players cannot write binding agreements because they have no access to an enforcement mechanism. The explanation was written by Elmar

Wolfstetter: 'Oligopoly games are viewed as noncooperative because oligopolists cannot use the machinery of law enforcement to enforce cartel agreement, simply because these are prohibited by antitrust law'.[23] The link between Cournot and game theory of John von Neumann and Oscar Morgenstern was that 'Cournot assumed that oligopolists set outputs as strategies and let a neutral auctioneer set the market clearing product price'.[24]

Game theory changes the old limit price paradigm; at the end of the 80s game theory reached a prominent position as a theoretical paradigm in the economic field, since the prices and quantities equilibrium into the markets began to be calculated through the framework of game theory. Therefore the behaviour of firms came to be analysed within a strategic game. Plenty of scholars from main universities published several theoretical articles about the use of game theory and the convenience of using it to explain market structures, agreements between firms, collusion and other less-accepted strategies of predominant firms in a market; as Gilbert wrote: 'Game theorists will recognize this assumption as Nash-Cournot behavior on the part of entrants, with the incumbent acting as a Stackelberg leader'.[25]

In 1987 Paul Milgrom and John Roberts wrote on the limits to the use of game theory in Industrial Organization issues. They said that the game using in competitiveness should be with informational asymmetries, the main example was used to demonstrate predatory pricing.[26] The methods of incomplete information game theory allow to the academy to model formally issues that are cornerstones of Industrial Organization, but some topics must be questioned. It seems necessary to assume a common knowledge base, robustness of the results, multiplicity of equilibria and difficulties in empirical implementation and testing. As they said: 'The type spaces in Asymmetric Information Games models rapidly become extremely complicated mathematical structures as the level at which the uncertainly is assumed to lie is pushed back'.[27] They pointed out that 'These models are new and have for the most part been developed by theorists; they may simply not yet have reached the empiricists' agenda',[28] in this line they recommended care, mainly with regard to case studies. On the other hand, game theory drives the analysis of market behaviour in a different way, as Hovenkamp wrote: 'More fundamental perhaps is the ideological consideration that game theory tends to undermine the Chicago School faith in the efficiency of markets and their superiority over regulatory alternatives'.[29]

The main change was a new framework, that of game theory. Some traditional barriers to entry began to be considered as strategic behaviour, rather then bad business practice. The new economic thought revolved around new barriers to entry, the demonstration of the existence of a new barrier and a model capable of confirming its existence. In a limit price model the features of industrial markets show barriers to entry, therefore, in the long run these barriers were worn down and overcome. It seems that only technological conditions and demand are barriers to entry in the long run.

One of the first models which included game theory in oligopolistic Cournot models is the work of Michael Spence, published in 1977; he was working under limit price assumptions or a Bain-Sylos-Modigliani framework. Some years later, in 1980, Therese Flaherty developed a dynamic noncooperative game in which firms choose output and cost-reducing investment sequences. Her model provides: 'A technical explanation of how industry structure can converge to a state in which firms has unequal market shares'.[30] At the same time, Avinash Dixit developed his model which improved upon Spence's original model. For Dixit: 'The basic point is that although the rules of the post-entry game are taken to be exogenous, the established firm can alter the outcome to its advantage by changing the initial conditions'.[31] Curtis Eaton and Richard Lipsey worked on durability of capital as a barrier to entry, using game theory, inevitably the point of their paper was: 'Not indivisibilities and decreasing cost per se which create barriers to entry. Rather, it is the inter-temporal commitment of specific capital to a market, in combination with decreasing costs which creates an entry barrier'.[32] The outcome of their model was that capital produces revenue for the firm by acting as a factor of production and as a barrier to entry. The reason why capital acts a barrier to entry is because product-specific capital is a natural vehicle for commitment and firms which use a large amount of capital will break with one important economic assumption: cost minimization.

The role of game theoretic analysis of firm behaviour improves the measure of market power, all of these methods allow a precise assessment of market power even in markets without dominant firms. Carl Shapiro, however, found the limits of games, he said that is difficult to select among the vast multiplicity of equilibria, and developed his argument as 'The huge number of supergame equilibria must be considered a major liability of this whole theoretical development. Certainly, game theory does not predict the collusive outcome; it simply indicates that such an outcome is supportable as a noncooperative equilibrium'.[33] The second of Shapiro's objections is that the Nash equilibrium is a self-enforcing agreement, in this case the punishment specified are not credible, and he asked himself: 'Is it credible never to renegotiate in order to prevent a reversion to a price war? If the firms have the opportunity to communicate fully at time zero, why do they not again have such an opportunity in the event of a defection?',[34] and then, he concluded that renegotiation occurs in cartel behaviour markets, also it is opportune to keep in mind that defection becomes attractive and hold collusion in the long run should be difficult. Game theory develops a corollary principle (named topsy-turvy)[35] to antitrust policies, which permits oligopolists to renegotiate and re-establish a collusive product in the case of a traitor may in fact weaken tacit collusion and then topsy-turvy promotes competition.

5.2. Old Barriers to Entry: New Discussion

In order to bear in mind how excess of capacity, industrial concentration and advertising work as a barrier to entry, we recommend you read the previous chapter. In the present one only new frameworks capable of confirming or disconfirming the existence of the specific barrier to entry are considered.

5.2.1. Excess of Capacity as a Barrier to Entry

Excess of capacity is considered one of the old barriers to entry; the framework, within capacity means deterring the entry of new incumbents in an industry, has been appreciated for decades. The use made by incumbents of their installed capacity into their industry garnered several criticisms nonetheless. During the 80s, game theory changed the mainstream able to demonstrate the existence of this barrier to entry. Under the lens of games began it became possible to assess the investments in front of the risk of losing money because of this decision itself. Keeping in mind this is a relevant decision of competitive strategy. In other words, during this decade the connection between capacity and concentration smoke straightly out, as we will analyse in the following pages. In this section we survey significant articles whose main target is to analyse excess of install capacity as barrier to entry in an industry.

In 1980 Carl Christian Von Weizsäcker published his book entitled *Barriers to Entry: a Theoretical Treatment*, at the same time as another article about barriers to entry and welfare analysis was published. Von Weizsäcker developed a theoretical model within the traditional Cournot equilibrium of suppliers. His model tried to argue how excess of capacity, the buildup of capital and economies of scale work as barriers to entry, following the path of Michael Spence. Von Weizsäcker argued that excesses of capacity are expensive and 'expenditures to deter entry are wasteful'.[36] On the other hand, the buildup of capital works as deterrent to entry only when the rate of interest is high; finally that economies of scale can become a barrier to entry hinges on the expansion of the market in which firm sells. Within the perspective of limit price theory, the point of Weizsäcker' research is:

> A more than infinitesimal effect of entry on the price, called Δp, implies a benefit to the consumers which is larger than -x Δp and thus the price reduction as such helps consumers more than it hurts competitors. On the other hand, if in the new equilibrium output of the competitors is smaller than without entry, the suppliers incur an additional loss, if price is above marginal cost, and hence output reductions imply more revenue loss than cost reductions. Which of the two effects is greater has to be investigated in a specific model.[37]

In 1982 Michael Porter and Michael Spence[38] worked on the case of Corn Wet Milling. This was a special case because they constructed a model from the final report. They tried to determine the capacity expansion of the industry analysed. Moreover, they had to establish the predictable behaviour of rivals, with approximately a dozen firms at work in the market. Altogether they consider two industry outputs, cornstarch and corn syrup. Using early game theory they draw alternative strategies as well, taking account the most likely capacity decisions for expanding markets, expectations of demand, the raise of market value and changes in the market structure during the time. They concluded with tables which offer multiple solutions for the industry. For the history of economic thought this is one of the first articles which uses game theory framework and it was put into practice as a business strategy.

From the Federal Trade Commission and following the path of Michael Mann, John Hilke wrote a paper which represents an exploratory effort to investigate empirically the prevalence and efficiency of excess capacity in deterring entry. The point is when excess capacity does not lead to creation of a credible threat; it may still act as a barrier to entry by shifting the risk–return perceptions of potential entrants enough to redirect the potential entrants' investments into other industries. This is the theory developed by Baumol and Willig in 1981, which takes into consideration that some fixed costs will be converted into sunk cost, in this case working as a barrier to entry.

The dependent variable, used by Hilke, was the sum of market shares obtained by domestic entrants and gains (or losses) in the market share of imports between 1950 and 1966. Assuming that entry decisions are not qualitatively different from other investment decisions, it can be a possible measure of the risk of predation signalled by excess capacity; that must be applied to pre-entry profit rates in estimating post-entry profit rates because of an incumbent firm's credible threats. Traditional barriers to entry are approximated by a trivariate dummy variable based on previous judgements of the old Mann's barriers to entry considered during the 60s. The main conclusion of Hilke was that he confirms his hypothesis whether price declined by more that predicted by using the Sylos-Labini theory, then production retaliation was assumed to have taken place and excess of capacity works as barrier to entry. The reason was that:

> Bain-Sylos limit price was calculated by adding a linear price trend from the three preceding years and the expected decline in price as a result of entry to the current price level. The expected decline in price is the result of multiplying the price elasticity of demand by the size of the entry relative to pre-entry capacity.[39]

William Brock and José Scheinkman,[40] in 1985, tried to build a supergame in order to establish the equilibrium price in an industry with capacity constraints. Telser's model developed during the 70s was used; but the scare flexibility and the lack of a specific game theoretic structure did not allow getting an accurate solution. In 1986 Bruce Lyons wrote about the use of excess of capacity as tool to deter entry in an industry. Using a game he noted that: 'In the presence of strategic behaviour any empirical measure based on prices and profits alone must be misleading',[41] because the monopolist (or collusive group of oligopolists) may choose to produce less than the capacity predicted by Modigliani's oligopoly.

Marvin Lieberman studied excess of capacity in depth; yet again this old barrier to entry was to find another empirical demonstration of its existence. Lieberman in 1987 began his article 'Excess Capacity as a Barrier to Entry' with the maintained hypothesis in his paper that excess capacity is non-strategic in nature. The main objection of traditional models is the *free rider* problem, because a free rider may reduce the incentives of incumbents to hold excess capacity. When the industry has not the threat of free rider, he argued: 'In the absence of strategic entry deterrence behavior, entrants and incumbents would exhibit similar thresholds for new plant investment'.[42] In order to confirm his hypothesis Lieberman applied his proposal to several American industries, organically chemicals, inorganic chemicals, synthetic fibers, metals. The dummy was built using an extended series of data, the period analyzed was 1952–82, despite the fact that in some industries the period was reduced. The conclusion of Lieberman was:

> Lack of statistical evidence that incumbents built plants pre-emptively to deter entry does not prove that such behavior never occurred. Conceivably, excess capacity may have served as an entry barrier for only a few products in the sample and therefore cannot be detected in the statistical analysis. To check this possibility, the data sample was screened to identify specific cases where excess capacity may have been maintained as a barrier to entry.[43]

He suggests that the potency of excess capacity as an entry barrier may be reconsidered mainly when the markets are growing, in the case of existence of free-rider problems and when demand-related effects appears. In the same year, Lieberman published an article that his theoretical model is empirically applied to the chemical industries. The main conclusion of this second article is parallel to the first; the size plant differential between entrants and incumbents is not correlated with seller concentration or rate of market growth. In other words, one little firm could enter in a market because the bigger installed competitors could not use their capacity to deter entry.

A few articles left which separate excess capacity as a barrier to entry itself, the tendency was to analyse capacity linked with economies of scale and scope as a strategy business decision. This barrier to entry deserves consideration in the antitrust policy until the Guidelines of 1992. After this date, the use of capacity as a weapon against competitor changed to the analysis of sunk cost. In other words, to build excess of capacity in a factory began to be analysed as a sunk cost, opening a new academic arguing about what exactly sunk costs means.

5.2.2. Industrial concentration as a barrier to entry

Industrial concentration is a controversial barrier to entry; it has scholars which defend it come hell or high water and cast-iron opponents as well. At this point, game theory became the most important theoretical framework to explain industrial concentration as a barrier to entry. The old assumptions of limit price theory were included in the models, but the traditional marginal cost analysis applied during decades give way to the strategic decisions of firms. It's true that economic theory works with marginal calculus, following Marshallian long-run equilibrium; however decision processes are increasingly based on profitability criteria, which furthers the role of game theory. One of the first models which included game theory in oligopolistic Cournot models is the work of Morton Kamien and Nancy Schwartz in 1975, followed by the Michael Spence article published in 1977. While Kamien and Schwartz worked in a traditional Cournot model with uncertain entry, Spence was working under limit price assumptions or a Bain-Sylos-Modigliani framework.

There have been analysed scale economies together with extra-profits gained by manipulation of price (limit price theory) and this manipulation was success-ful because of industry concentration or market power. A thin line divides the use of excess of capacity and industry concentration while both works to pre-vent new entry in an industry. In a Cournot model both could be considered in a similar way. Traditionally Bain-Sylos-Modigliani model separate capacity and concentration; capacity of production is an investment decision while concen-tration is a market structure. The first is a business issue, while the second is an industry consideration. Otherwise, the use of installed capacity in an industry is only successful in a concentrate industry.

In this decade we can see how industrial concentration analysis is mixed with installed capacity analysis. Mainly because investment decision and reduction of cost (scale economies) can work together, in this case both have influence in the industry price. In consequence both are pillars on which to build competitive strategy. In this section we survey the transformation of concentration as a bar-rier to entry in a strategic business decision.

Michael Spence traditionally worked on the subject of excess of capacity as a barrier to entry during the 70s. His article of 1980 entitled 'Notes of Adver-tising, Economies of Scale and Entry Barriers' built a model within limit price theory which considered advertising as a fixed cost; in this perspective, advertis-ing should be included in the curve of average cost, thus allowing its inclusion in the old models where economies of scale work as a barrier to entry. The only limit was that the model has to assume the existence of a homogeneous good within the industry. In his own words:

> If that production function is characterized by increasing returns to scale, then a firm's cost per dollar of revenue generated will decline with market share. Those increasing returns to scale will then have a role in creating entry barriers analogous to the role of ordinary returns to scale in the case of a homogeneous undifferentiated product.[44]

In the same vein, Avinash Dixit[45] built a model in which investment deters entry into an industry. Dixit's model attempted to develop the old Bain-Sylos-Modigliani model with improvements taken from Spence and his own research of the 70s. This proposal includes game theoretic aspects as well as strategic interactions of incumbent firms against a prospective entrant. The conclusion of Dixit was that where investment in sunk capital is made, the incumbent can lower its marginal cost and increase its post-entry equilibrium output. Roger Ware in 1985 built a new Dixit's model using inventory holding as a weapon able to deter entry in an industry. Ware notes:

> The problem I exactly analogous to that of finding a Nash equilibrium set of strategies for a monopoly owner of a fixed stock of an exhaustible resource, faced by the threat of entry from a single producer of a backstop technology, where the resource owner is also capable of producing the backstop at the same cost as the entrant.[46]

The question is how high a cost could deter a rival and reckon sunk cost which the company affords.

In the 80s, Richard Schmalensee changed his theoretical analysis of barriers to entry from advertising to economies of scale. He made a survey in the paper entitled 'Economies of Scale and Barriers to Entry' (1981), where he rethought the different theoretical assumptions made during the last thirty years, the models of Bain, Dixit, Spence and Eaton and Lipsey. Schmalensee's criticism was the theoretical consideration of scale economies. The estimations made in order to demonstrate that economies of scale work as a barrier to entry assume that national markets and products are homogeneous: he thought that this assumption was too strong.

Concerning incumbents' change of minimum efficient scale when rival threats become evident, Industrial Organization used different propositions: Bain's model assumed that incumbent firms maintain their levels of output after a new firm enters in the industry. Michael Spence assumed that established firms move their production from monopoly output to competitive output when they believe the threat of entry. Dixit assumed that incumbent firms in industry behave as if playing a noncooperative game in response to a new entrant. Eaton and Lipsey made the assumption that established firms manage to coordinate their investments following the goal of entry deterrence, and they advised that these strategies would be easy to detect in a world of static demand. All of them assumed that, in a way, the threats shown above are believed to be real. However as Schmalensee wrote: 'If entry is unattractive to outsiders, the flow of monopoly profits received by cooperating insiders cannot exceed the flow cost of capital assets embodied in a firm of minimum efficient scale, as long as industry demand is not strictly convex.'[47]

On the other hand, Kathryn Harrigan wrote about this topic in 1981; she built a dummy in order to explain the likelihood of successful entry into an industry. To test her model, she used data from the following American industries, for the period 1969–78: meatpacking, distilled liquors, cigarettes, hydraulic cement and aircraft manufacture. The independent variables were: capital scale economies, the age of physical assets, excess capacity, industry advertising, the number of firms in an industry, prices, sales and so on. Harrigan wrote in her conclusions:

> Structural barriers are generic to an industry to the extent that all potential entrants must invent a means of hurdling these obstacles to profitable performance in pursuing a new line of business, and as such, all face similar needs for the capital required to inaugurate sets of productive or distributive assets.[48]

The same year, Harrigan published another article entitled 'Deterrents to Divestiture' where she tests barriers to exit as barriers to entry. Indicators chosen to confirm her hypothesis were capital intensity, asset specificity, age of assets, technological or operating reinvestment requirements, and she got for sixty-one American firms from 1965 to 1978. The model established the likelihood of exit as a dependent variable, while structural and corporate inducements and deterrents to exit are the independent variables, measured by high-quality product image, strong customer industry, good distribution channel, favourable expectation of demand. She notes that barriers to entry are important because they can deter the firm's timing of exit from an industry, even suffering losses. Her conclusion to the manager was: 'this field of study can help the practicing strategist to assess the dynamics of the firm's competitive position with greater insights concerning the future barriers present investment can create.'[49]

In the same vein, Thorbjørn Waagstein worked on fixed costs, limit pricing and investment in barriers to entry. His paper was published in 1982. Working within the Bain-Sylos-Modigliani framework, Waagstein assumed that advertising and R&D are fixed costs in the following way:

> If the established firms ignore the threat of entry, then it would spend nothing in sales promotion and the like. But if it is limit pricing, it might do so. This is so because the optimal amount of advertising, R&D etc. enters in the potential entrant's considerations, when deciding to enter or not.[50]

The objective was to see barriers to entry as endogenous variables within the model. Therefore the analysis moved from barriers to rents, which means a return to monopoly analysis and to uncover the two sources of above-average profits: diversification advantages because of the knowledge of the market which incumbent firms have and the advantages of big business as receivers of cheaper credit, and power rebates or favourable government contracts which are profitable only for incumbent firms.

Henry Chappell, William Marks and Imkoo Park[51] worked on measuring entry barrier models. In 1983, they built a Switching Regression model whose equations assert that industry profitability is a function of industry concentration, a vector of variables indicative of entry barrier levels and a vector of variables which proxy elasticity of demand for each industry. They said that they can provide evidence as to which empirical measures seem to be the best indicators of the presence of entry barriers. They tested their theory in 209 American industries, where two-digit data with data from the 1967 Census of Manufactures. Their conclusions were not promising, and it seems necessary to improve the econometric models.

Steven Salop and David Scheffman in 1983 wrote a theoretical article entitled 'Raising Rivals' Cost'; they tried to demonstrate the behaviour of leader firm in an industry and production accommodation made by fringe firms. In this case, they worked with two demand curves with their own elasticity and a connection between firms in demand and supply. Their argument in defence of raising a barrier to entry was: 'Cost-increasing strategies are more credible than predatory pricing. Because these strategies do not require a sacrifice of profits in the short run, but allow profits to be increased immediately, the would-be predator has every incentive to carry out its threats'.[52] Their conclusion for antitrust analysis was that every exclusionary strategy made long-run profits to the leader firm, meanwhile competitors suffer, and last but not at least, this behaviour reduces consumer welfare through inefficiency.

Richard Caves began to work on competitive advantage in 1984; in fact, he worked with Michael Porter for years, but he always put the microeconomic vision before the business point of view. Caves notes important questions about an array of strategic decisions is complete; investment decisions, cost reduction through accumulated experience, research and design, quality control and differentiation. He wrote that: 'Strategy gives to organizational choices and to decision about acquiring and divesting assets that are selected for the efficient pursuit of this maximization plan'.[53] Despite strategic decisions pointed out below, Caves argues that commitments are relevant in a theoretic context of entry barriers and entry deterrence. In this way, entry barriers are therefore barriers to exit as well. Examples of relevant commitments are: production capacity, sales promotion, brand proliferation, vertical integration, and cost raising strategies that differentially disfavour entrants; Caves's conclusions about strategy and competition open a new door in the field of Industrial organization theory. He wrote: 'These models offer evident business -normative implications- how the firm can assess its relative advantage in pursuing some opportunity as well as degree of competition will prevail after successive rounds of commitment in its market'.[54] This is the beginning of new developments in the long-run competitiveness, and several academic literatures were written for and against the behaviour of firms in their own markets in the long run. In Chapter 3 of this book, the reader can found the two different opinions and hard debate which survive nowadays about the *long-run* in economics.

Ralph Braudburd and David Ross[55], in 1989, confirmed the strategic proposal of Caves and Porter, and Newman, refers to the market share is the key of profitability. Using 4,198 observations of data based on the Federal Trade Commission Line of Business survey for the year 1975 they found support for Porter's argument. Babu Nahata and Dennis Olson[56] published an article to examine the Bain and Stigler definitions of term barrier to entry and reconcile apparent differences between them. They worked with the Cournot model, where scale economies serve as a barrier to entry depend on demand, cost elasticities and the number of firms in the industry. The conclusion was that Bain and Stigler's definitions of barriers to entry coincide when the number of firms is increasing.

The last article of this decade is 'The Concentration Margins Relationship Reconsidered', by Michael Salinger,[57] which was improved upon by comments from Richard Caves and Sam Peltzman. Salinger argued on methodological issues; the main point was the use of cross-section data to analyse the industrial concentration as a barrier to entry. The question is discovering a positive relationship between concentration and price–cost margins, knowing this variable is a proxy for the return of sales. Following the path of Sam Peltzman who published in 1977 that no exist this relationship using data for 165 American industries from 1947–67. The conclusion is illustrative: 'The relationship between the level of concentration and cost and price changes may simply be a reflection of the economy in the 1970's rather than a standard pattern for industry dynamics'.[58] This is the abandonment of industrial concentration as barrier to entry, at least while the variable which demonstrates this proposal will be price-cost margins. The unique way, used by researchers in order to make use of industrial concentration as ugly behaviour of the firms, has been matched industrial concentration with economies of scale and converts it into a strategic business decision. As we wrote a few pages ago, excess of capacity and industrial concentration technically changed as barriers to entry. Excess of capacity turns into sunk cost and industrial concentration turns into market power exercise. Both enter in a new catalogue of capital requirements and therefore business strategy.

5.2.3. Advertising as a Barrier to Entry

Advertising has been considered a barrier to entry since the 70s. Richard Schmalensee began work in this topic in 1974, and as far as we know no article rejects this proposal. During the 80s advertising survived as a barrier to entry but the theoretical framework changed. The principal reason was the evolution of economic theory through the use of games in order to prove his proposals. Von Weizsäcker in his work on barriers to entry proposed a new analytical framework in order to analyse them; goodwill is the only barrier to entry therefore understanding the process left. The reason we consider this barrier to entry separately is due to its special characteristics. Goodwill can work as a barrier to entry or can work as an externality. Goodwill as a barrier to entry should be studied as an incentive for other firms to destroy information about the quality of the products sold by others firms in the market. Where goodwill is seen as an externality it should be analysed as a valuable asset, or the substitute for direct knowledge of quality. Von Weizsäcker chose the first option and concluded that: 'It is not useful to say that entrants are at a disadvantage as compared with established firms'.[59] In his book, this argument was further developed:

> Goodwill is not a barrier to entry, is necessarily only a partial solution of the quality information problem, this is due to quasi risk aversion of consumers. Barriers to entry would then only exist, if consumers do not form rational expectations, but are biased in favor of products of known quality.[60]

Schmalensee is the expert on advertising, although he wrote about other barriers to entry. He also accepts that advertising does not make it possible to protect those profits which accrue from the practice of monopoly power. In the same train of thought, John Cubbin wrote in 1981 'Advertising and the Theory of Entry Barriers'. He developed his model under limit price theory. Cubbin has a prima facie case for his proposition that advertising may contribute to an entry barrier effect: his point is that this effect does not cause fundamental asymmetries in cost of demand functions. In conclusion Cubbin wrote 'Entry barrier effect can exist as long as the entrant's prospective demand curve is made less favourable by the mere fact of the established firm's present advertising'.[61] From Chicago, Thomas Nagle[62] answered Richard Schmalensee who worked in MIT, about the role of advertising. Nagle assumes that repeat purchase behaviour, or brand loyalty, is the response to the lack of information about alternatives, keeping in mind that the cost of finding a better brand is high. In terms of Stigler's price theory, we are talking about information costs; In this case, advertising should be a correlation with profit rates for incumbents but otherwise for new entrant firms. Problems arise when it is not possible to separate profits from rates of return or monopolistic returns, in which case, there are no arguments in favour of the existence of barriers to entry. Nagle set his model out for thirty-seven American Industries. Nagle realized that cross-section data gives similar troubles shown with industrial concentration as barrier to entry. Whereas barriers to entry in general and particularly advertising should be tied to price–cost margins, the researchers are unable to distinguish the origin of profits. Technically it is not possible to separate the rate of return from return of investment, because rate of return does not necessarily mean extra profits for a monopoly. Monopoly profits are the only way to demonstrate the existence of a barrier to entry. In the same vein, Robert Ayanian, in 1983, wrote that the traditional barriers to entry hypothesis holds that heavy advertising expenditures create entry barriers, because they facilitate persistently above-average rates of return for firms in industries that advertise heavily. Testing this hypothesis on thirty-nine American industries (the same data pull that Comanor and Wilson used in 1974), Ayanian concluded that the theory that advertising creates entry barriers is not exact because 'Firms in industries with heavy advertising expenditures earn rates of return no greater than those in industries where advertising is light'.[63]

Joseph Farrell wrote a paper in 1986 which was influential up until the end of the decade. Farrell's model was built on game theory and he tried to disconfirm Schmalensee's proposal on customer discrimination between quality of goods. Farrell defined moral hazard as a barrier to entry as follows:

> If an industry is providing less consumer surplus than is possible, an entrant can make positive profits by offering buyers a slightly better deal than they are getting from incumbents firms. In some cases, however, an entrant's profits would be higher still if he "Cheated" by providing goods of low quality. In such a case, buyers with rational expectations would not be willing to buy form an entrant and entry will not occur. This is our entry barrier.[64]

He tried to demonstrate that the reputation of an incumbent doesn't offer incentives to new entrants in an industry. In this sense the first entrant into an industry faces at least severe moral-hazard problem, and moral hazard is higher than subsequent entrants do support, and this is exactly the way in which barriers to entry work.

In 1988, John Cubbin and Simon Domberger wrote an article entitled 'Advertising and Post-Entry Oligopoly'. The main issue was to demonstrate that advertising works as a barrier to entry, as well as how high this barrier is. They used a case study of markets with a heavily advertised consumer goods and services, primarily toothpaste, instant coffee, electric shavers, shampoos, deodorants and cigarettes mainly. His proposal was that post-entry behaviour may differ from pre-entry behaviour, thus effectively establishing whether there is prima facie evidence of predation. His conclusion returns to the old Bain assumption: 'The post-entry behaviour is likely influenced by pre-entry market structure.'[65]

Kyle Bagwell, following the path of Schmalensee and Comanor and Wilson, set up a game in order to demonstrate that inefficiency in quality can persist in the presence of informational product differentiation. He wrote in 1988 an article attempting to present informational product differentiation as a barrier to entry, keeping in mind that product differentiation had been classified as a barrier to entry since a long time ago. Bagwell's main idea was to demonstrate whether consumers are able to distinguish between the quality of products, in this case, advertising as informer and indicator of product differentiation works as a barrier to entry. Bagwell's improvement on this theory lies in his demonstration of the existence of equilibrium in the model with a low-quality incumbent, which is when an inefficient incumbent is able to permanently bar the entry of a high-quality, efficient competitor. This issue should be susceptible to being extended to infant-industries analysis, as Grossman and Horn did. He concluded that inefficiency in quality can persist, in other words, advertising deterrence entry of rivals in an industry, he notes 'We show that signalling equilibra exist in which a low-quality, inefficient incumbent is able to permanently bar the entry of a high quality, efficient entrant'.[66]

Gene Grossman and Henrik Horn, in 1988, tried to use the line of argument which assumes that the infant-industry typically endorses temporary protection until such a time as the domestic industry achieves equal footing with its foreign rivals. Their argument was:

> In industries with imperfect information, the lack of a reputation puts latecomers at a competitive disadvantage vis-à-vis established firms. We consider whether the existence of such informational barriers to entry provides a valid reason for temporarily protecting infant producers of experience goods and services. Our model incorporates both moral hazard in an individual firm's choice of quality and adverse selection among potential entrants into the industry.[67]

They notice that whereas the temporary protection doesn't reduce moral hazard problems, the distortion prevented adverse selection. Following the path of Farrell and Bagwell, they said: 'Even when information is a barrier to entry, the marginal firms that enter in response to an output subsidy may well lower the average quality of domestic products available on the market'.[68] Their contribution to the barriers to entry theory or deterrence theory is the extension of the moral hazard concept from microeconomics to macroeconomics.

In the 70s and 80s advertising was considered as a barrier to entry. The industrial structure analysis should considered advertising as a sunk cost, and it could also be analysed within game theory. Even advertising could be considered cost in promotion or consumers' information; in this case, advertising is investment or strategic decision. The sticky issue refers to the customer welfare; advertising should be assessing as a cost which increase price to the customers while is expelling new entrants in an industry, if this is true, then consumer's losses welfare because of advertising. Altogether, advertising could reduce the risk of moral hazard or asymmetric information into a market in two ways: entrants and incumbents, as well as producers and customers.

5.3. Sequential Entry Models

These entry models receive a separate consideration of capacity and concentration since Kamien-Schwartz's 1975 article; using the Cournot model, the output of the firm is considered the independent variable of the model. Kamien and Schwartz presented a model within the timing of rival entry, regarded as a random variable whose probability distribution is dependent on current industry price. They assumed that the potential rivals are attracted by the recent price rather than recent profit. The entry research improved the old Cournot model by the inclusion of movements in profits, conditions for comparative statics, even including a certain degree of collusion. The main target was to analyse the behaviour of the firm due the new framework, game theory, allowed relevant methodological improvements. The debate takes place in the field of oligopoly theory and the conditions of entry, relaxing the Cournot model by using games. It is interesting to keep in mind that Strategy[69] is winning its place as framework capable of giving the best solutions in order to exclude new entrants from a market.

In 1980, Jesus Seade[70] wrote a relaxing Cournot model in order to analyse effects of entry. Harold Demsetz tried to recapitulate about following barriers to entry, the traditional consumer sovereignty and creation of reputation, and spillovers of knowledge, he wrote:

> Whereas the existence of trademark protection is a barrier to greater production of known products, the absence of trademark protection is a barrier to invention of new products. It cannot be said there is a barrier in one case not (the potential of) a barrier in the other case.[71]

Predatory prices were also considered by Demsetz, because predatory and competitive prices are difficult to separate, 'The correct price is approximately the discounted value of the future higher price that is the objective of promotional selling'.[72] Demsetz's conclusion was tough for researchers, as concept barrier to entry is a successful policy, but it must distinguish among cases and connect values and weights to each other.

Paul Milgrom and John Roberts in 1982 wrote articles entitled 'Limit Pricing and Entry under Incomplete Information: an Equilibrium Analysis'[73] and 'Predation, Reputation and Entry Deterrence'. The first was dedicated to analysing contradictions of limit price theory mainly in pre-entry and post-entry prices, because both prices involved a strategic decision; they concluded that the game needs a multiperiod where predation is possible and where reputation are in production factor, therefore it would be an important extension of the analysis. In the second article they applied this proposal to analyse real companies' behaviour; they argued that predation may be rational if a firm is threatened, under a profit-maximizing strategy, because it yields a reputation which deters other entrants. Using documents come from US Department of Justice (*IBM, Proctor and Gamble* v. *Maxwell*) they built a game of complete and perfect information. The main assumption is that in the equilibrium, predation will never be practised, but in the short run, 'The logic still will lead the next entrant to anticipate not that past behavior will be repeated but rather that it entry will meet a nonaggressive response'.[74] They point out that predation can be a rational strategy and capable of deterring entry and supporting monopoly; meanwhile predation should be used in the antitrust regulatory system.

Following the path of developing new models in order to improve oligopoly theory, Avner Shaked and John Sutton[75] in 1983 developed a model with new conditions of entry that allow an arbitrary number of firms to coexist in an industry with positive market shares, and prices over the unit variable cost, at a Nash equilibrium in prices. Pankat Ghemawat and Barry Nalebuff,[76] in 1985, explored a Cournot competition model in a declining market in order to show which firms, smallest or biggest, are the first to exit the the industry. In 1984 Douglas Bernheim wrote a new and suggestive model of entry, which deserves special consideration. The target of the paper is quite interesting and controversial, 'The United States government possesses an arsenal of public policy instruments designed to foster competitive industrial structures'.[77] He included penalties, subsidization of entry, consent decrees, restructuring an industry by breaking up a dominant firm. Let me conclude the whole game with Bergheim's words:

> Initially, a certain number of firms operate within an industry, and face the threat of entry from a single potential competitor. Incumbent firms simultaneously choose investments in deterrence activities. The potential competitor then determines whether entry into the industry would be profitable. If he chooses not to enter, operating firms collect their profits and the game ends. If entry occurs, the group of operating firms is enlarged (one firm has been added). A new potential competitor then appears, all previous deterrence investments become obsolete, and the new group must undertake a similar decision.[78]

The model's solution must be found by Cournot and collusive oligopoly equilibrium. The author made an artificial construct, which he refers to as the *deterrence technology*. Through this technology, established firms can inflict costs upon the potential competitor if entry is attempted. The model is developed as:

> In particular, each incumbent firm i selects a level of deterrence investment I_i. This generates an entry cost of $D_n(I)$ where $I = \sum I_i$. The deterrence technology is intention-

ally ambiguous, since we wish to abstract form the complex issues which arise with regard to particular theories of entry deterrence. The most straightforward interpretation of D_n ($\cdot$) is that the established firm hires goon squads to break the thumbs of anyone who attempts to build a competing factory. Other commonly discussed practices, though less violent, often have the same essential features. These include:

1) Lobbying for legislative barriers to entry.
2) Advertising to establish brand name identification,
3) Choosing a non-optimal production technology which changes the nature of the duopoly solution.
4) Innovating constantly to keep entrants far down the learning curve.
5) Holding excess production capacity as a threat against entrants and
6) Practicing limit pricing.[79]

His conclusion is to bear in mind the difficulty of deterring entry, and to offer solutions for workable competition; joint with the hard work to maintain business' issues into legal rules, despite the arsenal of public policy instruments.

Economic oligopoly theory has a lot of new proposals to improve old models. Gilbert and Vives, for instance, used Dixit's model (developed in 1979), where Dixit distinguishes between capacity and output. Capacity would have a constant unit cost; output would have a constant marginal cost up to capacity and infinitely beyond that means Cournot's equilibrium, which results, at the same time, from the cost functions (capacities) chosen by the firms. Gilbert and Vives's model is included into Cournot equilibrium, when the entry costs are associated with entry preventing output. Because cartel industrial structures with an unnatural monopoly are rare. Nonetheless industry with high level of concentration maintains a cartel justified by technological conditions. Gilbert and Vives notice that:

> If entry was allowed, incumbents' equilibrium output would fall and entrants would hold back output resulting in a market price higher than the limit price. Thus incumbents' profits with entry can be higher than if entry is prevented while each incumbent firm chooses to prevent entry.[80]

And they concluded:

> One may conjecture that there will not be excess capacity in equilibrium since capacities costly and excess capacity does not deter entry; potential entrants ignore capacities that are not going to be use fully (i.e. capacities that are not credible). It would be profitable to keep an entrant out but it is not possible to do so because the output needed to prevent entry cannot be induced in Cournot equilibrium by any capacity choice of the incumbents.[81]

This model allows them to deduce that entry prevention is not exactly in the public good, because the result could be the opposite of what is needed. Following with entry and social efficiency, Gregory Mankiw and Michael Whinston wrote an article in 1986 arguing this topic. Their model established that entry can be settled in terms of outcome of the post-entry game played by entrants. In this model, an especial extension could be made to analyse entry within a homogeneous market, they said: 'Entry restrictions are often socially desirable, although, as we show, they become unnecessary as the fixed set-up cost becomes small'.[82]

At the end of the 80s, the old pricing limit theory was revived once again. The limit price model of Bain-Sylos-Modigliani plus games seems a good way to explain market structure, and therefore the noncompetitive behaviour of firms within their markets. Curtis Eaton and Roger Ware were the pioneers of this rescue: they wrote a paper entitled 'A Theory of Market Structure with Sequential Entry', in which they built a sophisticate mathematical model in order to demonstrate that in the long run equilibrium price of output in a industry tends to the limit price. Using the theoretical model of Spence, Dixit and newest article of Gilbert and Vives; Eaton and Ware built a model which technology is exogenous. As a conclusion Eaton and Ware wrote:

> In this article we have developed a theory of market structure suggested by the work of these earlier authors. Firms enter the market in sequence, each computing the reaction of all subsequent entrants to its own strategic investment decision. Only demand and cost conditions and the structure of the entry game are specified exogenously; the number of firms, their size distribution, and the market price are determined as the equilibrium to this entry game.[83]

In the same vein, Daniel Shapiro and R. Khemani using the 70s articles of Orr, Caves and Porter and Harrigan developed a model which investment in assets with sunk cost characteristics should be considered as a barrier to exit, and thus, gives an advantage to the incumbents in an industry ahead of new entry rivals. They found: 'A high positive correlation between entry and exit barriers across industries is observed because barriers to entry restrict displacement and exit'.[84]

In the same vein, Robert Masson and Joseph Shaanan[85] tested a vector of barriers to entry in 1987, following the path of Kamien and Schwartz, Baron, Gaskins and Orr. The vector had several variables, such as number of entrants, probability of i entrant, future industry value and the maximal number of potential entrants. The contrast of this vector was made with data from forty-three manufacturing industries in Canada during the period 1960–3. Statistical results were quite significant with Richard Caves' tests. Joseph Shaanan made another empirical study about the main barriers to entry, concentration, economies of scale and advertising. Thirty-seven manufacturing American industries were analysed during 1958–66, and his conclusion was that advertising didn't work as a barrier to entry; the market conditions tested empirically confirm the hypothesis of Structure-Conduct-Performance paradigm. Joachim Schwalbach applied the Masson-Shaanan's model to German industry using 122 four-digit German manufacturing industries from 1977–82, and his conclusion was: 'The incentive to enter new markets is reduced by entry barriers like scale economies, product differentiation and market risk'.[86] Meanwhile, Zoltan Acs and David Audretsch[87] tested the relationship between firm size and innovative activity. They used data come 172 innovative and forty-two highly innovative industries, for four-digit American Small Business Administration in 1982. They concluded that innovation rates have a significant effect on firm size as well in the industrial market structure.

Following the path of entry models, Timothy Bresnahan and Peter Reiss published a controversial article in 1987. They pointed out the low interest in strategic behaviour of the firms in the long run and a high interest in industrial concentration. In order to improve the strategic competitive theory they calculated entry thresholds ratios ETR, over the base of a ratio monopoly and duopoly. 'We treat price and quantity setting in monopoly and duopoly as a black box because we are interested only in the functions determining profits in industry equilibrium'.[88] Using American data from yellow pages, questions, telephones calls and so on, they assumed the threat of future entry should be led by a limit price. After a bitter discussion with George Stigler they admitted their short interest in normative implications, they answered that their only focus was to shed light on the distinction between competition subjects and market definition issues for posteriors studies of market entry.

One of the most innovative approximations to modern barriers to entry was made by Philippe Aghion and Patrick Bolton, working on contracts, and taking up Williamson's idea of labour costs, once again. Building on the assumption that informational asymmetry constrains the monopoly power of the incumbent and the buyer with respect to the entrant; in order to solve the problem of long run equilibrium they made use of the following principle:

> It is a well-known principle in economics that if agents engage in mutually advantageous trade, it is and their best interest to sign the longest possible contract. A long term contract can always replicate what a sequence of short-term contracts achieves.[89]

They built a game and concluded that a barrier to entry exists when the pre-entry profits are bigger than post-entry profits.

In 1988 Robert Smiley wrote an empirical study of strategic entry deterrence. His model was inspired by the older models of Bain, Spence, Dixit and Porter; in this way Smiley tried to test such barriers to entry as aggressive use of the learning curve, capacity expansion pre-emption, advertising, patents and R&D, reputation as an aggressive firm, the excessive filling of all product niches and the masking of single-product profitability. However he improved on the old framework using an opinion poll carried out on seven new products and eight existing product strategies and rent to the CEOs of the firms involved. Smiley wrote about the difficulties which he found doing this research:

> An additional difficulty in writing to CEOs is that they will rarely respond person-ally. Instead, they are likely to give the questionnaire to a public relations aide, or not respond at all. The problem of eliciting truthful answers is critical here, since the information desired is sensitive competitive information, and some of the strategies described might be in the grey zone of legality/illegality.[90]

The conclusion of this innovative research was that more than half the respond-ents reported that attempts to deter entry were comparable in importance to other strategic marketing and production decisions. Loyalty and advertising expenditures are often used by firms mainly the creation of product loyalty through advertising expenditures. Whereas application of limit pricing is used less often by companies; only for existing products do firms attempt to limit entry through filling all available product niches.

Timothy Dunne, Mark Roberts and Larry Samuelson[91] wrote, in 1988, about patterns of firm entry and exit in United States manufacturing industries. Using data coming from four-digit US manufacturing from 1963–82 they built a model whose main contribution to the analysis of structure market and non-competitive behaviour of the firm was that as many firms simultaneously operate in a number of industries, it is important to recognize several possible types of entry. The independent variable of their equation was taken as the number of firms over several years and the total output of firms within these years.

The pioneers in the study of market competition in Europe were Paul Geroski from the London School of Economics and Joachim Schwalbach from Wirstchaftszentrum Berlin für Sozialforschung. They published a document about barriers to entry and intensity of competition in European markets for the Commission of the European Communities in 1989. They used the Bain paradigm (S-C-P), and found special characteristics in the European industry, for example, the difficulty of understanding exactly what types of barriers cause high long-run profits,[92] some types of law create absolute cost advantages for incumbents firms (banking, 'purity laws' for beer in Germany, textile, autos, and so on). Geroski worked in this topic with Robert Masson in a framework named Dynamics of Market Structure. In this book, Geroski and Schwalbach argued, following Stigler caveats, that:

> 'Efficiency' used to be identify with the ability to survive and prosper, and to argue that if the market share of firms in a given size class falls, then that size of firm is not efficient ... This at least is consistent with the conclusions that scale advantages are unlikely to inhibit entry in general.[93]

They confirm their hypothesis with data come from eighty-five three-digit manufacturing industries in the UK and a specialist industry in Germany, brewery (6,000 individual businesses), during 1974–9 and 1983–4. They realized that the main problem is related to the data, in their words: 'Measuring particular barriers to entry is difficult at the best of times, and cross-section data is particularly limited in this respect'.[94] During the 90s, cross-section data changed to panel data, in an attempt to solve the econometrics problems due to the information gathering in cross-section way.

5.4. Consequences in Political Economy: 1984 Merger Guidelines

As specified at the beginning of this chapter, the 80s was a very convulsive period for our topic. Barriers to entry originated a lot of scientific production. This chapter concerns some of this production. In this selection we have not considered all the articles published during the decade, but every article deserves to be. The consequences of these big scientific publications meant an improvement in the oligopoly theory and the consecution of one important debate about the framework that economy gives to the courts; because the courts must decide about the existence of barriers to entry in a market, and as a consequence to pronounce them in order to ensure fair competition in American markets. For Europeans, during the eighties of the past century, the debate about the behaviour of the firms into their markets is at the beginning and does not deserve special consideration.

Following the tradition inaugurated by the 1968 guidelines; in 1982 Bill Baxter developed a new body of guidelines, following the concentration ratios improving with the Herfindahl index, and raised the level of market concentration necessary for the government intervention; altogether, he changed the strong consideration of economies of scale as a indicator of market power; Baxter used a flexible concept in order to consider efficiency and rationality in the factories production. The new guidelines were published in 1984.

As was done in Chapter 3 of the present book, the relevant issues will be reproduced, and the meanings of the 1984 merger Guidelines discussed.[95]

The unifying theme of the Guidelines is that mergers should not be permitted to create or enhance market power or to facilitate its exercise. The ability of one or more firms profitably to maintain prices above competitive levels for a significant period of time is termed *market power*. Sellers with market power also may eliminate rivalry on variables other tan price. In either case, the result is a transfer of wealth from buyers to sellers and a misallocation of resources. *Market power* also encompasses the ability of a single buyer or group to depress the price paid for a product to a level that is below the competitive price.

A market is defined as a product of group of products and a geographical area in which it is sold such that a hypothetical, profit maximizing firm, not subject to price regulation, that was the only present and future seller of those product in that area would impose a *small but significant and nontransitory* increase in price above currently prevailing or likely future levels. The group of products and geographic area that comprise a market will be referred to respectively as the *product market* and the *geographic market*.

The Department of Justice (hereafter, the Department) will first determine the relevant product market with respect to each product of each of the merging firms. In general, the Department will include in the product market a group of products such that a hypothetical firm that was the only present and future seller of those products (a monopolist) could profitably impose a *small but significant and nontransitory* increase in price.

The Department may use likely future prices when changes in the prevailing price can be predicted with reasonable reliability. Changes in price may be predicted on the basis of, for example, expected changes in regulations that directly affect price. In order to solve this issue, the Department will begin with the location of each merging firm (or plant of a multiplant firm) and ask what would happen if a hypothetical monopolist of the relevant product at that point imposed a *small but significant and nontransitory* increase in price.

The Department will consider all relevant evidence but will give particular weight to the following factors:

1) The shipment patterns of the merging firm and of those firms with which it actually competes for sales.
2) Evidence of buyers having actually considered shifting their purchases among sellers at different geographic locations, especially if the shifts corresponded to changes in relative price or other competitive variables.
3) Differences in the price movements of the relevant product or similarities in price movements over a period of years that are not explainable by common or parallel changes in factors such as the cost of inputs, income, or other variables in different geographic areas.
4) Transportation cost.
5) Costs of local distribution, and
6) Excess capacity of firms outside the location of the merging firms.

The Department determines horizontal merger as where the merging firms are in the same product and geographic area. Concentration affects the likelihood that one firm, or a small group of firms, could successfully exercise market power. It uses the Herfindahl-Hirschman Index of market concentration, and is calculated by summing the squares of the individual market shares of all the firms included in the market under the standards in Section 2 of these Guidelines (lack of information about small fringe firms is not critical because such firms do not affect the HHI significantly).

The Department will consider the likelihood and probable magnitude of entry in response to a *small but significant and nontransitory* increase in price. And the Department will consider the following factors, among others, as they relate to the ease and profitability of collusion; homogeneity-heterogeneity of the relevant product generally, degree of difference between the products and locations in the market and the next best substitutes, similarities and differences in the products and locations of the merging firms, information about specific transactions and buyer market characteristics, ability of small or fringe sellers to increase sales, conduct of firms in the market and efficiencies.

In evaluating the performance of a market, the Department will consider any relevant evidence, but will give particular weight to the following evidence of possible noncompetitive performance when the factors are found in conjunction:

a) Stable relative market shares of the leading firms in recent years.

b) Declining combined market share of the leading firms in recent years, and

c) Profitability of the leading firms over substantial periods of time that significantly excess that of firms in industries comparable in capital intensity and risk.

By definition, non-horizontal mergers (under traditional usage, such a merger should be characterized as either 'vertical' or 'conglomerate') involve firms that do not operate in the same market. Although non-horizontal mergers are less likely than horizontal mergers to create competitive problems, they are not invariably innocuous.[96] The theory of limit pricing suggests that monopolies and groups of colluding firms may find it profitable to restrain their pricing in order to deter new entry that is likely to push prices even lower by adding capacity to the market. In a footnote, the Guidelines acknowledged that when collusion is only tacit, the problem of arriving at and enforcing the correct limit price is likely to be particularly difficult.

In certain circumstances, the vertical integration resulting from vertical mergers could create competitively objectionable barriers to entry. Three conditions are necessary:

1. - The degree of vertical integration between the two markets must be so extensive that entrants to one market (the primary market) would also have to enter the other market (the secondary market) simultaneously.

2. - The requirement to entry at the secondary level must make entry at the primary level significantly more difficult and less likely to occur.

3. - The structure and other characteristics of the primary market must be otherwise so conducive to noncompetitive performance that the increased difficulty of entry is likely to affect its performance.

The Department will determine whether these conditions are satisfied. If there is sufficient un-integrated capacity in the secondary market, new entrants to the primary market would not have to enter both markets simultaneously. Also, if entry at the secondary level is easy in absolute terms, the requirement of simultaneous entry to that market is unlikely to adversely affect entry to the primary market, thus more capital is necessary to enter two markets than to enter one, so in evaluating the likelihood of increased barriers to entry resulting from increased cost of capital, the Department will consider both the degree of similarity in the essential skills in the primary and secondary markets and the economic life and degree of specialization of the capital assets in the secondary market. As a conclusion, barriers to entry are unlikely to affect performance if the structure of the primary market is otherwise not conducive to monopolization or collusion.

5.5. Guidelines Debate

At this time a new debate began to show the consequences of guidelines in the real economy. Until this moment, *workable competition* defined by Clark during the 50s and guidelines worked together as the best way to reach competitive markets in the USA. During the 80s, guidelines were questioned, because it seems possible that the way to catch competition could be turned into problems for companies; to respect established rules in guidelines, sometimes, could to take losses of competitiveness where the rules were not carefully designed.

Robert Willig[97] wrote a technical article in 1991 about the 1984 guidelines, whereas Salop and Scherer made some criticism. The analytical process to describe a merger follows a set with the following steps: delineation of the relevant product and geographic market, identification of firms included as participants in the relevant market, calculation and interpretation of market shares and concentration, assessing easy of entry, consideration of other factors and assessing efficiencies. Into a Cournot model and under the profit-maximizing monopoly supplier of the set would impose a small but significant and nontransitory increase in price (SSNIP) in this case the analysis assumes that:

> If a merger created a complete monopoly in an overlap relevant market, the analysis predicts that demand would permit the imposition of at least a small but significant and nontransitory price rise for the products and locations in this relevant market.[98]

The guidelines established the limit to increase the price by 5 per cent. This framework leaves considerable opportunity for influences beyond market delineation and concentration, even apart from efficiencies and entry. Collusion might be interpreted as some oligopolistic behaviour deviated in its outcome from perfect competition and into a game theory framework; tacit collusion is associated with supergames, a special case of dominant firm model (connected under the umbrella of Stigler) or a *carrot and stick* equilibrium of a repeated game.

Steven Salop wrote of the 1984 Guidelines that they were written under a contestable market framework; and for this reason they didn't included the more important variable: 'The guidelines do not state explicitly whether they are concerned with Stiglerian or Bainian barriers to entry',[99] because if there is an assumption the existence of sunk costs, they have a non-casual relationship with entry and pre-entry price. Salop argued that likelihood of entry because a SSNIP depends of factors clarified by Stigler and Bain long time ago: advantages of costs, timing, economies of scales and sunk cost. In the posterior comments Carl Shapiro congratulate with Willig' work about the analysis of price and market structure changes, and Shapiro defended that the data are able to show the price level to be the determinant of entry.

The most important change, in the 80s, was the role of microeconomics in the development of antitrust policy and litigation. Lawrence White[100] exposes clearly how relevant transformation happens:

> For the first time there were Federal Trade Commission Commissioners who were economist, including the Chairman during the first few year of the Reagan Administration ... An indication of the rising importance of economists in the mid 1980's was the redesignation of the Director of the Economic Policy Office as a Deputy Assistant Attorney General.[101]

Whereas the game theoretic framework is taking a significant role in the economic academy; there is not a successful defence of the same argument in the federal courts of antitrust, as Rudolph Peritz[102] wrote 'Judges do not understand the likelihood of harm to consumers that can result from aftermarket strategies'.[103] The main consequences in American antitrust law during the 80s were that Federal Courts have been opposed to finding antitrust legally responsible when evidence of agreements is entirely circumstantial.

The legacy of the Chicago and Harvard Schools survives; the controversy about the tools that economic science offers to the judges continued this decade. But the Federal Trade Commission, as the main court, took fair competition loss influence in the political field which approved of non-intervention in markets. As Schmalensee wrote in 1982:

> The industrial economics affects antitrust policy in three different ways. First, it is used in positive analysis aimed at determining whether or nor current law has been violated in specific cases and at assessing damages due injured parties. Second, it should be used in evaluating the desirability of relief that might be imposed in particular cases in order to alter structure or conduct if a violation is found. Finally, the

tools and results of industrial economics are important inputs in the formulation of
general rules of law.[104]

The limits of Industrial economics should be found in the fact that it provides a
large amount of market models, but no reliable tools for the empirical analysis of
particular industries; and this is the point, because if the economic theory is to
bring tools for courts, they have to be able to improve the judicial precedents.

While Richard Schmalensee published his article, William Baumol published
an article about how barriers to entry have been analysed within the framework
of industrial organization existing. Both authors surveyed research and in which
direction this research was headed. Beginning with the old controversy between
Joe Bain and George Stigler and following up with the limits of game theory to
improve the paradigm known as price limit theory, their intention was to set out
the theoretical arguments necessary to implement an antitrust policy. Baumol
rethought the proposal maintained in Areeda and Turner's article about predatory pricing of 1975, where they seek to find a distinction between predatory
and competitive prices; in other words, economists and lawyers must to be able
to differentiate between rents and profits in the industrial activities of the firms.
Baumol, Panzar and Willig wrote: 'A barrier to competitors may arise from the
superior efficiency of existing firms, in which case their low prices are precisely
what competitive markets are expected to bring forth'.[105] Baumol argued the
impossibility of distinguishing between competitive and collusive behaviour of
firms. Schmalensee reaches a similar conclusion to Baumol although using other
arguments, in order to keep the accurate sense of his words, there is pasted the
whole cite:

> The Harvard tradition initially condemned all tying arrangement as providing 'lever-
> age' that permitted the multiplication of monopoly positions. Chicago countered
> that the concept of leverage is without theoretical support, that tying is generally a
> form of price discrimination, and that ties should be legal because price discrimina-
> tion is generally efficiency enhancing ... Theoretical analysis suggest the non-existence
> of simple test that one could actually apply in particular cases to determine whether
> banning tying contracts would enhance efficiency.[106]

Under the assumptions defended above, Baumol's recommendation to policymakers was that: 'A plausible policy is to take the bird in hand now because none
may be in the bush tomorrow'.[107] Schmalensee confronted a similar dilemma:
when should economic analysis be transformed into antitrust laws which the
firms have to follow? He wrote: 'the sophistication of antitrust decisions will
surely rise more slowly than the sophistication of economic analysis and testimony'.[108] Two years later Bernheim defended a similar prudence, 'caution
when using simple economic models for making prescriptions about industrial

policy'.[109] In 1988 Vives[110] got the same conclusions, public authority has to be careful with measures to promote competition.

A controversial article was written by Samuel Loescher, in 1980, defending the convenience of returning to the old proposal of John Maurice Clark in 1940 and reviving the forces of potential competition, *workable competition* using Clark terminology. He thought that the predatory pricing theory developed by Areeda and Turner had a wide acceptation in the main courts in the United States, he wrote: 'Before a year had passed, their sweeping proposition was adopted virtually in Toto by the Fifth Circuit Court. Moreover, their central doctrine was adopted in at least six more federal cases during the following two years'.[111] He was quite worried about this theory, mainly because: 'Areeda and Turner neglect the serious negative impact that their liberalized coercive pricing rule will have upon new firms entry'.[112] The argument defended in the Areeda theory will accentuate corporate birth control, and under the idea of improved benefits through competitive performance there are speculative and indeterminate promises in the long run. Even in 1987 Kotaro Suzumura and Kazuharu Kiyono[113] built a theoretical model in order to demonstrate that more competition not necessarily increase welfare, against the traditional belief, if there should be necessary to add fuel to the fire.

Economic analysis improved during the 80s, despite theoretical controversy; Baumol, Panzar and Willig's book on contestable markets shed light about antitrust policies. They noted that whether the analysis of market structure change from Bain's S-C-P to contestable markets, the framework should be appropriate and the industrial performance could be better understood and, incidentally, the antitrust policymakers have a better weapon against the bad behaviour of firms, because: 'May be possible to isolate the portion of the industry's activities that cause the incontestability and regulate that portion, leaving the remainder of the industry's activities free from governmental interference'.[114]

But the whole of academy was not in agreement about the cautious use of economic tools to offer a good analytical instrument to the courts. Two articles were written about the consequences of deregulation: one by Shepherd and one by Bailey. William G. Shepherd who published in 1982 'Causes of Increased Competition in the U. S. Economy, 1939–1980', built his model with variables, some of which come from the Herfindahl index in order to specify standards of market structure. After he classified American Industries into three categories, such as pure monopoly, dominant firms and tight oligopoly, he analysed their rise in import competition. He met three criteria, more competitive industry, import share above 15 per cent of all US sales and imports genuinely competitive with US products rather than just brought in by US firms to be marketed under their own brand names. At the end of the paper Shepherd suggested policy lessons, such as that: 'Continued antitrust pressure is needed to retain the new level of competition ... free-trade policies are crucial to the continuation of effective import competition in a range of large industries'.[115] Elizabeth E. Bailey[116] wrote her article in 1986, entitled 'Prices and productivity change following deregulation: the US experience', she analysed the consequences emerged under deregulation in four businesses in the United States: Brokerage, Trucks and Rail, Communication and Airlines. During 1972–5, US brokers were required to charge fixed commissions for securities transactions; the Interstate Commerce Commission involved balkanization of authority, the regulation leaving rail with a low margin traffic and financial returns for rail averaging 2, 42 per cent during 1962–78, and the Federal Communications Commission received applications to enter in the telecommunications industries in competition with AT&T, in the same vein as air transportation and brokerage. Bailey pointed out that, after deregulation, in telecommunications the main consequence was lower prices, while the civil aeronautic board, later deregulation, the small local services expanded scope and scale; for trailers on flat car services, prices have risen by more than half between 1981 and 1984; and brokerage activity shows that the top ten firms in 1974 were still in the top in 1984. In short, the consequences of deregulation of markets were different, depending on the industry and connected with the market structure.

In the topic at hand predation and limit price theory explain to deterrence entry into a market, the controversy was quite relevant in political issues. The proposals made by Phillip Areeda and Donald Turner in 1975 are biased toward larger firms, there is no place for industries working in oligopoly market, there is not even reference to the Stigler umbrella and its consequences on market price. At the same time, founding a *reasonably anticipated* way to measure a price benchmark or price floor does not seem easy. On the other side Richard Posner's proposal would have practical problems as well, when demonstrating his model. The limit price in general is unable to explain how monopoly can prosper and exclude rivals despite empirical evidence presented by this theory's champions. McGee's theory about the mis-working of limit price theories is: 'The limit price is determined by the slope of industry demand, no matter how big the market is'.[117] In this issue, the intervention of markets found followers and detractors. However the health of this economic debate is a signal that economic theory was alive. While Marginalism's theory is changing to accommodate game theory, and the cost calculus is changing to games. The important debate during the 80s was centred in how to demonstrate the bad behaviour of firms within their own market performance. Two different frameworks are vying for prominence and several proposals fill the academic publications: strategic behavior and the neoclassical model; the relevance of the short run in economic theory, indeed, critical to business planning; in front of the neoclassical long run. Business' decisions took in the short run against the industry's equilibrium in the long run.

Conclusions

During the 1980s, the analysis of barriers to entry was improved by the introduction of games into the old limit price theory. The objective of researchers was the same, to find a theoretical framework capable of demonstrating the existence of barriers to entry. Armed with this new framework they will have arguments about how to change the behaviour of the firms through new interventions which have to be approved by policymakers.

At this time the old controversy between the Harvard and the Chicago Schools continue. Researchers from Harvard spend their time working within the Cournot theory of oligopoly, but inserting into their model more sophisticated statistical techniques and games theory. The Chicago School researchers worked in a irrefutable demonstration that barriers to entry do not survive in the long run. The controversy about survive of profits in the long run is one of the main debate at this moment. For the sake of not be repetitive, in this chapter it was not included again this topics, because it was analysed in the Chapter 4.

The extension of both branches happenened when Michael Porter, from Harvard, developed his theory about the competitive strategy of the firms, whereas William Baumol, Robert Willig and John Panzar developed their contestable market. The gap that existed between both Schools of thought grows. The only meeting point was that no one obtains their objective, that neither School reaches the goal that anybody's succeeded in providing a usable framework for policy markers.

At the end of the 80s, some researchers follow the path of Joe Bain, one by one each barrier revealed by empirical evidence. In the same vein, other researchers improve on the Bain-Sylos-Modigliani theoretical model by introducing games under the new heading of sequential entry. Scholars who work within the Stigler price theory paradigm follow their own path, pursuing markets' frictions.

In the 1980s new industrial organization tools, such as game theoretic approaches, allowed economists to examine the ways in which established firms behave strategically in relation to their actual and potential rivals, the distinction between credible and non-credible threats, also connected with predatory pricing. Game theory allows a theoretical demonstration of the bête noire of oligopoly theory: power market.

If the marginal cost theory was not able to offer worthwhile tools to courts in the United States, games theory, however, found more difficulties; strategic behaviour is considered such not deserving of punishment. Therefore, unworkable competition does not have successful framework relating to it that can be used in a court.

The main obstacle to competition theory appeared in this decade, the bastion of workable competition (i.e. guidelines), began to be questioned. The rules, long-negotiated and hardly implemented, are not more accepted without replication. To establish guidelines became the goal of research; small but significant and non-transitory increase in price, relevant evidence and likelihood began to be familiar words for researchers across America.

In Table 5.1, we have classified, in chronological order, the articles about barriers to entry analysed in this chapter. The columns correspond to the year of publication, author of the article, barrier or barriers analysed and, where available, the statistical variable used to confirm the hypothesis, predecessors' authors in order to give the reader a view of economic thought-line followed by the author in question including his framework of choice. The next column contains information about the empirical confirmation of the theory, such as main industries which data was used, and whee information was available we include the period and country of analysis. The last column shows the author's main conclusion.

6 BARRIERS TO ENTRY: CURRENT ANALYSIS

Introduction

During the last years of the twentieth century and the first few of the twenty-first century the scientific production of barriers to entry pivoted on three main points. The first was built following the Cournot model, developing theoretical models about sunk costs and the use of excess capacity as an entry barrier, using the price as indicator of workable competition, pursuing the difference between real price and marginal cost (the benchmark of competitive price). The second line of research followed the path of market power exercised by control of market production or market share between incumbents; the indicator of this behaviour is found in the Herfindahl-Hirschman Index and the consequences should be quantified by the Federal Trade Commission. The third scientific development should be considered entry models; which, using game theory, was able to demonstrate how firms could deter entry of rivals, through strategic decisions and strategic advantages.

The dominant framework, and powerful for the antitrust authorities, should be considered the Structure-Conduct-Performance paradigm; under its lens were drawn up the Merger Guidelines in 1992, 1997 and 2000. After a convulsive decade like the 1980s, a deep breath was drawn during the 1990s and 2000s. The analysis of the last research about barriers to entry and noncompetitive markets regarding the four old main branches: excess of capacity, industrial concentration, advertising and entry models. During this time excess of capacity as a barrier to entry included economies of scale and special treatment of sunk costs, the main contribution of the New Chicago School to the antitrust framework. The indicator of the use of excess of capacity by an industry to expel rivals has traditionally been considered the industry's price; 1992 Guidelines established the 5 per cent as the price increase that should be weigh up as dangerous and the intervention of Agency will be the consequence. Geroski, Christensen and Caves and Allen are the main authors worries about the treatment of the use of installed capacity as barrier to entry.

Industrial concentrations have special relevance in antitrust, not in vain is this the era of globalization, and now market power has not only reached domestic economy but also external economies as well. Market power has been considered a transfer of wealth from buyers to sellers and therefore a misallocation of resources. Bernheim, Whinston, Stenbacka, Geroski and Peteraf should be considered as the main champions of the exercise of market power as a barrier to entry.

Advertising, as a barrier to entry, changes in this period to be included in adverse selection models. This change makes sense because publicity and advertising have to run the risk in purchase customers, through the increasing of available information. Bagwell, Dell' Ariccia, Friedman and Marquez, and Scott Morton are researchers in this particular field, the use and development of signalling models and their utilization in empirical research is the main advance of this root.

The 90s was the decade of entry models. This kind of model could be included in two roots; business strategy and the Structure-Conduct-Performance paradigm. The choice between them could be finding peculiarities in each market. Knowing how to a market works leaves the door open to strategic decisions or the use of the weakness of incumbents. Specific information about barriers to entry determines which is the best strategy on how a market should be entered, while at the same time it gives a chance to new entrants, giving it the possibility of creating its own barrier.

This is the historical period when specialized business economists began to write a handbook on strategy, using case studies. These are not new; however, they begin to be relevant on both sides: in teaching in business schools and in reporting in competition trials for judicial requirements. The first field follows the path of Michael Porter, inaugurated in 1980 with his world-famous book, *Competitive Strategy*. At this time economic science kept an appropriate place in competition trials, Schmalensee and Bresnahan are the most cited reporters, as they published in scientific review their personal cases analysis. Fudenberg, Tirole, Pakes and Baumol focused their research on more theoretical issues.

Since the American Economic Review in 2004, Dennis Carlton[1] argued about the definition of a barrier to entry and its meanings. Carlton noted that *vigour of competition* should be helpful to understanding what are we thinking where we research an entry. The issue is that existence of barriers to entry is only a part of the non-workable competition, which seems convenient to widen the field of research. In order to help the Department of Justice and Federal Trade Commission, Carlton pointed out: 'What should matter to policymakers is how fast entry erodes any price increase caused by a merger, and not whether it eventually does so'.[2] Following the path to explain vigour of competition and to make a separate analysis of barriers to entry with other factors affecting timing to entry, in 2005 he wrote about the necessity of modelling explicitly the effect of uncertainty on entry or exit firm's decisions into their markets.

But every coin has two sides, and on the flipside of competition one book deserves a special consideration, *Competition Demystified*, by Bruce Greenwald and Judd Kahn. As the title shows they tried to reduce the analysis of competition as far as possible, noting: 'Understanding the significance of barriers to entry and how they operate is the key to developing effective strategy'.[3] If barriers to entry exist in any market, incumbents should be able to do things that potential rivals cannot. In the case of the rivals they have to identify the source of this advantage or barrier; looking at property rights in technologies, the way in which customers have been captured, and so on. Greenwald and Kahn taught that there are two telltale signs of the existence of a barrier to entry or competitive advantage. The stability of market share among firms and the profitability of firms within the sector; the way to assess this advantage is to collect information about after-tax returns on invested capital, if this is more than 15–25 per cent over a decade there is a clear evidence of the presence of barriers to entry. They wrote a manual for students with plenty of keys to understanding how to reach a barrier or advantage.

This chapter includes the main changes incorporated into the Guidelines; it is important to note that the inclusion of timelines, likelihood and sufficiency of entry could be considered as the first inclusion of game theory to analyse competition. Even though game theory has been used since the 80s to understand the behaviour of firms in their markets, the Agencies of American competition didn't pay sufficient attention to incorporate them into the Guidelines. Three complementary guidelines were published in this period, 1992, 2000 and 2006. They included relevant changes from the 1984 Guidelines, and in 2006 were included for R&D industries.

This chapter recounts a special discussion about antitrust, which took place at that time. For thirty years the battle of competition as confined in the academic field; how to demonstrate the existence of barriers to entry, how to assess extra profits, a predatory pricing in an industry exist, all these questions were debated for years in the most important American faculties of business and economics. At the beginning of the twenty-first century a new actor appeared in the arena, the courts where judges must to sentence for or against a firm behaviour, including penalties, strategic decisions and so on. Subsequently the discussion moved to trial resolutions; then showing the weakness of economic theory when helping judges, juries and courts. The theoretical models could be impeccable but not means necessarily sufficient proof for use in trials. The limits of economic theory in offering tools, without a possibility of question, are at the end of the present research and a new field which deserves future inquires.

6.1. Traditional Barriers, New Discussion

6.1.1. Excess of Capacity and Sunk Costs.

Since the 1990s the analysis of costs confused several issues, such as economies of scales and scope, excess of capacity, sunk costs, costs of distribution, transport and so on. The relevant evidence, used by the Guidelines in 1984, should generate likelihood and a probable magnitude of entry in response to a *small but significant and nontransitory* increase in price established as 5 per cent since 1992[4] and maintained in 2006[5]. This entry barrier should be demonstrated following the old limit price theory developed by Bain-Sylos-Modigliani at the end of the 1950; in this section are included new proposals of research mainly collected under the name of cost advantages.

Robert Cairns and John Galbraith wrote a paper in 1990 about the entry barriers in frequent flyer programmes. They built a Bertrand model in which equilibrium is not accounting for price alone but for price and the level of rebate offered by various firms. Cairns and Galbraith assumed that the rabbet-coupon works as a barrier to entry; not in the traditional sense of cost advantages, but through the link created by firms to demands for different goods or services, very close to a network of services. They concluded that:

> We have indicated circumstances in which a firm can create a barrier to entry in the absence of any absolute cost advantage; of any economies of scale, scope, or density; and of any other mechanism for ensuring that output can be produced at lower cost that an entrant could match.[6]

In this way they noted the convenience of researching new entry barriers other than the traditional cost advantages developed by firms which cause nonworkable competition.

Paul Geroski began to work with market dynamics in the 80,s and in 1991 published his book *Market Dynamics and Entry*. Geroski followed the models of strategic behaviour and he research within a framework which entry can often play a more significant and more important role in the evolution of markets. He worked on the old Bain-Sylos model but introduced fixed effects and he used panel data to confirm his hypothesis. He noted that: 'When incumbents do not respond to either potential or actual entry, the effects of entry on price occur only through induced changes in market structure.'[7] Regarding policymakers, he pointed out that holding down prices may limit the ability of entrants to finance their expansion and reduce the market penetration. Even in the cases which consider the residual market, understood as the difference between total market demand and total market offer by all entrants (in the past as well as the present), the burden should be held by the dominant firm, which must increase.

On this point Geroski concluded that: 'Limit price as a strategy seems uncompelling because it conveys little credible force'.[8]

Capacity installed is the most commonly discussed type of strategic investment; the effect of this is to alter the incumbent's marginal cost curve, in the words of Geroski, however, he did consider other barriers to analyse, for example, mobility barriers, scarce factors of production, a natural resource, patents, in short the existence of absolute cost advantages, because they are not exogenous to the competitive process. Finally Geroski argued that problems arose when the scientific community uses cross-section data to confirm scientific hypotheses and defends panel data as a better alternative in this field. Geroski confirm his hypothesis with data come ninety-five British industries during 1983–4; these are unique panel data; the other information used was cross-section data from seventy-nine West German four-digit industries, 1983–5; 141 Norwegian five-digit industries 1981–5; 73 Portugese industries, 1982–6; 109 Belgian three-digit industries, 1980–4 and sixty-two Korean four- or five-digit industries, 1977–81. Respecting the characterization of barriers to entry, Geroski noted that the pharmaceutical industry has product differentiation advantages. The airbus, coach, gas, polyester, metal box and photocopier industries have absolute cost advantages. While the beer, cigarette and network (IBM) industries enjoy advantages due to economies of scale.

In the same vein, in 1991, Sally Davies[9] examined the threat of entry by constrained pricing behaviour in a natural monopoly. She built a dynamic price competition model and concluded that product differentiation can have the social benefit of increasing competition in some markets. David Bunch and Robert Smiley wrote about the use of strategic entry deterrence in 1992; they consider capacity expansion responses as a pre-entry requirement. They wrote a questionnaire from forty-two different products and they share it among 296 managers. Assuming that managers are usually a busy people they introduced a statistic in order to adjust his point. They concluded that: 'Advertising is used to deter entry into concentrated markets and research-intensive into markets with small minimum efficient scale'.[10]

In 1993 Beth Allen wrote about investment in capacity as a barrier to entry. She built a game model on the use of prices, rather than quantities, as the strategic variables of firms can yield a better model of oligopoly. She concluded her model pointing out that: 'When entry is blockaded the incumbent can effortlessly maintain its monopoly position without the necessity of strategic action to prevent entry'.[11] She noted that capacity is better entry barrier that inventory, because the price is determined by marginal cost of production; while inventory must include storage cost. At the same time the election of installed capacity in a firm offer the possibility to sell a quantity equal to capacity.

Other literature was published in order to disconfirm the traditional use of the installed capacity as a barrier to entry. Jonathan Haskel and Christopher Martin[12] built in 1994 a theoretical model in order to confirm the use of capacity in the market competition; they tested results with data set is a panel of eighty-one manufacturing industries in the United Kingdom during 1980–9, and they concluded with a negative relationship between capacity and profits. They insist in the necessary discrimination between industries touching the capacity constraints.

The relevant case studies of the 80s, would become the case studies that burst onto the scene of antitrust in the 90s. Stephen Mathis and Janet Koscianski wrote about the excess of capacity as a barrier to entry in the US titanium industry. They work with the Spence, Dixit and Lieberman models of barriers to entry, but mainly Hilke who contends that investment in excess of capacity is worthy because it converts fixed costs into sunk costs for rivals. Their first problem is connected with cross-section data and it is because of this that they choose to use time series.[13] The titanium industry keeps singularities in respect to the other industries, being primary among them, titanium metal demand has been characterized by extreme fluctuations. This has primarily been due to the cyclical nature of the civilian aerospace industry and the unpredictability of government orders for aircraft, this is a central reason why the titanium industry must assume an excess of capacity, only to attend in time and form the government orders of purchase; as the authors noted: 'Clearly, excess capacity, to the extent that it serves as a barrier to entry, can create suboptimal performance results for society at large'.[14]

The pulp and paper industry was studied by Laurits Christensen and Richard Caves in 1997; the main idea supporting the study is the use of capacity by the incumbents to prevent rivalry from outsiders. They used the paper industry because the investment on capacity can increase the output in the short-run. They built a cheap-talk and auction model of investment rivalry, technically cheap-talk chose a game in which communication between players which does not directly affect payoffs. The period analysed to confirm the hypothesis was 1978–91. This initiative followed the old proposal of Lieberman from the 80s. They concluded that: 'We can explain very well which projects were and were not abandoned, so that any broadly relevant theoretical model should be consistent with the determinants that we find'.[15]

The sunk costs issue is deeply connected with investment in capacity and therefore with economies of scale. It is the core of the cost structure of a company. John Nachbar, Bruce Petersen and Inhak Hwangs wrote a theoretical paper about sunk costs and welfare in 1998; the proposal was that meanwhile non-sunk costs are accommodated the social welfare increase. From the point of view of policymakers it seems relevant to know how large sunk costs must be in order to improve the welfare effects of entry substantially. They set theories of entry deterrence out because they assumed that would give them the opportunity for a welfare assessment of entry. They pointed out that: 'As is well known, sunk costs introduce an asymmetry between the incumbent and the entrant, lowering the incumbent's marginal cost in the post-entry game and thereby making the incumbent less accommodating'.[16] They noted as Spencer, von Weizsäcker, Mankiw and Whinston said previously that market performance could be improved by regulating entry. Dennis Carlton and Jeffrey Perloff[17] from the Chicago School, in their book, *Modern Industrial Organization*, developed a long-run barrier to entry, because Stigler's model paid no attention to sunk cost. The main objection to Stigler's definition of barrier of entry is that it does not help describe the post-entry equilibrium. Because Stigler definition of a barrier to entry implies that it's transitory, even if he spoke about the sunk costs. Some years later, on sunk cost, Carl Shapiro noted that: 'We are able to identify quite a large number of strategic considerations that come into play when there are large firms and enough sunk cost so that threats of entry are not the primary determinate of industry behavior, at least for the short to medium run'.[18] This discouraged conclusion about the area of strategic investment is balanced with the Shapiro's thoughts about the economic understanding of the strategic role of many business practices, and he pointed out the convenience of further tests of the empirical validity of every strategic behaviour theory. In 2004 the American Economic Review published three articles about barriers to entry; two of them arguing about sunk cost, Richard Schmalensee wrote one; Preston McAfee, Hugo Mialon and Michael Williams were the authors of the second article. Sunk cost could be considered the cornerstone of the analysis of market structure in terms of excess of capacity and economies of scale as barriers to entry in an industry.

In 2001, Daniel Rubinfeld wrote about competition when a company develops a new product, he pointed that the rule of thumb should be to assume that competition exists when more than one firm are in the same market developing new products, furthermore this assumption should be consistent with Law and Guidelines. However, it is convenient to keep in mind that market power, due to scale economies in production, will come from both the demand side and the supply side, especially in contractual practice, Rubinfeld wrote: 'Albeit with the risk that market power will be used for exclusionary purposes'.[19]

6.1.2. Industrial Concentration and Market Power

Industrial concentration is one way to exercise market power, which means industrial output control drive to control the market price. The Guidelines of 1992, maintained in 2006, established that the control of 35 per cent of the total product in an industry is enough to be considered market power, and two years maintaining this control is considered a stable market share. When collusion in a market allows the control of not only market share but market price as well, the market is analysed as a monopoly market.

Douglas Bernheim and Michael Whinston tried to demonstrate that in the case of geographic markets with high transportation costs bargaining is the usual horizontal agreement among the incumbents. Their model is a set of subgame perfect equilibria, in their words: 'May also be viewed as the set of credible nonbinding agreements available to firms, since any element of this set specifies actions that are in each firm's individual self-interest at all times'.[20] They develop a multimarket that allows the creation of *spheres of influence*, meaning that incumbent firms in a market, through these spheres, can improve profits and prices. In this way, they established a link between multimarket contact and collusive behaviour, and they remark that: 'Multimarket contact relaxes the incentive constraints governing the implicit agreements between firms, and that this has the potential to improve firms' abilities to sustain collusive outcomes'.[21] In order to measure this proposal they share in different markets with homogeneous products and they analysed the price competition from each other. They concluded that they can demonstrate horizontal reciprocal output agreement in the studied market. That means, in this kind of market it is possible to demonstrate when firms operate outside the parameters of the Sherman Act. This is exactly a case where the agreement is obvious, but game theory doesn't offer a worthwhile tool for courts. In the same vein Rune Stenbacka[22] used trigger strategies, where the collusive outcome is considered as a credible threat of decline of the industry, this assumption allows the building of a supergame model with free entry.

In 1992 Paul Geroski studied both vertical and horizontal strategies of integration, primarily in the R&D cartels; he argued about different business strategies in the UK and made a contrast with Japanese R&D industries. He noted that the innovation is a product of rivalry into markets, and frequently happens at the same time that waves of entry. Geroski also pointed out that correlation between firm size and innovation is weak, but seems to improve between market concentration and innovation. His conclusions was: 'In contrast to horizontal strategies, vertical strategies often combat two types of market failures simultaneously, and this suggests that they may have a more profound effect on incentive to innovate, and fewer undesirable side effects'.[23] His political recommendations were clear and accurate: 'Antitrust policy can be used to discourage horizontal mergers in sectors where horizontal strategies are unlikely to yield dividends, and to discourage vertical integration in sectors where less formal vertical relations are likely to be desirable'.[24]

During the 90s the usual published articles began to refer to the analysis of a special case. The airline industry seemed a good candidate to be one of the first concentrated industries which deserve consideration. Under the influence of Bain, but within the context of Baumol's contestable market, Margaret Peteraf and Randal Reed built a strategic model capable of demonstrating that into airlines industry, the incumbents have to invest in assets which could be sunk cost because of the difficulty to replicate this asset investment. They concluded that: 'It appears that the number and concentration of potential entrants have an even weaker effect on pricing than they do in more competitive markets'.[25]

6.1.3. Advertising and Product Differentiation

Advertising is considered a barrier to entry at the end of the twentieth century. During this century, information is considered more and more as a specific expensive asset; in terms of competition turns in a barrier to entry. Kyle Bagwell[26] keeps the baton of the edge in research advertising. In 1990 he wrote a paper about how product differentiation works as a barrier to entry. He noted that inefficiency in quality can continue in front of informational product differentiation, this is the way in which differentiation should be considered a barrier to entry. Bagwell developed a signalling equilibria model in order to demonstrate that the inefficient incumbent into an industry could maintain entry deterrence of a high quality to the rivals. Following this path Giovanni Ariccia, Ezra Friedman and Robert Marquez[27] built a model in 1999; which adverse selection should be considered as a barrier to entry in the banking industry. The conclusion is clear: asymmetric information works as a barrier to entry, in the banking market structure prices or costs are less significant than information.

Fiona Scott Morton[28] applied a model of entry decisions into a market with patent expiation, which allows her to examine the role of pre-expiation brand advertising as a barrier to entry able to deter generic entry, the conclusion was not. Limit pricing is a well-known approach to deterring entry and she used the relationship among entry, price changes, and advertising to demonstrate her conclusion.

6.2. Entry Models

As shown in Chapter 4, in 1975 Kamien and Schwartz presented a model in which the timing of rival entry is regarded as a random variable whose probability distribution is dependent on current industry price. They assumed that the potential rivals are attracted by recent price rather than recent profit. The entry research improved the old Cournot model by the inclusions of movements in profits, conditions for comparative statics, even including certain degree of collusion. This article should be considered as the primary article written to explain models of entry. Even in the classical Cournot model, allowing inclusion of several variables to get more information about how markets work. This proposal, under the lens of game theory, allows reaching scientific advances and further price and product equilibrium than the classical models. Mainly there are three different models to prevent entry: the first, named top dog behaviour, is optimal in their case whether or not entry is actually prevented. The second, named fat cat behaviour, supposes that reaction curves are upward sloping as in the case of Bertrand competition with differentiated products. In addition, suppose that more investment makes the incumbent soft. And the last one, named the puppy dog ploy, is underinvestment in order to make the incumbent firm appear friendlier to a new entrant.

During the 80s it was the branch of Industrial Organization which deserved greater consideration; Chapter 5 of this book includes several articles that follow this vein, most of which were brought forth in the 80s. This fruitful field of research in workable competition markets is also related to the entry models in the 90s. Ioannis Kessides built a specific and testable model for entry behaviour and the factors that influence entry decisions; he found that sunk costs are a prime impediment to contestability. Using four-digit American Manufacturing cross-section data from 1972 to 1982, he concluded that: 'The market performance depends continuously on the degree of imperfection in its contestability'.[29]

In 1990 Timothy Bresnahan and Peter Reiss[30] developed a new empirical model of market concentration from game-theoretic models of entry. The main two measures of the effects of entry were one statistic summarizing the competitive cost of entry and a statistic measuring the presence of entry barriers or differences in entrants' fixed costs. The model was contrasted in 149 isolated automobile markets. They explain how the number of automobile dealers alters in as concentrate retail market; knowing that market demand changed fast.

Adam Brandenburger and Stuart Harborne in 1996 developed a new model to expose business strategy. Their inspiration was Michael Porter but they widened the old business strategy under the lens of *value creation*. They assumed that value is created by such a vertical chain of players: suppliers, firms and buyers. They tried to determine how value is divided up among the different players in the chain. The next step was to discover how a firm gets a positive added value; the answer is through the creation of asymmetry between itself and other firms, each asymmetry should be considered a *value-based* strategy for the firm. Within noncooperative game theory, the value created is equal to the willingness to pay minus the opportunity cost. The natural extension of this theory should be through a theory of appropriation, because it makes sense to consider both creation and appropriation, could happens together. As they noted: 'Examples of this type of situation can be found in the area of market entry. Often, a potential entrant finds that it has an unfavourable asymmetry with respect to an incumbent (measured as willingness to pay)'.[31] They concluded that to choose a sufficiently small capacity that the incumbent decides to cede some buyers to the entrant, and then to avoid getting drawn into a competition that would spoil the whole market. This is an example of the use of the natural wild life into the business strategy model, sometimes it is better to share the prey than begin a fight which could harm all parties.

Telecommunications is a peculiar industry; operators can use or invest in capacity to expel new competitors, which is similar to using a model of blockade to entry by prices. This is the case study made by Jean Laffont, Patrick Rey and Jean Tirole in 1997; they analysed a hypothetical unregulated network competition to the telecommunications and they argued about the liberalization of telecom operators. They concluded that: 'The setting of a reciprocal access charge by an incumbent firm can be a powerful instrument to blockade entry as long as entrants cannot quickly achieve a high coverage of the market'.[32]

In the path to deter entry of new entrants in an industry, analysis of strategic decisions remains relevant. The timing of entry could be considered as a business strategy; in order to demonstrate how this management decision must be made, Richard Makadok[33] built a game following Porter's theory. Following Mueller proposals about the survival of profits in the long run, he made a study of the persistence of entry barriers, or other competition impeding features of industry structure. Makadok tested his hypothesis with data from 132 Money Market Mutual Fund Industries, during the period 1972–91, and across 233 different found families. He pointed out the possibility of extending remarks to the cigarettes and off-patent pharmaceuticals. The political application was that knowing the estimated rate of erosion high enough that the first mover advantages will be completely eliminated by the entry of a number of competitors that the market can actually support, the target must be to erase the advantages of first and early incumbents, which require a large number of new entrants; it seems convenient to keep in mind that it is necessary that more entrants can be supported by the specific product category.

Models to entry offer researchers a good way to be creative; this is the case with Joel Podolki and Fiona Scott Morton, who developed a model in which reputation is a good reason for predation. They noted that: 'High social status entrants are significantly less likely to be preyed upon by the incumbent cartel than the low social status entrants. We also find that the strength of the social status effect declines with the age of the entrant firm'.[34] They checked the possibility of three kinds of predation, namely, first: predation, where the game is explicitly dynamics and allows an incumbent to create a reputation through an aggressive behaviour able to deter entry further happens. Second: Long purse, where the asymmetric information and agency cost start a situation where firms can be driven out of the market for lack of capital. Third: Signalling, where the incumbent may need firm-specific information such as low demand or low cost to the entrant; the goal of this behaviour should be merging with the entrant in order to get a favourable price and control industry capacity. The authors confirm their hypothesis using data of British Shipping cartels from 1879 to 1929.

The results indicate that: 'The social status of an entrant was an important factor in the success of the entrant's attempt to break in to a shipping cartel',[35] and then it seems necessary to consider that the absence of an explicit means of enforcing cooperation would be an even more important basis for inferring the likelihood of cooperative behaviour of a firm into a market.

In the mould of the Structure-Conduct-Performance paradigm Anita McGahan[36] proposed the use of the Tobin's q in order to improve the Porter's strategic model. The idea is that traditional market structure is not completely responsible for performance, it is almost not more sustainable than competitive advantage. Whereas Tobin's q is the ratio of the market value of financial claims on a corporation the replacement value of the corporation's assets. She confirms her proposal with panel data of American four-digit businesses during 1981–94, and concluded by remarking on the necessity of understanding the performance of the industries over time.

In 2000, Drew Fudenberg and Jean Tirole developed a model of complete information limit pricing, 'Based on the idea that the installed base of a network good can fill a pre-emptive role similar to that of investment in physical capacity'.[37] They assumed that when a new entrant reaches the goal of entering, it should be welcomed as a new incumbent, and the old incumbent leaves share market to the new entrant in the next year within a Bertrand equilibrium model.

Following the argument of Geroski that the size and age of a company are correlated with the survival of entrants, Rajsheree Agarwal and David Audretsch[38] wrote a paper about size and firm survival. The argument which supports their proposal is clear, as the larger the firm, the higher the likelihood of survival for any given growth rate. And they developed a model of entry for 3,431 pool firms, which take advantage of the market niches. They concluded that for small and large firms survival chances are variable, because entrants responding to different stimulus in the formative stages of the life cycle than in the mature stages.

6.3. The Consequences in Political Economy: 1992–2000 Merger Guidelines

Since 1992, the Guidelines and the merger enforcement policy of the Department of Justice and the Federal Trade Commission were made by the Agency (henceforth) improving position since 1984, when it was still called the Department. Technically the specific standards set forth in the Guidelines must be applied to a broad range of possible factual circumstances; mechanical application of those standards may provide misleading answers to the economic questions raise under the antitrust laws. Guidelines included a special emphasis in that they do not attempt to assign the burden of proof.

It is equally accurate to say that in 1984 the Guidelines pursue the market power, as defined in 1984, as the ability of one or more firms profitably to maintain prices above competitive levels for a significant period of time is termed *market power*. The Guidelines understood that the exercise of market power is a transfer of wealth from buyers to sellers or a misallocation of resources.

As in Chapters 3 and 6 of the present book, we discuss the relevant issues, and the meanings of 1992 merger Guidelines.[39]

In 1992 the Guidelines describe the analytical process that the Agency will employ in determining whether to challenge a horizontal merger.

1. The Agency assesses whether the merger should significantly increase concentration and result in a concentrated market, properly defined and measured.
2. The Agency assesses whether the merger should, in light of market concentration and other factors that characterize the market, raises concern about potential adverse competitive effects.
3. The Agency assesses whether entry would be timely, likely and sufficient either to deter or to counteract the competitive effects of concern.
4. The Agency assesses any efficiency gains that reasonably cannot be achieved by the parties through other means.
5. The Agency assesses whether, but for the merger, either party to the transaction would be likely to fail, causing its assets to exit the market.

The process of assessing market concentration, potential adverse competitive effects, entry efficiency and failure is a tool that allows the Agency to answer the ultimate question in merger analysis: whether the merger is likely to create or enhance market power or to facilitate its exercise.

In considering the likely reaction of buyers to a price increase, the Agency will take into account all relevant evidence, including, but not limited to, old evidences such as the shifting patterns of buyers and sellers. As well as new evidences such as the influence of downstream competition faced by buyers in their output markets, timing and costs of switching products. In 1992 the classical *small but significant and nontransitory* increase of price, defined in 1984, was changed to the use of a price increase of 5 per cent lasting for the foreseeable future. Now the courts have a referential *small but significant and nontransitory* increase of price.

The Agency defined sunk costs in the analysis of markets as a significant sunk cost is one which would not be recouped within one year of the commencement of the supply response. In some instances it may be difficult to calculate sunk costs with precision. Accordingly, when necessary, the Agency will make an overall assessment of the extent of sunk costs for firms likely to participate through supply responses.

The Guidelines of 1992 respect the Herfindahl-Hirschman Index of *market concentration* and take into account that a merger may diminish competition by enabling the firms selling in the relevant market more likely, more successfully, or more completely to engage in coordinated interaction that harms consumers. Coordinated interaction is comprised of actions by a group of firms that are profitable for each of them only as a result of the accommodating reaction of the others. This behaviour includes tacit or express collusion, and may or may not be lawful in and of itself. In this case, the Agency will examine the extent to which post-merger market conditions are conducive to reaching terms of coordination, detecting deviations from those terms, and punishing such deviations. Deviation from the terms of coordination will be deterred where the threat of punishment is credible. Credible punishment, however, may not need to be any more complex than temporary abandonment of the terms of coordination by other firms in the market.

A merger may diminish competition even if it does not lead to increased likelihood of successful coordinate interaction, because merging firms may find it profitable to alter their behaviour unilaterally following the acquisition by elevating price and suppressing output. This proposal needs a practical application, the 1992 Guidelines consider that where market concentration data falls outside the safe harbour region established with HHI, the merging firms have a combined market share of at least 35 per cent. Thus it is a significant share of sales in the market accounted for by consumers who would be adversely affected by the merger. Keeping in mind that HHI is calculated by summing the squares of the individual market shares of all the firms included in the market under the standards in Section 2 of these Guidelines (the lack of information on small fringe firms is not critical because such firms do not affect the HHI significantly). The HH Index below 1,000 means unconcentrated market, between 1,000 and 1,800 means moderately concentrated market and above 1,800 the Agency regards markets in this region to be highly concentrated. Market share of at least 35 per cent, merged firms may find it profitable to raise price and reduce joint output below the sum of their premerger outputs because the lost markups on foregone sales may be outweighed by the resulting price increase on the merged base of sales.

The **entry analysis** in the 1992 Guidelines began contending that a merger is not likely to create or enhance power or to facilitate its exercise if entry into the market is so easy that market participants, after the merger, either collectively or unilaterally could not profitably maintain a price increase above premerger levels. The committed entry treated is defined as new competition that requires expenditure of significant sunk costs of entry and exit. The Agency employs a three-step methodology to assess whether committed entry could deter or counteract a competitive effect of concern.

1. Agency assesses whether entry can achieve significant market impact within a timely period.
2. Agency assessed whether committed entry would be a profitable and, hence, a likely response to a merger having competitive effects of concern. The profitability of such committed entry must be determined on the basis of premerger market price over the long run.
3. Agency assesses whether timely and likely entry would be sufficient to return market prices to their premerger levels.

The Agency established three analysis, timelines, likelihood and sufficiency defined as:

Timelines of entry. Generally the Agency will consider timely only those committed entry alternatives that can be achieved within two years form initial planning to significant market impact.

Likelihood of entry. An entry alternative is deemed likely if it would be profitable at premerger prices, and if such prices could be secured by the entrant. Entry is unlikely if the minimum viable scale is larger than the likely sales opportunity available to entrants. Minimum viable scale is the smallest average annual level of sales that the committed entrant must persistently achieve for profitability at premerger prices.

Since the 2000 Guidelines, the Agencies evaluate the likelihood of entry based on the extent to which potential entrants have 1) core competencies that give them the ability to enter into competing R&D, and 2) incentives to enter into competing R&D.

Sufficiency of entry. Defined as entry that, although likely, will not be sufficient if, as a result of incumbent control, the tangible and intangible assets required for entry are not adequately available for entrants to respond fully to their sales opportunities.

In 1997 the guidelines changed point 4, on efficiencies, in order to include that competition usually spurs firms to achieve efficiencies internally. While efficiencies generated through merger can enhance the merged firm's ability and incentive to compete, this may result in lower prices, improved quality, enhanced service, or new products. It concluded that efficiencies almost never justify a merger to monopoly or near-monopoly.

In 2000 the guidelines included *competitor collaboration*, defined as types of agreement that have been held per se illegal, including agreements among competitors to fix prices or output, rig bids or share or divide markets by allocating customers, suppliers, territories or lines of commerce. The courts conclusively presume such agreements, once identified, to be illegal, without inquiring into their alleged business purposes, anticompetitive harms, precompetitive benefits, or overall competitive effects. The Department of Justice prosecutes participants in hardcore cartel agreements criminally.

The Department of Justice assumed, that given the great variety of competitor collaborations, rule of reason analysis entails a flexible inquiry and varies in focus and detail depending on the nature of the agreement and market circumstances. Focusing special attention in agreements of a type that always or almost always tend to raise price or reduce output are per se illegal.

Under the rule of reason, the Agency's analysis begins with an examination of the nature of the relevant agreement, since the nature of the agreement determines the types of anticompetitive harms that may be of concern. The nature of the agreement is relevant to whether it may cause anticompetitive harm. For example, by limiting independent decisions on price, output or other competitively sensitive variables, an agreement may create or increase market power or facilitate its exercise through the collaboration, its participants or both. An agreement may also increase the likelihood of an exercise of market power by facilitating explicit or tacit collusion, either through facilitating practices such as an exchange of competitively sensitive information or through increased market concentration.

The **relevant agreements** that limit independents decision making or combine control or financial interests are:

- Production collaborations (agreements jointly to produce a product sold to others or used by the participants as an input)
- Marketing collaborations (agreements jointly to sell, distribute or promote goods or services that are either jointly or individually produced)
- Buying collaborations (may involve agreements jointly to purchase necessary inputs)
- Research and development collaboration.

Agencies consider that each of the types of competitor collaboration outlined above can facilitate collusion. Also, consider the relevant markets affected by collaboration: goods, technology, R&D. Agencies noted that factors relevant to the ability and incentive of the participants and the collaboration to compete are those where the nature of the agreement and market share and market concentration data reveal a likelihood of anticompetitive harm. The Agencies examine more closely the extent to which the participants and the collaboration have the ability and incentive to compete independent of each other. For instance, exclusivity, control over assets, financial interest, control of the collaboration's competitively significant decision making, likelihood of anticompetitive information sharing, duration of the collaboration.

6.4. Debate over guidelines

During the 90s a new debate takes place in this economic field; the debate over the Guidelines, because at this time they included restrictive lines of control of antitrust. Both are pillars of this controversy, the first is considered an increase of price used to be *small but significant* since 1992, it is 5 per cent; the second is the concept of *nontransitory* which, since 1992 has meant two years. Technically these accurate numbers should be helpful for courts, both had to reduce the discretion of the Judge in the application of the purposes of the Guidelines. However, the increase of the price of steel seems not perfectly comparable with the price of orange juice. Two years is not too much time for an industry in which amortization time of investments in equipment is over ten years, otherwise two years of agreement in the mattress market can destroy the profits of the company out the game.

George Stigler wrote a suggestive article in 1992 entitled 'Law or Economics?' He showed that a change happened in economic thought before Coase published 'The Problem of Social Cost' and he noted that human behaviour is not as rigorously deterministic as a multiplication table. Stigler said that the economic definition of efficiency: 'Accepts private market judgments on the values of goods and services, and, in policy analysis, one may legitimately employ an alternative definition of efficiency that rests on the goals adopted by the society through its government'.[40] He wrote that the Sherman Act today is the culmination of 100 years of judicial decisions, influenced as well by actual cases and the changing economic, legal and political circumstances of that century. That drive to the core of the antitrust law, courts solved cases, individual or corporative cases, which means, the antitrust has been made by jurisprudence. Stigler concluded that economics has two roles to play in law: provide of tools requested by the lawyers and study the legal institutions and doctrines.

In 1993 Andrew Kleit and Malcolm Coate wrote an article entitled 'Are Judges Leading Economic Theory?' the reason was the argument written by Judge Clarence Thomas who wrote for the Court of Appeals for the District of Columbia Circuit, Kleit and Coate wrote that Judge Thomas:

> Rejected the Government's approach, concluding that it is unrealistic to expect such strong proof in the context of a merger case an even if a firm never enters a market, the threat of entry can stimulate competition. Thus, one could conclude that some showing of entry barriers is now a necessary condition for a merger to violate the antitrust laws.[41]

This paragraph offers to Kleit and Coate the possibility of arguing about the scope of the Guidelines. They built a game Bertrand model with positive sunk costs, and therefore considered scales economies as a barrier to entry. The model focused on the threat of entry, rather in the probability of entrance. The contribution of this article was to confirm whether judges consider the threat of entry sufficient to maintain competition; using thirty observations from twenty courts' opinions reporting some form of entry barriers and ten without. The conclusion is that: 'Recent court decisions clearly show that the judiciary recognizes many of these concepts'.[42] Two years later Coate widened his research, introducing more observation, until forty, of which twenty-five were Republican courts whereas fifteen were Democratic courts. Coate did not find a different structure of legal decisions dependent on party affiliation, neither among Reagan–Bush era. This issue established a new point of view about antitrust, including its analysis and conclusions out the political affairs. Both Coate's articles confirm that the path of antitrust follows competitive markets and that understanding how markets works independent of the political affiliations of courts.

At the same time Steven Berry and Ariel Parkes wrote a theoretical article about the limitations of Industrial Organization in the merger analysis. They built a model that included product differentiation and price differentiation, they argued that: 'Differentiating the first order condition shows that prices can be strategic substitutes in price-setting models if price cost margins are high enough and if an increase in a rival's price steepens the own price demand curve'.[43] They made a model centred on demand conditions in order to demonstrate how troubling the merger analysis can become.

John McGee developed a reputation for predatory behaviour in 1958, Lester Telser in 1966 noted that the predator receives rents once exit occurred and this money is sufficient to compensate for the reduction in profits during the predatory episode, then predatory is both feasible and rational. Areeda and Turner established in 1975 a rule which explains predatory price: 'A monopolistic pricing below marginal cost should be presumed to have engaged in a predatory or exclusionary practice',[44] ahead of the traditional belief that presumes a price above the average cost as predatory. A company that wants to be predatory must have capacity available (or a transitory surplus of demand). Areeda and Turner pointed out that:

> Recognizing that marginal cost data are typically unavailable, we conclude that: a price at or above reasonably anticipated average variable cost should be conclusively presumed lawful. And a price below reasonably anticipated average variable cost should be conclusively presumed unlawful.[45]

This is the starting point of William Baumol in 1996, his argument was appropriate:

> The courts have accepted the view that marginal cost is exceedingly difficult to determine in practice, so that, *faute de mieux*, one must apologetically accept average variable cost as an imperfect proxy. Even though one knows full well that the magnitudes of the two costs can differ substantially.[46]

Baumol defines a predatory price which meets all three conditions:

> First, the choice of that price must have no legitimate business purpose. Second, that price must threaten the existence or the entry of rivals that are at least as efficient as

the firm that has adopted the price at issue. Third, there must be a reasonable prospect of recoupment of at least whatever initial cost to firm F were entailed in the company's adoption of the price in question, that recoupment taking the form of monopoly profits made possible by reduction (as a result of price P) in the number of competitors facing F.[47]

This is a worthwhile argument for courts: prices below marginal costs constitute a presumption that the act is without legitimate business purpose, otherwise a price above marginal cost doesn't keep a conclusive argument of a legitimate business purpose. The other type of costs considered are sunk costs, understood as costs which a company can not escape in the short run, because of a contract or because it has already signed a contract to buy the item whose cost is sunk. At this moment it seems convenient to include the difference between sunk cost and fixed cost: fixed costs are costs that must be borne by firms, whatever the output, and do not vary when the magnitude of output changes. These costs are not variable either in the short or the long run. Any cost that is not fixed is defined to be variable. Baumol offers an appropriate example to keep in mind:

> The investing for one airplane to fly for Boston to Los Angeles, is fixed whose amount, does not vary with number of passengers until capacity is reached. Thus, this cost is fixed, and does not become variable even in the long run, because one cannot run an airline on the route with zero airplanes. In contrast, this cost is not sunk because, if traffic between Boston and Los Angeles, declines drastically, the plane can be shifted to serve another route. A large factory with a 10 year useful life, however, constitutes a cost that is sunk for that period, but it need not be fixed because at the end of 10 years it may be desirable to produce less then before, using a smaller factory whose investment cost is lower. The distinction is not mere semantics; the two types of cost have very different implications for market performance and economic efficiency.[48]

William Baumol tried to clarify the economic ideas of cost, whichever type is under discussion, to the courts; his goal is to distinguish between predatory and non-predatory behaviour of a firm in an instance where it has short-run losses. He concluded that: 'Surely, the average variable cost test is the appropriate way to deal with the dilemma, that is, a price that exceeds average variable cost as defined here cannot be predatory, even if it does not maximize short-run profit'.[49] The exception of the Areeda-Turner rule should be the case when a firm doesn't cover the opportunity cost, in this case investment can be considered a threat to a more efficient rival.

In 1982 Paul Milgrom and John Roberts[50] developed a model for signalling predation which was improved upon during the 80s, they contended that in the presence of incomplete information any firm has two incentives to increase output: one being to induce the exit of rivals, and the other to induce the rival to curtail its production if it doesn't leave. There exists another possibility, raising a rival's costs, Janusz Ordover and Garth Saloner give the next example 'Signing of an exclusive dealing contract in which the supplier of an input agrees not to supply the rival firms ... Or taking actions that raise the price at which the rival can obtain the resources',[51] technically create a disadvantage for entrants, in the real world these happened in the Aspen and Alcoa cases. Under the lens of antitrust authorities, this theoretical model of predation provides a limited guidance for policymakers.

Not every article written at this time had as its objective the improvement of the Guidelines, or helping courts defend the convenience to erode antitrust policy. The next article should be considered representative of this way of thought. In 1996, Daniel Deneffe and Peter Wakker built a three stage bargaining model in order to explain how legal factors affect the corporate problem. They argued that antitrust policy has been more tolerant with conglomerates than towards horizontal mergers. Due to the relevance of the argument, it seems convenient to cite the whole paragraph using the words of authors in order to keep their own sense:

> One of the ways a conglomerate merger can be condemned is due to its harm to 'actual potential competition' (Department of Justice, Guidelines 1984). Under this theory, if the acquiring firm could enter directly the conglomerate merger is condemned because it fails to increase competition. However, the Supreme Court and some circuit courts have put the burden on the government to prove that the acquiring firms could actually enter via internal development if conglomerate acquisition was somehow prohibited. This proof is extremely difficult for two reasons. First, the acquirer has no incentive to reveal the feasibility of diversification via internal development to the government (but it does have such incentive toward the incumbent). Second, in its 1984 guidelines, the Department of Justice has required "particularly strong" evidence of the likelihood of entry via internal development before challenging a merger. The courts have, however, required the government to prove that entry via internal development is feasible. Given the formidable evidentiary requirements, the government has not been very successful at blocking conglomerate mergers and only a few have been blocked on the basis of the actual potential competition doctrine.[52]

The authors concluded that under the Reagan Administration, and because of the relaxation of antitrust, American society saved resources, and increased welfare through the elimination of rent-seeking expenditures.

In 1999 Jonathan Baker and Daniel Rubinfeld reviewed and critiqued the use of empirical methods in antitrust litigation. They argued that: 'The greater judicial willingness to evaluate evidence about the economic effects of mergers and the effect of alleged anticompetitive practice rather than relying exclusively on presumptions about the anticompetitive consequences that flow from a particular industrial structure',[53] and this is the core of a relevant article about the limits of economic theory being useful in litigations. Baker and Rubinfeld explained how economists advise the courts to calculate prices using traditional equations of demand and supply. But equations should include dummies, and this is the point, under the point of view of defendants this 'result was not causal but rather was the misleading artefact of omitting unobservable cost variable'.[54] The conclusion is that the apparent relationship between high prices and the absence of superstore competition in a metropolitan area arose because rival entry was deterred by the same cost factors leading to higher prices. Defendants argued that when reduced form price equations are employed to distinguish between anticompetitive and alternative explanations for high prices then is not possible to distinguish between absence of competitors and cartel behaviour. In other words it is not possible to separate market structure consequences from anticompetitive conduct.

When economists gave to the courts auction models, the lawyers said: 'They may be useful in informal bidding situations when there are not sufficient market data to estimate demand functions directly, but it is possible to find out a good deal about the winning and losing bids'.[55] The antitrust analysis differs from academic empirical industrial organization research in four important ways. First: the data sets the argument should be:

> Firms involved in antitrust cases may be motivated to plumb their confidential business records in order to come up with evidence that might persuade an enforcement agency or court, and to take the time to explain their data to economists analyzing it. These rich data sets come at a cost.[56]

Secondly: documents and deposition or oral testimony and then:

> The range of qualitative evidence that can be brought to bear is typically greater in the antitrust enforcement and litigation context than in academic work, because a wide rage of documentary evidence from firms files and testimonial evidence from executives and other industry experts is generally available. Third: In antitrust analyses the goal is to understand the industry and the practices at issue in the case, and find the best answer possible. In contrast, in the academic world, some studies are conducted with the primary objective of illustrating a methodological problem or the application of a new technique.[57]

The main problem resulting from these limitations should be that small errors in the computerization of the information, even with a little effect, without more importance in the academic world, can erode the credibility in court.

Under lens of economic theory, since the mid-1990's courts begun to use the analytical perspectives in trials, almost in cases of collusion between firms, searching techniques worthwhile to made a factual analysis able to compete with the traditional *rule of reason* current in Guidelines. As William Kovacic and Carl Shapiro pointed out in 2000:

> Government efforts to combat collusion in the 1990's have applied game theory in two notable ways. First, the Justice Department adopted a policy that gives criminal

immunity to the first cartel member to reveal the cartel's existence ... second; govern-ment has prosecuted behavior that facilitates coordination.[58]

Kovacic and Shapiro concluded with the special government interest in follow bad behaviour in cyberspace.

Dennis Carlton, in 2007 explained how economic theory can help the courts, in his words: 'Economists would try to estimate demand systems econo-metrically to get a sense of substitution patterns amongst different products and then use that knowledge to estimate the effect of a merger or some other ques-tioned business practice'.[59] In this vein, he said that it is not possible to know the competitive price in any industry, however sophisticated the statistical tools allowing modelling demand as a function of both price and quality and then to solve the problem.

This section would not be complete if we didn't mention an article about *capture models*, the origins of the firms capturing state belongs to George Stigler and was developed a long time ago, but in 2001 Roger Noll put this topic in the core of competition, his hypothesis was: 'The coercive power of the states causes transactions costs and information imperfections to be lower for government action that for private negotiations'.[60] Then, he said that entrants are likely to be less effectively represented in the political process. In this case, predation must be considered in three different ways. First, predation as relaxation of regula-tion, including some combination of lower wages and harder financial times for regulated firms. Second, predation as all forms of regulation are likely to retard entry by new firms either directly by franchising or indirectly by imposing higher costs on potential entrants and third, predation as regulation will depart from efficiency only when it is necessary to create and divide rents among represented interests. Noll concluded with the idea of the existence of: 'Coalitional basis of government and the role of organized interests in shaping government policy'.[61]

Doubtlessly, about the main trial in decades was *The United States* v. *Micro-soft Corporation*; several experts were called to report on the anticompetitive practices of Microsoft. In 1995 the US antitrust authorities published *Antitrust Guidelines for the Licensing of Intellectual Property*, especially for industries with a high R&D activity, and in 1998 began the Microsoft case. One of the experts called to report the Microsoft case was Richard Schmalensee, he argued over this case in three main roots: monopoly power, market definition and predatory pricing. He noted that the traditional test of market power is not appropriate in the case of Microsoft because: 'When the innovation is rapid, market shares that depend almost entirely on intellectual property are likely to lack predictive power'.[62] In this vein, it seems convenient to look for barriers to entry able to secure a monopoly behind them, otherwise the plaintiffs were right if Window's market position were not fragile. Referring to market definition, he noted that it is unlikely to be critical measuring monopoly power, and then Schmalensee's conclusions are that in the case of software, the likelihood of market power should be found in tying and predatory product design. In this case, plaintiff's case assumes that Netscape and Java might have attracted enough application to displace Windows; but in author's opinion: 'They would have had to surmount the "applications barrier to entry"'.[63].

At the same time as the Microsoft case, Richard Schmalensee wrote with David Evans a very interesting working paper about antitrust in the new technological industries. Some issues must be taken into account. It seems convenient to point out that the Structure-Conduct-Performance paradigm which is based on the antitrust analysis should be changed to analyse dot-com industries. They noted that the market power analysis has to consider the relevant market with products and regions and the share market of each company selling in the market; both together are worthwhile to inferring the market power into the favourite threshold for the courts, 60 per cent.

Predatory pricing is still difficult to prove in the majority of the cases, since the first definition of predator, several articles was written arguing over the same theory:

> Until the early 1980's predatory cases were a nightmare. Defendants are charged with maintaining monopoly by lowering price temporary to prevent the entry or force the exit of a troublesome rival or set of rivals. It is generally irrational not to cut price in the face of new competition, but price cuts large enough to be effective might open the door of Lawsuits. Lacking economic standards, judges and juries came to rely on evidence of injury and intent to determine whether or not price cuts were predatory.[64]

One of the last definitions of predation was made by Dennis Carlton and Jeffrey Perloff.[65] they said that the Government use of predation is stringent, they argued that the Agencies measure predation by profit-maximizing the returns from increased monopoly profits.

Conclusions

This chapter analysed the three branches of barriers to entry, discussed in the preceding chapters: excess of capacity, industrial concentration and advertising. The use of excess of capacity as a barrier to entry and economies of scale holds special attention in the academy. While there is an improvement in the analysis of sunk costs and developing new models able to distinguish sunk cost from other kinds of costs. Sunk cost deserves special consideration to the empirical economic theory and in case studies. This barrier to entry is measured within price models and keeping in mind that guidelines consider 5 per cent as *small but significant and nontransitory increase of price.*

Industrial concentration and market power is centred on the case study; the reason is that demonstrating the existence of market power should be confined to an industry that necessarily knows its market structure. This barrier to entry should be analysed under the benchmark of 35 per cent as the limit of product or seller concentration by the Guidelines.

Advertising moved from barrier to entry to adverse selection models, this is enough to reduce its place during this period. A good promotional campaign is not a barrier to entry; technically everyone can do it. Only the use of advertising to break the rival's reputation should be considered a barrier to entry, but it is absolutely impossible to find evidence that would be useful in a trial.

Entry models are included in a separate epigraph, new games were built to improve entry and exit in a market: top dog, fat cat, puppy dog ploy and signalling. This is the way to follow, building theoretical models into games theory, is a good way to explain how markets work, if economic science is able to do it, and offer accurate tools to courts, the goal should be reached.

Guidelines changed few things during the last eighteen years of this study, except the inclusion of entry analysis. As was suggested above, game theory takes a place in the traditional Structure-Conduct-Performance paradigm prevailing over forty years. This is the reason that at this time there is open discussion about guidelines and how courts, judges and juries need to learn game theory and to become familiar with timelines, likelihood or sufficiency of entry. They need judicial proofs, and the article written by Baker and Rubinfeld in 1999 shows this necessity.

It is not my intention to be pessimistic at the end of the analysis of barriers to entry. The old model defined in the 60s is used nowadays by courts in the USA to settle agreements in trials. Firm behaviour must be in keeping with guidelines, otherwise companies will turn to strategy; we do not believe in attaining profit by any means necessary, but as far I know, economic science has to improve its tools. Because if economists will be able to build an objective framework, of which every firm knows the limits, then arbitrary court decisions will diminish at the same time. This chapter included several improved economic models in strategy, sunk cost, entry and deterrence, economic science is hardworking when following theoretical frameworks which explain workable competition, scientific production, pursuing debate, and confirming and disproving assumptions and possible evidence. The point is not how many articles are published; the question is how much help we are able to offer to the courts. Because this is our objective, to give tools in order to help the objective decisions of judges.

Several opinions head in this direction 'Unfortunately, economists have not yet been able to reach broad consensus over the definition of an entry barrier, and this has probably hindered the development of efficient antitrust policy'.[66] Dennis Carlton wrote in the same vein, 'Disagreement over whether a barrier exists or not can matter in terms of the outcome of an antitrust trial or regulatory proceeding, even if there may not be disagreement among economists about a market's equilibrium'.[67]

This chapter is supported by Table 6.1, which classifies the articles on barriers to entry chronologically. We have separated the analysis into four different types, Excess of capacity, industrial concentration, advertising and entry. The columns include year of publication, author of the article and barrier or barriers analysed. When we have the information on the statistical variables used to confirm the hypothesis, and the authors' predecessors are included in order to give the reader an idea of the economic thought-line of the author and even his choice of framework. The next column contains information on the empirical confirmation of the theory; as well the main industries concerned, which data was used and when the information became available, we have included period and country of analysis. We have added one further column, with the author's main conclusion.

CONCLUSION

Market price is the main approach that the economy as a science employs as an indicator of scarcity or abundance of supply or demand in every market. The problem appears when price is manipulated by one side of the market, when price loses its status as an indicator, which means the market doesn't work freely. This is due to the fact that we lose the right information about each market in question. Market price has given rise to a lot of written opinions since scholastics' just price, amongst them that of Adam Smith, who in 1776 wrote about the difference between price of competition and monopoly price:

> The price of monopoly is upon every occasion the highest which can be got. The natural price, or the price of free competition, on the contrary, is the lowest which can be taken, not upon every occasion, indeed, but for any considerable time together. The one is upon every occasion the highest which can be squeezed out of the buyers, or which, it is supposed, they will consent to give; the other is the lowest which the sellers can commonly afford to take, and that the same time continues their business.[1]

Economists are looking for a way to demonstrate which price has been reached in a competitive market and is, therefore, fair, and which price responds to a monopolistic market because suppliers are getting extra profits due to market control. The idea is not difficult to understand, indeed, the difficulty lies in demonstrating who are the agents and how they are controlling the market. The second step has to be to put the market in balance again. The limit price theory was developed by Joe Bain in the 40s and widely diffused the notion of barriers to competition. Since 1956 he tried to shed light on this issue. Bain and the Harvard School assumed that every instance market friction could be detected by looking at unfair market prices. Whether true or not, they suspected the existence of barriers to entry for rivals erected by incumbents; while economists will be able to demonstrate the existence of a barrier to entry, which could then be prosecuted and corrected. Technically the idea is simple but not naïve. The correction of markets is not gratis, several agents are involved, and some of them have to change their regular behaviour in order to adapt it to new rules, and that could mean a lot of money.

The price limit developed by Bain-Sylos was never an equilibrium price but a disequilibrium price, which means that intrinsically it is not stable, in physical sense, this weakness plus the special characteristic which establishes a limit price for every company within every industry created a controversy between the economic and legal academies. There is a need to know the accurate price limit of the industry in order to have arguments against a company.

In the beginning of the twentieth century, John Bates Clark, John Maurice Clark, Joe Bain and Edward Mason considered the convenience to offer a tool box to courts in order to help them with economic issues. Both could reach the political spheres and they had the opportunity to see their economic theory reflected in Guidelines of workable competition. They assumed that certain market structures, especially industrial ones, are susceptible to exercise market power: expel new entrants and raise the price to customers, basically. This is the origin of a large amount of papers and books; being the existence of barriers to entry within an industry which quite articles have been written to demonstrate them. On the other side, from Chicago University, George Stigler and Richard Posner tried to explain the opposite idea continue, in the sense that maintaining a barrier to entry constitutes a higher cost than allowing competition within the market.

Barriers to entry are not always the same, since firms are interested in different kinds of agreements to exclude competition. These will vary according to time and place. From an academic point of view it would be extremely interesting to understand how firms over time alter their behaviour towards competition. As a consequence of this adaptability it appears to be easy to set up barriers to entry and just as quickly make them disappear when competitors legally denounce them. One example of this behaviour is a barrier to entry which was not even questioned in the 1960s, the fixed percentage of production shared out amongst the five major firms in an industry. The theoretical argument in favour of this barrier maintained that the five firms exercised a kind of positive market power which enabled them to control and impose retail prices. There were even legal sentences which obliged firms not to grow, and keep to their market share on pain of punishment. Today opinion has shifted and we feel that the size of a firm is not a matter for a regulator to decide, since any limit imposed on size would imply a limitation on the ability to compete in ever larger, more globalized markets.

This book tries to show the evolution of the academic debate about which kind of tools are capable of demonstrating the existence of barriers to entry in a market and its academic controversy: econometric models, microeconomics improvements, strategic thought, game theory. Parallel to the economic debate, the Guidelines were implemented and included within them successive changes and improvements according to the economic contributions.

Of all the barriers to entry presented by Joe Bain in 1956, three of them had been widely demonstrated: the concentration of the industry, excess capacity and advertising. At least until the 80s, the critics failed to take into account their views. In fact, until the 1984 guidelines there is no serious attempt to change the Structure-Conduct-Performance paradigm as the unquestionable way to assess the American antitrust. Only since the methodological change, did the limit price theory on game theory and with it a broad discussion about the judgments lead to changing the structures of some industries.

In the early 70s, the game theory was not widespread in the economy. It was necessary to wait until the 80s when the revolution of games extended modelling in economics, and with it the models that showed how difficult it is for a company that wants to enter a market, despite barriers specific to that industry, and that minimum efficient production and technological progress should be added impediments of incumbents. Economic models known as entry models discussed this issue and demonstrate the behaviour of certain markets, on the company's side mainly, which create friction and impede fair competition.

The 80s would be the decade of coexistence of the model Structure-Conduct-Performance with games theory; a coexistence that remains to this day. Game theory is becoming increasingly important but faces severe limitations for use in an antitrust trial. Theoretical economics advanced far in this decade but we cannot say the same thing about game theory as a theoretical device that provides irrefutable evidence in the trials of business.

Finally, the last decade was characterized by the fusion of models showing that the two traditional barriers to entry, industrial concentration and capacity existed within a single theoretical framework, i.e. business strategy. For over twenty years, all decisions that related to business investment, were considered within the strategic decision-making and therefore, if used to expel competitors should be questioned with a cost-benefit analysis, implying that any of the cost for a company to address this should be less than the benefit they expect.

Whether American economists developed successful tools in order to explain how markets work, lawyers, judges and courts put in practice these theories with uneven results. Economists could see bad behaviour in market absolutely clearly. They could make a perfect econometric model which demonstrates this conduct; however, the point is to convert this model into evidence. A simpler model easily could more easily be applied in the real world, but business is not a simple task. Economic theory would have to be as flexible as companies are, in which case theory would lose objectivity and allow us to solve one trial which would probably then have no further applications, meaning it would be jurispruden-tially limited.

Today academic interests have broadened. Firstly thanks to a new generation of business studies specialists and to businessmen themselves showing greater interest in how markets work. Secondly, there is now more interest in the rela-tionship between economics and law, the workings of the economy and the legal framework, and thirdly there is a growing literature on barriers to entry and international trade. Business studies specialists have found in the studies of barriers to entry a theoretical framework which allows them to distinguish between legitimate strategic business behaviour and illegal practices designed to control markets. Those interested in the interrelationships between economics and law will find in the literature of barriers to entry case studies in which firms win or lose a lawsuit brought by another competing firm. The detailed analysis of such cases, where a firm denounces another for prejudicial behaviour, will be of great use in understanding how in the past such evaluative judgments have been made. Finally regarding the terms of international trade, the literature on barriers to entry shows how globalization has eliminated many long-term barriers to entry, above all those explicit and implicit national agreements which shared out domestic markets. Similarly, the literature provides cases where, thanks to national legislation specifically passed to protect specific firms, some barriers to entry have managed to survive the effects of globalization.

By way of conclusion we can cite Adam Smith, when he wrote that: 'People of the same trade seldom meet together, even for merriment and diversion, but the conversation ends in a conspiracy against the publick, or in some contrivance to raise prices'.[2] The point is that we cannot demonstrate it, unless with our actual tools. In the twentieth century, economists developed a good way to build a market structure, and this is the contribution of Joe Bain and Harvard School to the economic theory. The second step must be connected to an especial market structure with an illegal conduct, economic theory shows several limits offered to courts of an analytical framework capable of being used as a proof in trials.

During this century the main improvements have been to change the per se rule to the rule of reason. Market Structure per se generates a conduct and the consequence of this is the performance of market prevail four decades (from 1956 until 1992) when rules change in order to be reasonable in recommendations to companies, to be flexible and implement the rule of reason, which means that case to case analysis has become prevalent and the search for generalist frameworks is over. Economic theory includes the benefit of doubt in business behaviour.

Economists have to realize that when our models, dummies, games and so on are much closer to the mathematics than looking for generalizations that seem to stay far from reality and therefore we are heading in the opposite direction to that of the courts, judges cannot to assume anything (the magic key of economics) they need empirical, tangible proof. We are at the beginning of an era when economists must to play the role of analysts for every case in litigation, using theoretical tools, not looking for universally useable jurisprudential conclusion.

The American system of competition where every firm detects ugly behaviour or non-workable competition comes freely to court and its damages are better than the European ones, where only the biggest companies can afford to have a trial. Also American customers are protected by Federal Trade Commission working with the Department of Justice, together these form a big agency able to fight against huge companies, in this way the rights of American consumers are defended better than those of their their Europeans counterparts.

So far as I know we have to learn a lot about competition, the European Tribunals to defend competition need to use more referees and experts, and to be transparent in trials and sentences.

Another consequence of this research is that I would like more companies to offer the same product in a market. As a customer I like to have the possibility to choose and to change companies when I am not satisfied with one of them. When I need a plumber I look for one close to home, I can change plumbers any time I wish, and in four or five years, I will have gathered enough information to choose the best plumber. The reader should be with me whether I noted that this is not exactly the case when we talk about the electricity company, the telephone company, a big company which demands a minimum fee for their services, or a company which keeps the patent of an innovation, or a company which doesn't let me use a new product or service if I don't pay for another of their products or services which I don't need.

The field of competition under the lens consumers is an area of passionate research, as a firm playing in a market; its point of view should be quite different. I can imagine if one is a company and its main goal would be to sell as much as possible and to get as much money as possible, this is a basic economic principle, knowledge as profits maximization. This controversy is older than the notion economics as science. The appropriation of the welfare customers by firms also appears in Adam Smith's *Wealth of Nations*, but to give an opportunity to customers to bargain the market price is the aspiration of American Federal Trade Commission. I am committed to the discovery of how I can improve my welfare as a customer following the principle of maximization like companies do. The only way to reach my goal is through the promotion of several companies offering a rane of products and services, and giving me opportunities to choose the price, and the company from which I purchase the output, because this is the only bargaining power I have in terms of market price.

APPENDIX: TABLES

Table 2.1

Year	Author	Barrier to entry	Predecessors	Industries analysed	Conclusion	Country
1955	Edwards, H.R.	Excess capacity		Theoretical model	Positive	Australia
1956	Bain, J.	Main barriers to entry		Bigger American industries	Positive	EEUU
1957	Sylos-Labini, P.	Index of concentration, Gini coefficient		Steelworks and rolling mills, electrical machinery, petroleum refining, lumber and timber products, shipbuilding and iron and steel.	Positive	EEUU
1958	Modigliani, F.	Limit price theory		Theoretical model	T	
1958	Andreano, R. and Warner, S.	Bain proposals	Bain	20 manufacturing industries	Positive	EEUU
1958	McGee	Predatory price cutting		Theoretical model Standard-oil case	Negative Case study	
1959	Kahn, A.	Different prices for different clients.	Robinson, Coase	Ford and Chrysler against Champion Spark Plug company and General Motors and Electric Auto-Lite	Positive Case study	EEUU
1963	Williamson, O.	Excess capacity	Bain and Modigliani	Theoretical model	T	
1963	Weiss, L. W.	Factor in changing concentration	Kalecki, Bain	134 industries, four digit 1947–54	Not completely	EEUU
1964	Telser, L.	Advertising	Kaldor	44 thee digit industries 1947–58	Positive	EEUU
1964	Caves, R.	Market structure	Bain	Main industries 1954	Positive	EEUU
1966	Mann, M.	Seller concentration Scale-economy Product differentiation Absolute cost Capital requirement	Bain	30 industries, 1950–1960 Sulphur industry in alberta Canadian nickel Us pharmaceutical industry aluminum industry 1945–58 Biscuit makers Glass container industries Baking Midwestern coal industry Brewers	Positive	EEUU and Canada

Year	Author	Barrier to entry	Predecessors	Industries analysed	Conclusion	Country
1967	Mann, M. H. Henning, J. A. Meehan J. W.	Advertising and concentration	Telser Weiss	40 industries 1952–65	Positive	EEUU
1967	Comanor, W. and Wilson, T.	Advertising	Bain	41 industries, 1942–57	Positive	EEUU
1968	Stigler, G.	Oligopoly theory		Theoretical model	T	
1968	Williamson, O	Tradeoffs		Theoretical model	T	
1968	Stigler, G.	Control of needed resources, commercial disloyalty such as a reduction of price, bribery, and coercion of clients, fomenting resentment among workers, starting rumours regarding the inferiority of competing products and sabotage		Theoretical model	T	
1969	Mueller, D and Tilton, J	Research and Development cost	Schumpeter	Petroleum, Steel, Big Steel, Oxygen Steel, Pharmaceutical, Electronic Capital Goods, Viscose, and others. Data: the accumulation of patents	Positive	EEUU

Table 4.1

Year	Author	Barrier to entry	Predecessors	Industries analysed	Conclusion	Country
Excess capacity as barrier to entry						
1971	Wenders, J.	Excess capacity	Sylos Labini and Pashigian	Theoretical model	T	
1971	Pyatt, G.	Profit maximization	Chamberlin and Harrod	Theoretical model	T	
1972	Kamien, M. and Schwartz, N.	Limit price theory	Osborne and Mansfield	Theoretical model	T	
1972	Qualls, D.	Concentration, barriers to entry, long run economic profit margins	Bain and Mann	20 industries for period 1936–40 and 1947–51. Automobiles, cigarettes, liquor, typewriters, fountain pens, steel, farm machinery, petroleum, soap, shoes, gypsum products, metal containers, canned fruits, cement, flour, meat packing, rayon, tires and tubes 30 industries for period 1950–60 Cited above more nickel, sulphur, chewing gum, ethical drugs, flat glass, beer, baking, etc	Negative Impossible to assess	EEUU
1973	Osborne, D.	Limit price theory	Modigliani, Scherer, Wenders and Kamien and Schwartz	Theoretical model	T	
1974	Orr, D.	Index of entry barriers	Bain, Mann and Rhoades	Smelting and refining, Aircraft, Breweries, Petroleum, Toilet, Cement, Iron, Distilleries, Cotton, Tobacco Battery, Pharmaceuticals, Motor	Positive but caution with conclusions	Canada
1975	Caves, R. Khalilzadeh-Shirazi and Porter, M.	Scale economics	Comanor and Wilson Bain,	42 American industries and 59 British industries	Positive	EEUU and UK
1975	Vany, A. de	Capacity Utilization	Chamberlain, Kaldor	Case study Taxi Markets	Positive	EEUU
1975	Vany, A. de	Capacity and efficiency.	Douglas and Miller, White	Case study airlines	Positive	EEUU
1977	Caves, R. and Porter, M.	Corporate strategy	Bain	Major Home Appliance industry, US Computer industry, Petroleum industry, Aluminium Industry	Positive	EEUU
1977	Spence, M.	Limit price theory	Bain and Mann	Theoretical model	Positive	
1979	Dickson V. A.	Sub optimal capacity	Bain Shepherd	1961–6 146 manufactured industries	Positive	Canada

Year	Author	Barrier to entry	Predecessors	Industries analysed	Conclusion	Country
1979	Salop, S.	Innocent entry barrier and strategic entry barrier	Eaton and Lipsey, Spence, Schmalensee and Williamson	Theoretical model	Positive	
1979	Dixit, A.	Limit price theory and Nash	Gaskins, Wenders and Scherer	Theoretical model	T Depends	

Industrial concentration as barrier to entry

Year	Author	Barrier to entry	Predecessors	Industries analysed	Conclusion	Country
1970	Rhoades, S.	Industrial concentration	Bain and Mann	23 industries (included in Mann's study)	Negative depends	EEUU
1973	Demsetz, H.	Market rivalry and rates of return		95 industries in 1963	Negative	EEUU
1973	Baron, D.	Potential entry and barriers to entry	Bain, Mann, Kamien and Schwartz, Osborne, Sylos Labini and Modigliani	Theoretical model	Negative Difficult to demonstrate	
1974	Duchesneau, T.	Industrial concentration	Bain and Mann	From 1947 to 1967 Motor Vehicles, Cigarettes, Flat glass, Cereals, Chewing gum, Soft drinks, Liquor, Cement, Copper, Steel, Alkaline, Hard Surface Floor Coverings, Petroleum refining, Gypsum, Metal Cans, Glass Containers, Wet Corn Milling, Beer, Flour, Bread and Meat Packing.	Positive	EEUU
1974	Berry, C. H.	Corporate diversification and market structure	Shepherd, 1970	461 four digit large industries 1961–1966	Negative	EEUU
1977	Pelzman, S.	Industrial Concentration	Weiss, Bain and Stigler	1947–1967. Four digit Standard Industrial Classification 165 industries, half of US manufacturing sales Theoretical model	Negative	EEUU

Year	Author	Barrier to entry	Predecessors	Industries analysed	Conclusion	Country
1979	Scherer, F.	Changes Industrial concentration	Bain, Mann and Stigler	From 1947 to 1967 Household Laundry equipment, Greeting card publishing, cutlery, Watch-cases, Fine earthenware food utensils, Motor vehicles, pressed and blown glass, beer brewing, cigars, industrial leather belting, flavoring extracts and syrups, printing trades machinery, chewing gum, paper industries machinery, motorcycles and bicycles, corsets and allied garments, vitreous china food utensils and marking devices	Negative Statistical difficulties	EEUU

Advertising as barrier to entry

Year	Author	Barrier to entry	Predecessors	Industries analysed	Conclusion	Country
1974	Schmalensee, R.	Brand loyalty	Bain, Caves and Scherer	Theoretical model	Positive	
1974	Siegfried, J. and Weiss L. W.	Advertising, profits and Corporate taxes revisited	Comanor and Wilson	Theoretical model 1958–1963 38 consumer good industries and 10 large advertisers	Positive	EEUU
1973	Vernon, J. and Nourse, R.	Profit rates and advertising/sales ratios	Comanor and Wilson, Weiss, Needham	1963–1968 105 companies ranked by *Fortune* magazine on the basis of their 1969 sales	Positive	EEUU
1976	Needham, D.	Non-price aspect of firm's behaviour	Sylos Labini, Osborne and Schmalensee	Theoretical model	Positive	
1978	Schmalensee, R.	Entry deterrence (monopolization) and game theory	Salop and Willing	Theoretical model applied to Breakfast Cereal Industry	Positive	EEUU
1979	Schmalensee, R.	Product differentiation		Realemon case	Positive	EEUU
1979	Comanor, W. and Wilson, T.	Effects of advertising	Schmalensee and Martin	Theoretical model	T	
1979	Demsetz, Harold	Accounting for Advertising	Bain, Mann Weiss Comanor and Wilson	77 industries 1958–1967	T	EEUU
1979	Martin, S.	Advertising and industrial concentration	Phillips, Nelson and Winter, Schmalensee and Orr	209 industries from input-output tables 1967	Positive	EEUU

Entry and market structure as barrier to entry

Year	Author	Barrier to entry	Predecessors	Industries analysed	Conclusion	Country
1974	Hay and Kelley	Collusion	Stigler	49 cases 1961–70	T	EEUU

Year	Author	Barrier to entry	Predecessors	Industries analysed	Conclusion	Country
1975	Kamien, M. and Schwartz, N.	Entry and demand of a industry	Garkins Bhagwati, Kamien and Schwartz, Baron and Fisher	Theoretical model	T	
1975	Gorecki, P.	Determinants of entry	Bain, Hines	1958–1963 51 UK industries	T	UK
1975	Areeda and Turner	Predatory pricing	Bain	Theoretical model	Depends	
1976	De Bond	Uncertain entry and Entry lag	Kamien and Schwartz, Baron and Gaskins	Theoretical model	T	
1977	Friedman, J. W.	Non-cooperative behaviour	Bain	Theoretical model	Positive	
1978	Levin, R.	Technological progress and conditions of entry		Theoretical model	T Depends of hypothesis	
1978	Newman, H.	Strategic groups	Bain, Caves	Theoretical model	Positive	
1979	Spence	Investment strategy and growth	Von Stackelberg	Theoretical model	Positive	
1979	Joskow, P. and Klevorick, A	Predatory pricing	Penrose, Baumol. Posner, Scherer, Bork	Theoretical model	Positive	
1979	Weiss, L.	Brand loyalty	Bain, Stigler	Ibm case	Positive	EEUU
1979	Salop, S.	Strategic entry deterrence	Cournot, Bain	Theoretical model	T	

Table 5.1

Year	Author	Barrier to entry	Predecessors	Industries analysed	Conclusion	Country
Strategy						
1980	Porter, M	Strategy	Caves, Spence	New Paradigm.– Competitive Strategy	Positive	EEUU
1982	Yip, G.	Market structure, business –level Corporate-level	Porter	59 entrants in 31 markets	Positive	EEUU
1987	Gelfard, M. and Spiller, P.	Rival's threat	Stigler, Areeda and Turner, Porter, Schmalensee	Banking system	Positive	Uruguay
1987	Lanning, S.	Cheating	Porter	Theoretical model	Positive	EEUU
1989	Mascarenhas, B and Aaker, D.	Mobility barriers Brand name, loyal customer base, distribution channels, long term contracts, managerial pride	McGee, Porter	Personal interviews with industrial officials of oil-drilling industry And 142 firms Period 1973–81.	Positive	EEUU
Contestable markets						
1981	Baumol W. and Willing R.	Sunk cost	Bain, Caves and Porter, Salop, Spence, Stigler, Von Weizsäcker, Dixit	Theoretical model	Positive even in the long run	
1982	Baumol W., Panzar, J. and Willig R.	Market structure	Bain, Stigler, von Weizsäcker	New paradigm.– Contestable markets	T	
1989	Hurdele, Johnson, Joskow, Werden Williams	Concentration, scale economies and sunk cost	Baumol, Spence	Case study Airline industry, 867 non-stop cities pair.	Positive Case study	EEUU
Excess capacity						
1980	Von Weizsäcker, C.C.	Differences between externalities and barriers to entry	Bain Stigler, Spence, Gaskins, Schmalensee	Theoretical model	No	
1982	Porter and Spence	Capacity expansion	Their own	Theoretical model, game theory Case of Corn Wet Milling	Case study	EEUU
1984	Hilke, J.	Excess capacity	Wenders, Spence, Dixit and Schmalensee	Four- or five-digit level of industry classification	Positive	EEUU
1985	Brock and Scheinkman	Capacity constraint	Telser	Theoretical model, games	T	

Year	Author	Barrier to entry	Predecessors	Industries analysed	Conclusion	Country
1986	Davidson and Deneckere	Long-run competition in capacity, short run competition in price	Bertrand and Cournot		Positive	
1986	Lyons	Excess capacity	Wenders, Spence	Theoretical model	Positive	
1987	Lieberman, M	Excess capacity	Wenders, Spence, Eaton and Lipsey.	Long Series of data 1952–82 Organical chemicals, inorganic chemicals, synthetic fibers, metals.	Positive	EEUU

Industrial concentration

Year	Author	Barrier to entry	Predecessors	Industries analysed	Conclusion	Country
1980	Spence, M.	Advertising as fixed cost and economies of scale	Comanor and Wilson, Dixit and Porter	Theoretical model	Positive	
1980	Dixit, A.	Investment or capacity	Spence	Theoretical model with games	Positive	
1980	Flaherty, T.	Market share	Kamien and Schwartz	Games theory	T	
1980	Eaton, B. And Lipsey R.	Durability of capital	Caves and Porter, Dixit, Schmalensee, Spence	Theoretical model	Positive	
1981	Schmalensee, R.	Economies of scale	A Survey	Limit price theory	Positive	
1981	Harrigan, K.	Industry Structure	Bain	540 observations Meat packing, distilled liquors, cigarettes, hydraulic cement and aircraft manufacture 1969– 1978	Positive	EEUU
1981	Harrigan, K.	Exit	Bain	61 firms 1965–1978	Positive	EEUU
1982	Waagstein, T.	Investment in R&D, sales promotion	Bain, Caves and Porter,	Theoretical model	Positive	EEUU
1983	Chappell, H. Marks, W. and Park, I.	Scale economies Advertising, minimum efficient scale, cost disadvantage ratio	Bain, Mann, Martin	209 American industries from the 1967census of Manufactures	Positive	EEUU
1983	Salop and Scheffman	Raising rivals' costs	Bain, Williamson	Theoretical model	Positive	
1984	Caves R.	Competitive advantage	Bain, Newman Porter	Theoretical model	Positive	EEUU
1985	Ware, R.	Inventory Holding as a strategic weapon	Dixit,	Theoretical model,	T	

Year	Author	Barrier to entry	Predecessors	Industries analysed	Conclusion	Country
1989	Braudburd Ralph M. and Ross David R.	Market share	Porter, Caves	4198 observations of data based on the Federal Trade Commission Line of Business survey for the year 1975	Positive	EEUU
1989	Nahata B and Olson D.	Scale economics	Stigler against Bain	Theoretical model	Positive	
1990	Salinger	Industrial con-centration	Bain, Caves, Peltzman	Theoretical model	Negative	
Advertising						
1980	Von Weizsäcker, C.	Goodwill	Bain, Stigler	Theoretical model	Negative	
1981	Cubbin, J.	Advertising	Salop, Dixit, Scherer, Needham, Schmalensee.	Theoretical model	Positive even in the long run	
1981	Nagle, T.	Advertising	Bain, Robinson and Comanor and Wilson,	37 industries.	Negative	EEUU
1983	Ayanian, R.	Advertising	Telser, Comanor and Wilson, Demsets	39 industries	Depends	EEUU
1986	Farrell, J.	Moral hazard	Schmalensee, Baumol, Panzar and Willing, Von Weizsäcker.	Games theory	Positive	
1988	Cubbin, J. and Domberger, S.	Advertising and Post-Entry Oligopoly Behaviour	Orr, Yip	Industries heavily advertised consumer good and services	Positive	EEUU
1990	Bagwell, K	Product differen-tiation	Farrell, Schmalensee	Game theory	Positive	EEUU
1988	Grossman, G. and Horn, H.	Infant-industry protection	Farrell, Schmalensee	Games theory	Positive	
Entry Conditions: Sequential						
1980	Seade	Entry	Cournot, Bain Sylos	Theoretical model	T	
1982	Demsetz, H.	Information Knowledge Predatory	Posner, Survey		Positive With atten-tion	
1982	Shepherd, W.	Causes of Increased Competition in the U.S. Economy,	Stigler	1939–1980	Positive	EEUU
1982	Milgrom and Roberts	Predation, reputation	Selten, Kreps and Wilson	Theoretical model	Positive	

Year	Author	Barrier to entry	Predecessors	Industries analysed	Conclusion	Country
1983	Shaked, A. and Sutton, J.	Coexistence of firms		Theoretical model	T	
1984	Berheim, D	Strategic deterrence	Gaskins, Schmalensee, Spence	Game theory	Positive	
1985	Ghemawat P., Nalebuff B.	exit	Fudenberg, Tirole	Game theory	T	
1986	Gilbert, R. and Vives, X	Free rider and entry deterrence	Dixit, Bain, Sylos, Spence,	Games theory	Positive	
1986	Mankiw, G. and Whinston	Free entry	Spence, Dixit, Stiglitz, won Weizsäcker, Perry	Theoretical model	T	
1986	Fudenberg, Tirole	Signal-Jamming Theory of predation	McGee Areeda and Turner	Theoretical model Limit price-predation	Positive	
1987	Eaton C. and Ware, R.	Sequential entry	Spence, Dixit, and Gilbert and Vives	Mathematical model Market structure	Positive	
1987	Shapiro, D. and Khemani, R	Sunk cost	Orr, Caves and Porter, Eaton and Lipsey	Entry and exit barriers across industries	Positive	
1987	Masson, Shaanan	Vector of entry barriers	Kamien Schwartz	43 manufacturing industries 1960–1963	Positive	Canada
1987	Schwalbach, J.	Barries to entry	Geroski and Orr	122 german industries from 1977–1982	Positive	Germany
1987	Acs, Z. J. and Audretsch, D. B.	Scale, concentration, differentiation	Schumpeter Galbraith, Scherer	247 four digit SIC industries	Positive	EEUU
1987	Breshahan, T. and Reiss, P.	Entry conditions across markets	Stigler, Willig	Market structure	Positive	EEUU
1987	Aghion, Ph and Bolton P.	Contracts	Caves, Spence, Dixit. Williamson	Theoretical model	Depends	
1987	Cubbin, J and Geroski, P.	Mobility barriers	Porter, Caves and Schmalensee	217 large UK firms 1951–1977	Positive	UK
1988	Smiley, R.	aggressive use of the learning curve, capacity expansion pre-emption, advertising, patents and R&D, reputation as an aggressive firm, excessive filling of all product niches, and masking single product profitability	Bain, Spence, Dixit, Comanor and Wilson	Deterrence, test made to firms Strategy 171 firms	Positive	EEUU

Year	Author	Barrier to entry	Predecessors	Industries analysed	Conclusion	Country
1988	Dunne, T, Roberts, M. and Samuelson, L.	Entry and Exit	Orr, Gorecki	Four-digit US manufacturing 1963–82	T	EEUU
1988	Suzumura, K. and Kiyono, K.	Regulation-Welfare	Dixit	More competition not increase welfare	Positive	
1988	Shaanan	Market conditions	Kamien and Schwartz, Baron,	37 manufacturing American industries 1958–66 Minimum efficient scale: yes Advertising: no	Depends	EEUU
1989	Geroski P and Schwalbach J.	Conditions of entry	Bain, Stigler	85 three-digit manufacturing industries in the UK Beer industry in Germany. 6,000 types 1974–9 and 1983–4	Positive	UK and Germany

Table 6.1

Year	Author	Barrier to entry	Predecessors	Industries analysed	Conclusion	Country
Excess of capacity and sunk cost						
1990	Cairns and Galbraith	Cost advantages	Von Weizsäcker	Airlines companies	Positive	Canada
1991	Geroski	Markets dynamics	Bain, Salop	Pharmaceutical, Airbus, Coaches, gas, banking, bier, cigarettes, network 95 UK industries 1983–4 panel data 79 West Germany four-digit industries 1983–5 141 Norway five-digit industries 1981–5 73 Portugal industries 1982–6 109 Belgium three-digit industries 1980–4 62 Korea four or five-digit industries 1977–81	Positive	UK Germany Norway Portugal Belgium Korea
1991	Davies	Sunk costs, entry	Limit pricing	Theoretical model	Positive	
1992	Bunch and Smiley	Capacity , R&D	Smiley	296 managers and 42 products	Positive	EEUU
1993	Allen	Capacity, pre-commitment	Ware		Positive	
1994	Haskel, Martin	Capacity	Dixit, Masson, Shanahan Shapiro, Tirole	81 manufacturing industries	Negative	UK
1996	Mathis Koscianski	Capacity	Spence, Dixit. Hilke	Titanium industry 1962–91	Positive Case study	EEUU
1997	Chris-tensen and Caves	capacity	S-C-P	Pulp and paper industry 1978–91	Positive Case study	EEUU
1998	Nachbar, Petersen and Hwang	Sunk costs	Von Weizsäcker Mankiw and Whinston, Spencer	Theoretical model, regulation	Positive	
Industrial concentration and market power						
1990	Berheim Whinston	Market concen-tration	Caves, Abreu	Theoretical model	Positive	
1990	Stenbacka	Market concen-tration	Friedman, Abreu	Theoretical model	Positive	
1992	Geroski	Integration strategies		1960–70 machine tools	Positive	UK
1994	Peteraf and Reed	Concentration, rivalry	Bain, Baumol	Airline markets	Negative	EEUU
Advertising and product differentiation						
1990	Bagwell	Advertising	Schmalensee Signalling model		Positive	

Year	Author	Barrier to entry	Predecessors	Industries analysed	Conclusion	Country
1999	Dell' Ariccia, Friedman and Marquez	Adverse Selection, Asymmetric information	Stiglitz, Schmalensee	Banking	Positive	EEUU
2000	Scott Morton	Advertising	Spence, Telser Schmalensee, and Caves	Pharmaceutical industry 98 drugs patent 1986–92	Positive	EEUU

Entry models

Year	Author	Barrier to entry	Predecessors	Industries analysed	Conclusion	Country
1990	Kessides	Entry	Willing, Geroski, Dennis Mueller, Spiller.	Four-digit US manufacturing industries, cross section data 1972–82	Positive	EEUU
1990	Bresnahan, Reiss	Entry	Milgrom	149 geographically isolated US automobiles markets	Positive	EEUU
1990	Stenbacka	Collusion Trigger strategies	Friedman Abreu' MSSP Harrington		T	
1997	Loffont, Rey, Tirole	Deterrence price	---	Telecom operators	Case study	---
1998	Makadok	Timing of entry	Porter	132 Money Market Mutual fund Industries. Across 233 different found families 1972–91	Positive	US EEUU
1999	Podolny, Scott Morton	Social status	Becker, Montgomery and Greif	Shipping cartels, 1879–1929	Positive	UK
1999	McGahan	Market structure	Porter	Four digits Business firms 1981–94	Positive but not completely	EEUU
2000	Fudenberg and Tirole	Pricing a network	Maskin Tirole	Theoretical model	T	
2001	Agarwal, Audretsch	Firm size	Geroski, Porter, Caves	3,431 firms	Positive	EEUU
2005	Greenwald Kahn	Strategy	Porter	Case studies; Coke and Pepsi, Kodak and Polaroid,	Positive	EEUU

NOTES

Introduction

1. W. E. Kovacic and C. Shapiro, 'Antitrust Policy: A Century of Economic and Legal Thinking'. *Journal of Economic Perspectives*, 14:1 (2000), p. 47.
2. M. Whinston, 'Antitrust Policy toward Horizontal Mergers', in *Handbook of Industrial Organization* (Amsterdam: Elsevier, 2007) vol. 3, ed. M. Armstrong and R. Porter, p. 2390.
3. D. Carlton, 'Does Antitrust Need to be Modernized?', *Journal of Economic Perspectives*, 21:3 (2007), p. 173.
4. Ibid., p. 173.
5. Ibid., p. 173.
6. F. H. Easterbrook, 'The limits of antitrust', *Texas Law Review*, 63:1 (1984), p. 10.
7. E. S. Mason, 'Market Power and Business Conduct: some Comments', *American Economic Review*, 46: 2 (1956), p. 476.
8. Ibid., p. 474.
9. Ibid., p. 476.
10. Easterbrook, 'The Limits of Antitrust', p. 10.
11. D. Turner, 'Conglomerate Mergers and Section 7 of the Clayton Act', *Harvard Law Review*, 78 (1965), pp. 1313–95, p. 1317.
12. Ibid., p. 1340.
13. Ibid., p. 1354.
14. Ibid., p. 1356.
15. Ibid., p. 1363.
16. Ibid., p. 1380.
17. Ibid., p. 1364.
18. Ibid., p. 1395.
19. G. Stigler, *The Organization of Industry* (Illinois: Richard D. Irwin, 1968), p. 67.

1 The imperfect competition into the economic theory before 1956

1. The Federal Trade Commission webpage include an interesting paper, written by Marc Wineman about the history and jurisprudence in the early period of FTC.
2. Antoine Augustin Cournot, French economist, he published in 1838 his duopoly model where he sets up a mathematical model with two rival producers of a homogeneous product.

3. G. Stigler, 'Perfect Competition, Historically Contemplated', *Journal of Political Economy*, 65: (1957), pp. 1–17, p. 15.
4. Joseph Louis François Bertrand, French mathematician. Bertrand reworked Cournot's duopoly model using prices rather than quantities as the strategic variables. Depends of industries the adjust is better in prices or productions; if output and capacity of the industry are difficult to adjust, then Cournot is generally a better model.
5. Heinrich Freiherr von Stackelberg, German economist. He is the precursor of the use of games theory in economics. His relevant contribution was that when a firm holding excess capacity is another means of responsability.
6. D. Fudenberg and J. Tirole, 'Noncooperative Game Theory for Industrial Organization: an Introduction and Overview', In R. Schmalensee and R. Willig. *Handbook of Industrial Organization* (Amsterdam: Elsevier Science B.V, 2001), vol. 1, p. 268.
7. F. H. Knight, *Risk, Uncertainly and Profits* (Boston, MA: Houghton Mifflin Company, 1921), 7th impression (London: Replika process, 1948), p. 15.
8. Ibid., p. 17.
9. Ibid., p. 18.
10. A. Pigou, *The Economics of Welfare* (London: Macmillan and Co., 1920).
11. P. Sraffa, 'The Laws of Returns Under Competitive Conditions', *Economic Journal*, 144: 36 (1926), pp. 535– 50.
12. E. H. Chamberlin, *The Theory of Monopolistic Competition* (Cambridge, MA: Harvard University thesis 1927), 1st edn (Cambridge: Harvard University Press, 1933), 6th edn (London: Geoffrey Cumberlege and Oxford University Press 1949), p. 48.
13. Ibid., p. 50.
14. Ibid., p. 50.
15. Stigler, *The Organization of Industry*, p. 315.
16. D. Fudenberg and J. Tirole, 'Noncooperative Game Theory for Industrial Organization: an Introduction and Overview', in R. Schmalensee and R. Willig. *Handbook of Industrial Organization* (Amsterdam: Elsevier Science B.V, 2001), vol. 1, p. 278.
17. J. Robinson, *Economics of Imperfect Competition* (London: MacMillan and Co. Limited, 1942 (c1933)), p. 307.
18. E. H. Chamberlin, *The Theory of Monopolistic Competition* (Cambridge: Harvard University thesis 1927), 1st edn (Cambridge: Harvard University Press, 1933), 6th edn (London: Geoffrey Cumberlege and Oxford University Press 1949), p. 200.
19. R. F. Harrod, 'Doctrines of Imperfect Competition', *Quarterly Journal of Economics*, 48:3 (1934), p. 455.
20. Ibid., p. 460.
21. A. P. Lerner, 'The Concept of Monopoly and the Measurement of Monopoly Power', *Review of Economic Studies*, 1: 3 (1934), p. 166.
22. Italics come from Lerner.
23. Ibid., p. 175.
24. F. Knight, *The Ethics of Competition and Other Essays* (London: G. Allen & Unwin, 1935), 2nd edn (New York : Harper & Brothers, 1936).
25. Coase was educated in the London School of Economics.
26. R. Coase, 'The Nature of the Firm', *Economica*, 16:4 (1937), p. 390.
27. Ibid., p. 393.
28. J. R. Hicks, *Value and Capital: an Inquiry into Some Fundamental Principles of Economic Theory* (Oxford: Clarendon Press, 1939), p. 62.
29. Ibid., p. 133.

30. Kenneth Boulding obtained his degree at Oxford and he emigrated to United States in the thirties.

31. K. Boulding, 'The Theory of the Firm in the Last Ten Years', *American Economic Review*, 32:4 (1942), p. 792.

32. Machlup's PhD at the University of Vienna and he emigrated to United States.

33. F. Machlup, Machlup, 'Marginal Analysis and Empirical Research', *American Economic Review*, 36:4 (1946), p. 524.

34. Italics are my own.

35. Italics are my own

36. F. Machlup, 'Theories of the Firm: Marginalist, Behavioural, Managerial', *American Economic Review*, 57:1 (1967), p. 6.

37. E. Penrose, *The Theory of the Growth of the Firm* (Oxford: Basil Blackwell, 1959).

38. J. Bain, *Literature and Price Policy and Related Topics, 1933–1947* (Berkeley, CA: University of California Press, 1947).

39. R. L. Hall and C. J. Hitch, 'Price Theory and Business Behaviour', *Oxford Economic Papers*, 2 (1939), p. 32.

40. Machlup, 'Theories of the Firm: Marginalist', *American Economic Review*, 57:1 (1967), p. 9.

41. R. M. Cyert and J. G. March, *A Behavioral Theory of the Firm* (Englewood Cliffs, N.J.: Prentice-Hall, 1963), 2nd edn (Malden, Mass: Blackwell Publishers, 1992), p. 193.

42. Ibid., p. 31.

43. Ibid., p. 214.

44. W. Baumol, 'Reasonable Rules for Rate Regulation: Plausible Policies for an Imperfect World', In A. Phillips and O. Williamson (eds.), *Prices: Issues in Theory, Practice, and Public Policy* (Philadelphia, PA: University of Pennsylvania Press, 1964), p. 172.

45. J. Woodward, *Industrial Organization, Theory and Practice* (Oxford: Oxford University Press, 1965), p. xviii.

46. O. Williamson, 'A Dynamic Theory of Interfirm Behaviour', *Quarterly Journal of Economics*, 79: 4 (1965), p. 582.

47. R. Cyert and G. Pottinger, 'Toward a Better Micro Economic Theory', *Philosophy of Science*, 46:2 (1979), p. 218.

48. R. Caves, 'Industrial Organization, Corporate Strategy and Structure', *Journal of Economic Literature*, 18:1 (1980), p. 88.

49. O. Williamson, 'Antitrust Enforcement: Where it has been; Where it is going', *Saint Louis University Law Journal*, 27 (1983), p. 313.

50. Ibid., p. 294.

51. W. Baumol, *Growth, Industrial Organization and Economic Generalities* (Cheltenham: Edward Elgar, 2003), p. 22.

52. P. Ghemawat, 'Competition and Business Strategy in Historical perspective', *Business History Review*, 76 (2002), p. 66.

53. D. Carlton, 'Why Barriers to Entry are Barriers to Understanding', *American Economic Review*, 94:2 (2004), pp. 466–70, p. 466.

54. John Bates Clark is one of the pioneers in Marginalist revolution in United States. The annual medal with his name give to young economist to have made a significant contribution to economic thought and knowledge is considered the prelude of the Nobel price.

55. John Maurice Clark is the son of John Bates; during his live he changed his economic theoretical preferences from the marginalism to the institutionalism.

56. J. B. Clark and J. M. Clark, *The Control of Trusts* (New York: Augustus M Kelley Publishers, 1912), p. 26.
57. Ibid., p. 59.
58. Ibid., p. 141.
59. Ibid., p. 149.
60. Ibid., p. 202.
61. More information about the history of FTC could be found in http://www.ftc.gov/ftc/history/docs/origins.pdf
62. A. Pigou, *The Economics of Welfare* (London: Macmillan and Co., 1920), 4th edn (Edinburgh: R. & R. Clark, 1932), p. 21.
63. Ibid., p. 273.
64. Ibid., p. 273.
65. D.H. Wallace, 'Monopolistic Competition and Public Policy', *American Economic Review*, 26:1 (1936), p. 82.
66. Ibid., p. 81.
67. Ibid., p. 88.
68. E. S. Mason, 'Monopoly in Law and Economics', *Yale Law Journal*, 47:1 (1937), p. 34.
69. Ibid., p. 35.
70. Ibid., p. 45.
71. Ibid., 49.
72. J. M. Clark, 'Toward a Concept of Workable Competition', *American Economic Review*, 30:2 (1940), p. 241.
73. Ibid., p. 243.
74. Ibid., p. 246.
75. Ibid., 253.
76. He won the Nobel price in 1982 mainly because of his contributions to market analysis with incomplete information.
77. G. Stigler, *The Theory of Price: An Enlarged Edition of the Theory of Competitive Price* (New York: Macmillan, 1946), p. 21.
78. Ibid., p. 209.
79. Ibid., p. 211.
80. Ibid., p. 279.
81. J. Bain, 'The nrmative Problem in Industrial Organization', *American Economic Review*, 33:1 (1943), p. 55.
82. Ibid., p. 57.
83. Ibid., p. 64.
84. Ibid., p. 63.
85. J. Bain, 'Workable Competition in Oligopoly: Theoretical Considerations and Some Empirical Evidence', *American Economic Review*, 40:2 (1950), p. 39.
86. J. Bain, *Price Teory* (New York: Henry Holt and Company, 1952), p. 286.
87. J. Bain, 'The nNrmative Problem in Industrial Organization', *American Economic Review*, 33:1 (1943), p. 441.
88. E. S. Mason, 'The Current Status of the Monopoly Problem in the United States', *Harvard Law Review*, 62: 8 (1949), p. 1269.
89. Ibid., p. 1281.
90. J. Bain, 'A Note on Pricing in Monopoly and Oligopoly', *American Economic Review*, 39:2 (1949), p. 455.

91. G. Stigler, 'Monopoly and Oligopoly by Merger', *American Economic Review*, 40:2 (1950), pp. 23–34, p. 25.
92. Ibid., p. 34.
93. J. Bain, 'Workable Competition in Oligopoly: Theoretical Considerations and Some Empirical Evidence', *American Economic Review*, 40:2 (1950), p. 40.
94. Stigler, 'Monopoly and Oligopoly by Merger', p. 63.
95. Inverted commas of Chamberlin
96. J. M. Clark, 'Competition and the Ojectives of Government policy', in E. Chamberlin, *Monopoly and Competition and their Regulation* (London: McMillan and Co LTD, 1954), p. 325.
97. G. Stigler, 'Mergers and Preventive Antitrust Policy', *University of Pennsylvania Law Review*, 104 (1955–6), p. 182.
98. E. S. Mason, 'Market Pwer and Bsiness Cnduct: some Comments', *American Economic Review*, 46: 2 (1956), p. 479.
99. The National Science Foundation is an independent federal agency created by Congress in 1950; its objectives are to promote the progress of science; to advance the national health, prosperity, and welfare, among others.
100. H. H. Hines, 'Effectiveness of "Etry" by Aready Etablished Frms', *Quarterly Journal of Economics*, 71:1 (1957), p. 150.
101. E. H. Chamberlin, *The Theory of Monopolistic Competition*, p. 109.
102. J. M. Cassels, 'Excess Capacity and Monopolistic Competition', *Quarterly Journal of Economics*, 51:3 (1937), p. 427.
103. N. Kaldor, 'Professor Chamberlin on Monopolistic and Imperfect Competition', *Quarterly Journal of Economics*, 52:3 (1938), p. 515.
104. Ibid., p. 516.
105. K. Bagwell, 'The Economic Analysis of Advertising', in M. Armstrong and R. Porter (eds) *Handbook of Industrial Organization* (Amsterdam: Elsevier, 2007), vol. 3, p. 1710.
106. Ibid., p. 1710.
107. D. Braithwaite, 'The Economic Effects of Advertising', *Economic Journal*, 38:149 (1928), p. 23.
108. K. Bagwell, 'The economic analysis of advertising', in M. Armstrong and R. Porter (eds.) *Handbook of Industrial Organization* (Amsterdam: Elsevier, 2007), vol. 3, p. 1711.
109. N. Kaldor, 'The Economic aspect of Advertising', *Review of Economic Studies*, 18:1 (1950– 1), p. 20.
110. Ibid., p. 21.
111. K. Bagwell, 'The Economic Analysis of Advertising', in M. Armstrong and R. Porter (eds.) *Handbook of Industrial Organization* (Amsterdam: Elsevier, 2007), vol. 3, p. 1712.

2 Barriers to Entry: the Late 1950s and 1960s

1. J. Bain, *Barriers to New Competition, their Character and Consequences in Manufacturing industries* (Cambridge, MA: Harvard University Press, 1956), p. 3.
2. Stigler, *The Organization of Industry*, p. 10.
3. Bain, *Barriers to New competition*, p. 6.
4. Ibid., p. 1.
5. In order to know this changes in the Bain theory more deeply, references are Gaskins (1971) and Masson, Shaanan (1987)

6. F. Modigliani, 'New Developments on the Oligopoly Front', *Journal of Political Economy*, 66: 3 (1958), p. 216.
7. Ibid., p. 218.
8. Ibid., p. 226.
9. H. R. Edwards, 'Price Formation in Manufacturing Industry and Excess Capacity', *Oxford Economic Papers*, 7:1 (1955), p. 116.
10. Ibid., p. 480.
11. R. Gilbert, 'Mobility Barriers and the Value of Incumbency', in R. Schmalensee and R. Willig (eds), *Handbook of Industrial Organization*, vol. 1 (Amsterdam: Elsevier Science B.V., 2001), p. 116.
12. Bain, *Barriers to New Competition*, p. 67.
13. R. I. Andreano, and S. I. Warner, 'Professor Bain and Barriers to New Competition', *Journal of Industrial Economics*, 7: 1 (1958), p. 76.
14. Ibid., p. 71.
15. A. H. Kahn, 'Discriminatory Pricing as a Barrier to Entry: The Spark Plug Litigation', *Journal of Industrial Economics*, 8: 1 (1959), p. 10.
16. This note comes from the Trial Record, p. 234, quoted from Kahn, see next note.
17. A. H. Kahn, 'Discriminatory Pricing as a Barrier to Entry', p. 12.
18. O. E. Williamson, 'Selling Expense as a Barrier to Entry', *Quarterly Journal of Economics*, 77:1 (1963), p. 117.
19. O.E. Williamson, 'Economies as an Antitrust Defense: the Welfare Tradeoffs', *American Economic Review*, 58:1 (1968), p. 34.
20. L. W. Weiss, 'Factor in changing concentration', *The Review of Economics and Statistic*, 45:1 (1963), p. 77.
21. At this time, Michael Mann worked in the Bureau of Economics, which was director in the seventies. Bureau of Economics belong to the Federal Trade Commission
22. Lester Telser was professor in Chicago University.
23. L. G. Telser, 'Advertising and Competition', *Journal of Political Economy*, 72:6 (1964), p. 551.
24. H. M. Mann, J. A. Henning and J. W. Meehan, 'Advertising and Concentration: an Empirical Investigation', *Journal of Industrial Economics*, 16: 1 (1967), p. 39.
25. William Comanor is professor in UCLA and from 1978 through 1980 was Chief Economist and Director of the Bureau of Economics at the U.S. Federal Trade Commission in Washington.
26. Thomas Wilson was Adam Smith Professor of Political Economy, 1958–1985 in the University of Glasgow
27. W. Comanor and T. Wilson, 'Advertising Market Structure and Performance', *Review of Economics and Statistics*, 49:4 (1967), p. 423.
28. Ibid., p. 438.
29. Dennis Mueller is professor of economics in the University of Wien.
30. John Tilton is professor of the School of Mines in Colorado.
31. For more information about guidelines request, http://www.ftc.gov/
32. O. E. Williamson, 'The Merger Guidelines of the U.S. Department of Justice – In perspective', 2007, http://www.usdoj.gov/atr/hmerger/11257.htmpp. p. 11.
33. R. H. Bork, 'Antitrust and Monopoly the Goals of Antitrust Policy', *American Economic Review*, 57:2 (1967), p. 250.
34. Kovacic and Shapiro, 'Antitrust Policy', p. 52.

3 The Harvard and Chicago Schools:
Two Ways of Studying Barriers to Entry

1. Bain, *Barriers to New Competition*, p. 60.
2. O. Williamson, *The Economics of Discretionary Behavior Managerial Objectives in a Theory of the Firm* (Englewood Cliffs, N.J., Prentice-Hall, 1964), p. 133.
3. F. M. Scherer, *Industrial Market Structure and Economic Performance* (Chicago, IL: Rand McNally & Company, 1970), p.2.
4. R. Posner, 'The Chicago School of Antitrust Analysis', *University of Pennsylvania Law Review,* 127 (1978–9), p. 929.
5. M. Porter, 'The Contributions of Industrial Organization to Strategic Management', *Academy of Management Review*, 6: 4 (1981), p. 614.
6. T. Bresnahan and R. Schmalensee, *The Empirical Renaissance in Industrial Economics* (New York: Basil Blackwell published in cooperation with The Journal of industrial Economics, 1987), p. 2.
7. Ibid., p. 3.
8. D. Rubinfeld, 'Antitrust Policy', *International Encyclopaedia of Social and Behavioural Sciences*, 1 (2001), p. 556.
9. L. J. White, 'Economics, Economists, and Antitrust: A Tale of Growing Influence', in J. J. Siegfried (ed.), *Living Better through Economics* (Cambridge: Harvard University Press, forthcoming 2009).
10. This book collects several articles he written in a ten years period and it includes some pages such as the introduction of chapters and new contributions in competition theory
11. Stigler, *The Organization of Industry*, p. 67.
12. Ibid., p.15.
13. Ibid., p. 21.
14. J. McGee, 'Predatory Pricing Revisited', *Journal of Law and Economics,* 23:2 (1980), p. 290.
15. Phillip Areeda was Assistant Special Counsel to President Eisenhower in 1958. In 1969 returned to Washington as Executive Director of the president's Cabinet Task Force on Oil Import Control and from 1974– 75 he was a counsel to President Ford.
16. Donald Turner was Chief of America's Antitrust Division in 1975.
17. P. Areeda and D. Turner, 'Predatory Pricing and Related Practices under Section 2 of the Sherman Act', *Harvard Law Review*, 88 (1975), pp. 697–733, p. 697.
18. Ibid., p.703.
19. Ibid., p. 704.
20. Ibid., p. 706.
21. Ibid., p. 711.
22. R. A. Posner, *Antitrust Law: An Economic Perspective* (Chicago, IL: Chicago University Press, 1976), p. 29.
23. Ibid., p. 41.
24. Ibid., p. 62.
25. Ibid., p. 936.
26. Ibid., p. 938.
27. Ibid., p. 948.
28. J. McGee, 'Predatory Pricing Revisited', p. 293.
29. Ibid., p. 289.

30. Ibid., p. 300.
31. H. Hovenkamp, 'Antitrust Policy after Chicago', *Michigan Law Review*, 84:2 (1985), p. 229.
32. Ibid., p. 231.
33. W. Baxter, 'Posner's Antitrust Law: An Economic Perspective', *Bell Journal of Economics*, 8:2 (1977), p. 610.
34. D. Mueller, *Profits in the Long Run* (Cambridge: Cambridge University Press, 1986), p. 224.
35. Ibid., p. 231.
36. A. Pakes, 'Review: Mueller's Profits in the Long Run', *RAND Journal of Economics*, 18:2 (1987), p. 328.
37. C. L. Davidson and R. Denckere, 'Long-run Competition in Capacity, Short-run Competition in Price, and the Cournot model', *RAND Journal of Economics*, 17:3 (1986), p. 413.
38. J. Cubbin and P. Geroski, 'The convergence of profits in the Long Run: Inter-firm and Inter-industry Comparisons', *Journal of Industrial Economics*, 35:4 (1987), *The Empirical Renaissance in Industrial Economics*, p. 441.
39. P. Geroski and R. T. Masson, 'Dynamic Market Models in Industrial Organization', *International Journal of Industrial Organization*, 5 (1987), p.5.
40. Ibid., p. 5.
41. P. Geroski and A. Jacquemin, 'The Persistence of Profits: a European Comparison', *Economic Journal*, 391: 98 (1988), p. 385.
42. P. Ghemawat, 'Competition and Business Strategy in Historical Perspective', *Business History Review*, 76 (2002), p.54.
43. I. Schmidt and J. Rittaler, *Chicago School of Antitrust Analysis* (Boston, MA: Kluwer Academic Publishers, 1989), p. 51.
44. R. Posner, 'The Chicago School of Antitrust Analysis'. *University of Pennsylvania Law Review*, 127 (1978–9), p. 932.
45. A. Demsetz, 'Barriers of Entry', *American Economic Review*, 72:1 (1982), p. 51.
46. H. Hovenkamp, 'Antitrust Policy after Chicago', *Michigan Law Review*, 84: 2 (1985), p. 231.
47. H. Hovenkamp, 'The Neoclassical Crisis in U.S. Competition Policy, 1890–1955', *http://ssrn.com/abstract=1156927*, 2008, p. 47.
48. S. Rosen, 'George J. Stigler and the Industrial Organization of Economic Thought', *Journal of Political Economy*, 101:5 (1993), p. 813.
49. Ch. Hsiao, *Analysis of Panel Data* (Cambridge: Cambridge University Press, 2003), p. 7.
50. T. Bresnahan and R. Schmalensee, *The Empirical Renaissance in Industrial Economics*, p. 4.
51. R. Schmalensee, 'Inter-industry Studies of Structure and Performance', in R. Schmalensee and R. Willig (eds), *Handbook of Industrial Organization* (Amsterdam: Elsevier Science B.V., 2001) vol. 2, p. 960.
52. Ch. Hsiao, *Analysis of Panel Data*, p. 5.
53. Kovacic and Shapiro, 'Antitrust Policy', p. 53.
54. D. Rubinfeld, 'Antitrust Policy', *International Encyclopaedia of Social and Behavioural Sciences*, 1 (2001), p. 556.
55. O. Williamson, 'Antitrust Enforcement', *Saint Louis University Law Journal*, 27 (1983), p. 293.
56. Kovacic and Shapiro, 'Antitrust Policy', p. 54.

4 Barriers to Entry, the 1970s

1. J. T. Wenders, 'Excess Capacity as a Barrier to Entry', *Journal of Industrial Economics*, 20:1 (1971), p. 15.
2. Ibid., p. 320.
3. M. I. Kamien and N. L. Schwartz, 'Uncertain Entry and Excess Capacity', *American Economic Review*, 62:5 (1972), p. 926.
4. G. Pyatt, 'Profit Maximization and the Threat of New Entry', *Economic Journal*, 81:322 (1971), p. 254.
5. D. K. Osborne, 'On the Rationality of Limit Pricing', *Journal of Industrial Economics*, 22:1 (1973), p. 79.
6. D. Qualls, 'Concentration, Barriers to Entry, and Long Run Economic Profit Margins', *Journal of Industrial Economics*, 20:2 (1972), p. 158.
7. R. Caves, J. Khalilzadeh-Shirazi and M. Porter, 'Scale Economics in Statistical Analyses of Market Power', *The Review of Economics and Statistics*, 57:2 (1975), p.133.
8. Ibid., 134.
9. Ibid., 135.
10. V. A. Dickson, 'Sub-optimal Capacity and Market Structure in Canadian Industry', *Southern Economic Journal*, 46:1 (1979), p. 216.
11. R. Caves and M. Porter, 'From Entry Barriers to Mobility Barriers: conjectural decisions and Contrived Deterrence to New Competition', *Quarterly Journal of Economics*, 91:2 (1977), p. 261.
12. Michael Spence won the Nobel Prize for Economics in 2001 for his analyses of markets with asymmetric information.
13. M. Spence, 'Entry, Capacity, Investment and Oligopolistic Pricing', *Bell Journal of Economics*, 8:2 (1977), p. 542.
14. F. Scherer, *Industrial Market Structure and Economic Performance*, p. 100.
15. Ibid., p. 130.
16. Ibid., p.157.
17. Ibid., p. 178.
18. H. Demsetz, 'Industry Structure, Market Rivalry and Public Policy', *Journal of Law and Economics*, 16:1 (1973), p. 3.
19. D. P. Baron, 'Limit Pricing, Potential Entry and Barriers to Entry', *American Economic Review*, 63:4 (1973), p. 669.
20. Ibid., p. 670.
21. T. D. Duchesneau, 'Barriers to Entry and the Stability of Market Structures: a Note', *Journal of Industrial Economics*, 22:4 (1974), p. 319.
22. S. Pelzman, 'The Gains and Losses from Industrial Concentration', *Journal of Law and Economics*, 20:2 (1977), p. 263.
23. F. Scherer, *Industrial market Structure and Economic Performance*. p. 207.
24. R. Schmalensee, 'Brand Loyalty and Barriers to Entry', *Southern Economic Journal*, 40:4 (1974), p. 579.
25. J.M. Vernon and R. E. M. Nourse, 'Profit Rates and Market Structure of Advertising Intensive Firms', *The Journal of Industrial Economics*, 22:2 (1973), p.12.
26. D. Needham, 'Entry Barriers and Non-price Aspects of Firms' Behaviour', *Journal of Industrial Economics*, 25:1 (1976), p. 41.
27. R. Schmalensee, 'On the Use of Economic Models in Antitrust: The Realemon Case', *University of Pennsylvania Law Review*, 127 (1979), p. 1000.

28. Idid., p.1033.
29. S. Martin, 'Advertising, Concentration, and Profitability: the Simultaneity Problem', *Bell Journal of Economics*, 10:2 (1979), p. 646.
30. H. Demsetz, 'Accounting for Advertising as a Barrier to entry', *TJournal of Business*, 53:3 (1979), p. 357.
31. W. Comanor and T. Wilson, 'The Effect of Advertising on Competition: A Survey', *Journal of Economic Literature*, 17:2 (1979), p. 472.
32. R. Levin, 'Technical Charge, Barriers to Entry and Market Structure', *Economica*, 45:180 (1978), p. 347.
33. R. R. de Bondt, 'Limit Pricing, Uncertain Entry, and the Entry Lag', *Econometrica*, 44:5 (1976), p. 945.
34. J. W. Friedman, 'On Entry Preventing Behavior and Limit Price Models of Entry', in J. Gabszewicz and J.-F. Thisse (eds), *Microeconomic Theories of Imperfect Competition, Old Problems and New Perspectives* (Northampton: Edward Elgar Publishers, 1999).
35. H. Newman, 'Strategic Groups and the structure-Performance Relationship', *Review of Economics and Statistics*, 60:3 (1978), p. 419.
36. P. Joskow and A. Klevorick, 'A Framework for Analyzing Predatory Pricing Policy', *Yale Law Journal*, 89:2 (1979), p. 218.
37. Ibid., p. 219.
38. L. W. Weiss, 'The Structure-Conduct-Performance Paradigm and Antitrust', *University of Pennsylvania Law Review*, 127:4 (1979), p. 1133.
39. Ibid., p. 1118.
40. Kovacic and Shapiro, 'Antitrust Policy', p. 55.
41. P. Joskow and A. Klevorick, 'A Framework for Analyzing Predatory Pricing Policy', p. 238.
42. In order do not unnecessary reiterations, the Areeda and Turner article does not analysed twice. Look epigraph 3.2.
43. W. Baumol, J. Panzar, and R. Willig, *Contestable Markets and the Theory of Industry Structure* (New York: Harcourt Brace Jovanovich, 1982), p. 27.
44. W. G. Shepherd, 'Causes of Increased Competition in the U.S. Economy, 1939–1980', *Review of Economics and Statistics*, 64: 4 (1982), p. 624.

5 Barriers to Entry: the 1980s

1. Michael Porter during the eighties worked with Richard Caves, and Michael Spence. Whereas the core of Caves research was exit barriers with a microeconomics approach and Michael Spence worked for Federal Trade Commission, Michael Porter focused his work on business behaviour.
2. M. Porter, *Competitive Strategy: Techniques for Analyzing Industries and Competitors* (New York: The Free Press, 1980), p. 7.
3. Ibid., p. 9.
4. These costs are different to sunk cost, which Porter defined as those cannot be recovered if a firm decides to leave a market; they therefore increase the risk and deter entry.
5. M. Porter, *Competitive Strategy*, p. 10.
6. Ibid., p. 11.
7. Ibid., p. 14.
8. Ibid., p. 20.

9. G. S. Yip, 'Diversification Entry: Internal Development versus Acquisition', *Strategic Management Journal*, 3: 4 (1982), p. 334.

10. B. Mascarenhas and D. Aaker, 'Mobility Barriers and Strategic Groups', *Strategic Management Journal*, 10:5 (1989), p. 485.

11. M. Gelfand, and P. Spiller, 'Entry Barriers and Multiproduct Oligopolies', *International Journal of Industrial Organization,* 5 (1987), pp. 101– 13.

12. S. G. Lanning, 'Cost of Maintaining a Cartel', *The Journal of Industrial Economics*, 36:2 (1987), p. 172.

13. William Baumol was professor of economics in Princeton University from 1949 to 1992.

14. Robert Willig was professor of economics in Princeton University and he has served as a consultant and advisor for the Federal Trade Commission and the Department of Justice on antitrust policy.

15. John Panzar was professor of economics in Northwestern University

16. W. Baumol, 'Contestable Markets: an Urising in the Theory of Industry Structure', *American Economic Review*, 72:1 (1982), p. 3.

17. Ibid., p. 8.

18. W. Baumol, J. Panzar and R. Willig, *Contestable Markets and the Theory of Industry Structure* (New York: Harcourt Brace Jovanovich, 1982). p. 3.

19. Ibid., p. 4.

20. Ibid., p. 9.

21. W. Baumol, 'Contestable Markets', p. 7.

22. G. Hurdle, R. Johnson, A. Joskow, G. Werden and M. Williams, 'Concentration, Potential Entry, and Performance in the Airline Industry', *Journal of Industrial Economics*, 38:2 (1989), p. 137.

23. E. Wolfstetter, *Topics in Microeconomics: Industrial Organization, Auctions and Incentives.* (Cambridge: Cambridge University Press, 1999), p. 66.

24. Ibid., p. 67.

25. R. Gilbert, 'The Role of Potential Competition in Industrial Organization', *The Journal of Economic Perspectives,* 3:3 (1989), p. 108.

26. Predatory pricing was analysed in Chapter 4.

27. P. Milgrom and J. Roberts, 'Informational Asymmetries, Strategic Behaviour, and Industrial Organization', *American Economic Review*, 77:2 (1987), p. 189.

28. Ibid., p.191.

29. H. Hovenkamp, 'Law and Economics in the United States: a Brief Historical Survey', *Cambridge Journal of Economics*, 19:2 (1995), p. 347.

30. M. T. Flaherty, 'Industry Structure and Cost-Reducing Investment', *Econometrica,* 48:5 (1980), p. 1187.

31. A. Dixit 'The Role of Investment in Entry-Deterrence', *Economic Journal*, 90:357 (1980), p. 96.

32. B. C. Eaton and R. G Lipsey, 'Exit barriers are entry barriers: the durability of capital as a barrier to entry', *Bell Journal of Economics,* 11:2 (1980), 722.

33. C. Shapiro, 'Theories of oligopoly behaviour', in R. Schmalensee and R. Willig (eds), *Handbook of Industrial Organization.* (Amsterdam: Elsevier Science B.V., 2001) vol. 1, pp. 329– 414, p. 379.

34. Ibid., p. 405.

35. The topsy-turvy principle implies that large capacities allow firms to behave very competitively and hence support collusion.

36. C. C. von Weizsäcker, *Barriers to Entry, a Theoretical Treatment* (Berlin: Springer Verlag, 1980), p. 405.
37. Ibid., p. 408.
38. M. Porter and M. Spence, 'The Capacity Expansion Process in a Growing Oligopoly: the Case of Corn Wet Milling', in John McCall, *Economics of Information and Uncertainty*. (Chicago, IL: The University of Chicago Press, 1982), pp. 259–316.
39. J. C. Hilke, 'Excess Capacity and Entry: Some Empirical Evidence', *Journal of Industrial Economics*, 33: 2 (1984), p. 236.
40. W. Brock, and J. Scheinkman, 'Price Setting Supergames with Capacity Constraints', *Review of Economic Studies*, 52:3 (1985), pp. 371–82.
41. B. R. Lyons, 'The Welfare Loss due to Strategic Investment in Excess Capacity', *International Journal of Industrial Organization*, 4 (1986), p. 119.
42. M. B. Lieberman, 'Excess capacity as a barrier to entry: an empirical appraisal', *The Journal of Industrial Economics*, 35: 4 (1987), p. 613.
43. Ibid., p. 621.
44. M. Spence, 'Notes of Advertising, Economies of Scale, and Entry barriers', *Quarterly Journal of Economics*, 95: 3 (1980), p. 505.
45. Several references of this paper have been included previously.
46. R. Ware, 'Inventory Holding as a Strategic Weapon to Deter entry', *Economica*, 205:52 (1985), p. 96.
47. R. Schmalensee, 1981: 'Economies of Scale and Barriers to Entry', *Journal of Political Economy*, 89:6 (1981), p. 1234.
48. K. R. Harrigan, 'Barriers to Entry and Competitive Srategies', *Strategic Management Journal*, 2 (1981), p. 412.
49. K. R. Harrigan 'Deterrents to Divestiture', *Academy of Management Journal*, 24:2 (1981), p. 322.
50. T. Waagstein, 'Fixed Cost, Limit Pricing and Investment in Barriers to Entry', *European Economic Review*, 17 (1982), p. 77.
51. H. Chappell, W. Marks and I. Park, 'Measuring Entry Barriers using a Switching Regression Model of Industry Profitability', *Southern Economic Journal*, 49:4 (1983), pp. 991–1001.
52. S. C. Salop and D. T. Scheffman, 'Raising Rivals' Cost', *American Economic Review*, 73:2 (1983), p. 267.
53. R. Caves, 'Economic Analysis and the Quest for Competitive Advantage', *American Economic Review*, 74:2 (1984), p. 128.
54. Ibid., p. 131.
55. R. Braudburdand and D. R. Ross, 'Can Small Firms Find and Defend strategic Niches? A Test of the Porter Hypothesis', *Review of Economics and Statistics*, 71:2 (1989), pp. 258–62.
56. B. Nahata and D. Olson, 'On the Definition of Barriers to Entry', *Southern Economic Journal*, 56:1 (1989), pp. 236–9.
57. Michael Salinger is Director of Bureau of Economics of the Federal Trade Commission since 2005.
58. M. Salinger, R. Caves R. and S. Peltzman, 'The Concentration-Margins Relationship Considered', *Brookings Papers on Economic Activity, Microeconomics* (1990), p. 319.
59. C. C. von Weizsäcker, 'A Welfare Analysis of Barriers to Entry', p. 418.
60. E. Wolfstetter, *Topics in Microeconomics*, p. 124.

61. J. Cubbin, 'Advertising and the Theory of Entry Barriers', *Economica*, 48:191 (1981), p. 296.

62. T. Nagle, 'Do Advertising-Profitability Studies Really Show that Advertising Creates a Barrier to entry?', *Journal of Law and Economics,* 24: 2 (1981), pp. 333– 49.

63. R. Ayanian, 'The Advertising Capital Controversy', *Journal of Business,* 56:3 (1983), p. 363.

64. J. Farrell, 'Moral Hazard as an Entry Barrier', *RAND Journal of Economics*, 17:3 (1986), p. 41.

65. J. Cubbin and S. Domberger, 'Advertising and Post-Entry Oligopoly Behaviour', *Journal of Industrial Economics,* 37: 2 (1988), p. 138.

66. K. Bagwell, 'Informational Product Differentiation as a Barrier to Entry', *International Journal of Industrial Organization*, 8 (1990), pp. 208.

67. G. M. Grossman and H. Horn, 'Infant-industry Protection Reconsidered: The Case of Informational Barriers to Entry', *Quarterly Journal of Economics*, 103:4 (1988), p. 767.

68. Ibid., p. 786.

69. The father of Strategy is Michael Porter. He worked for years with Richard Caves. Both are considered relevant authors of the Harvard School. Harvard heritage is showing it head as clearly as Porter's theory evolution is.

70. J. Seade, 'On the Effects of Entry', *Econometrica*, 48:2 (1980), pp. 479–89.

71. H. Demsetz, 'Barriers of Entry', *American Economic Review,* 72:1 (1982), p. 52.

72. Ibid., p. 53.

73. P. Milgrom and J. Roberts, 'Limit Pricing and Entry under Incomplete Information: an Equilibrium Analysis', *Econometrica*, 50:2 (1982), pp. 443–59.

74. P. Milgrom and J. Roberts, 'Predatory, Reputation and Entry Deterrence', *Journal of Economic Theory*, 27 (1982), p. 283.

75. A. Shaked and J. Sutton, 'Natural Oligopolies', *Econometrica*, 51:5 (1983), pp. 1469– 83.

76. P. Ghemawat and B. Nalebuff, 'Exit', *RAND Journal of Economics*, 16:2 (1985), pp. 184– 94.

77. D. B. Bernheim, 'Strategic Deterrence of Sequential Entry into an Industry', *RAND Journal of Economics*, 15:1 (1984), p. 1.

78. Ibid., p. 2.

79. Ibid., p. 3.

80. R. Gilbert and X. Vives, 'Entry Deterrence and the Free Rider Problem', *Review of Economic Studies*, 53 (1986), p. 81.

81. Ibid., p. 82.

82. G. Mankiw and M. Whinston, 'Free Entry and Social Inefficiency', *RAND Journal of Economics*, 17:1 (1986), pp. 48–58, p. 57.

83. B. Eaton and R. Ware, 'A Theory of Market Structure with Sequential Entry', *RAND Journal of Economics,* 18:1 (1987), p. 14.

84. D. Shapiro and R. S. Khemani, 'The Determinants of Entry and Exit Reconsidered', *International Journal of Industrial Organization,* 5 (1987), p. 25.

85. E. Masson and J. Shaanan, 'Optimal Oligopoly Pricing and the Threat of Entry', *International Journal of Industrial Organization*, 5 (1987), pp. 323– 39.

86. J. Schwalbach, 'Entry by Diversified Firms into German Industries', *International Journal of Industrial Organization*, 5 (1986), p. 48.

87. Z. J. Acs and D. B. Audretsch, 'Innovation, Market Structure and Firm Size', *Review of Economics and Statistics*, 69:4 (1987), pp. 567–74.

88. T. Bresnahan and P. Reiss, 'Do Entry Conditions vary Across Markets', *Brookings Papers on Economic Activity,* 3 (1987), p. 838.

89. P. Aghion and P. Bolton, 'Contracts as a Barrier to Entry', *American Economic Review,* 77:3 (1987), p. 389.

90. R. Smiley, 'Empirical Evidence on Strategic Entry Deterrence', *International Journal of Industrial Organization,* 6 (1988), p. 169.

91. T. Dunne, M. Roberts and L. Samuelson, 'Patterns of Firm Entry and Exit in U.S. Manufacturing Industries', *RAND Journal of Economics,* 19:4 (1988), pp. 495– 515.

92. There is an extended arguing about profits in the long run as a section in Chapter 3.

93. P. Geroski, J. Schwalbach, *Barriers to Entry and Intensity of Competition in European Markets* (Commission of the European Communities, 1989), p. 16.

94. Ibid., p. 26.

95. http://www.usdoj.gov/atr/hmerger/11249.htm.

96. Caveat: This sentence should be confusing as it has been written in contradictory ways. It is possible to find theoretical articles where the vertical mergers have been considered more likely to create competitive problems, but not in this case.

97. Robert Willig worked for Department of Justice in 1991.

98. R. Willig, S. Salop, and F. Scherer, 'Merger Analysis, Industrial Organization Theory, and Merger Guidelines', *Brookings Papers on Economic Activity: Microeconomics,* 1991, p. 284.

99. Ibid., p. 314.

100. Lawrence White was the Chief Economist in the Antitrust Division of the US Department of Justice, 1982– 1983.

101. L. White, 'Economics, Economists, and Antitrust: A Tale of Growing Influence', in J. J. Siegfried (ed.), *Living Better through Economics* (Cambridge, MA: Harvard University Press, forthcoming 2009).

102. Rudolf Peritz is professor in New York Law School and Senior Research Scholar in the American Antitrust Institute.

103. R. J. R. Peritz, 'Antitrust Policy and Aggressive Business Strategy: A Historical Perspective on Understanding Commercial Purposes and Effects', *Journal of Public Policy & Marketing,* 21:2 (2002), p. 239.

104. R. Schmalensee, 'Antitrust and the New Industrial Economics', *American Economic Review,* 72:2 (1982), p. 24.

105. W. Baumol, J. Panzar and R. Willig, *Contestable Markets and the Theory of Industry Structure* (New York: Harcourt Brace Jovanovich, 1982), p. 52.

106. R. Schmalensee, 'Antitrust and the New Industrial Economics', *American Economic Review,* 72:2 (1982), p. 26.

107. W. Baumol, J. Panzar and R. Willig, *Contestable Markets and the Theory of Industry Structure* (New York: Harcourt Brace Jovanovich, 1982), p. 56.

108. R. Schmalensee, 'Antitrust and the New Industrial Economics', *American Economic Review,* 72:2 (1982), p. 25.

109. D. B. Bernheim, 'Strategic Deterrence of Sequential Entry into an Industry', *RAND Journal of Economics,* 15:1 (1984), p. 11.

110. X. Vives, 'Sequential Entry, Industry Structure and Welfare', *European Economic Review,* 32 (1988), pp. 1671– 87.

111. S. M. Loescher, 'Intrafirm Grants and the New Legitimation of Coercive Competition: the Areeda–Turner rule In perspective', *Journal of Economic Issues,* 14:4 (1980), p. 962.

112. Ibid., p. 964.

113. K. Suzumura and K. Kiyono, 'Entry Barriers and Economic Welfare', *Review of Economic Studies*, 54:1 (1987), pp. 157– 67.

114. W. Baumol, J. Panzar and R. Willig, *Contestable Markets and the Theory of Industry Structure* (New York: Harcourt Brace Jovanovich, 1982), p. 466.

115. W. G. Shepherd, 'Causes of Increased Competition in the U.S. Economy, 1939–1980', *Review of Economics and Statistics*, 64:4 (1982), p. 624.

116. E. Bailey, 'Price and Productivity Change Following Deregulation: the US Experience', *Economic Journal*, 96 (1986), pp. 1– 17.

117. J. S. McGee, 'Predatory Pricing Revisited', *Journal of Law and Economics,* 23:2 (1980), p. 312.

6 Barriers to Entry: Current Analysis

1.   Dennis Carlton since 2007 is Deputy Assistant Attorney General for Economic Analysis, Antitrust Division, US Department of Justice.

2.   Carlton, 'Why Barriers to Entry are Barriers to Understanding', p. 469.

3.   B. Greenwald and J. Kahn, *Competition Demystified* (New York: Porfolio, 2005), p. 20.

4.   At the end of this chapter is included a detailed resume of the Guidelines of 1992.

5.   The last Guidelines published in 2006 will be analysed at the end of this chapter.

6.   R. Cairns and J. Galbraith, 'Artificial Compatibility, Barriers to Entry and Frequent-Flyer Programs', *Canadian Journal of Economics*, 23:4 (1990), p. 814.

7.   P. Geroski, *Markets Dynamics and Entry* (Cambridge: Blackwell, 1991), p. 111.

8.   Ibid., p. 113.

9.   S. Davies, 'Dynamic Price Competition, Briefly Sunk Costs, and Entry Deterrence', *RAND Journal of Economics,* 22:4 (1991), pp. 519–30.

10. D. S. Bunch and R. Smiley, 'Who Deters Entry? Evidence on the use of Strategic Entry Deterrents', *Review of Economics and Statistics*, 3:74 (1992), p. 518.

11. B. Allen, 'Capacity Precommitment as an Entry Barrier for Price-setting Firms', *International Journal of Industrial Organization*, 11 (1993), p. 69.

12. J. Haskel and C. Martin, 'Capacity and Competition: Empirical Evidence on UK panel Data', *Journal of Industrial Economics*, 42:1 (1994), pp. 23– 44.

13. These difficulties may be manifested through the problem of heteroscedasticity, leading to the generation of inefficient least squares estimates in a statistical analysis. The use of time series data for a single industry provides an approach which circumvents this dilemma.

14. S. Mathis and J. Koscianski, 'Excess Capacity as a Barrier to Entry in the US Titanium Industry', *International Journal of Industrial Organization*, 15 (1996), p. 279.

15. L. R. Christensen and R. Caves, 'Cheap Talk and Investment Rivalry', p. 71.

16. J. Nachbar, B. Petersen and I. Hwangs, 'Sunk Costs, Accommodation, and the Welfare Effects of Entry', *Journal of Industrial Economics*, 46 (1998), p. 319.

17. D. Carlton and J. Perloff, *Modern Industrial Organization* (New York: Harper Collins College Publishers, 1994).

18. C. Shapiro, 'Theories of Oligopoly Behaviour', in R. Schmalensee and R. Willig (eds), *Handbook of Industrial Organization.* (Amsterdam: Elsevier Science B.V., 2001) vol. 1, p. 409.

19. D. L. Rubinfeld, 'Antitrust Policy', *International Encyclopaedia of Social and Behavioral Sciences*, 1 (2001), p. 559.

20. D. Bernheim and M. D. Whinston, 'Multimarket Contact and Collusive Behavior', *RAND Journal of Economics*, 21:1 (1990), pp. 1–6, p. 2.

21. Ibid., p. 3.

22. R. L. Stenbacka, 'Collusion in Dynamic Oligopolies in the Presence of Entry Threats', *Journal of Industrial Economics*, 34:2 (1990), pp. 47– 154.

23. P. Geroski, 'Vertical Relations Between Firms and Industrial Policy', *Economic Journal*, 410:102 (1992), p. 143.

24. Ibid., p. 144.

25. M. Peteraf and R. Reed, 'Pricing and Performance in Monopoly Airline Markets', *Journal of Law and Economics*, 37 (1994), p. 210.

26. K. Bagwell, 'Informational Product Differentiation as a Barrier to Entry', *International Journal of Industrial Organization*, 8 (1990), pp. 207– 23.

27. G. dell Ariccia, E. Friedman, and R. Marquez, 'Adverse Selection as a Barrier to Entry in the Banking Industry', *RAND Journal of Economics*, 30:3 (1999), pp. 515– 34.

28. F. Scott-Morton, 'Barriers to Entry, Brand Advertising and Generic Entry in the US Pharmaceutical industry', *International Journal of Industrial Organization*, 18 (2000), pp. 1085– 104.

29. I. Kessides, 'Towards a Testable Model of Entry: a Study of the US Manufacturing Industries', *Economica*, 57:226 (1990), p. 234.

30. T. Bresnahan and P. Reiss, 'Entry in Monopoly Markets', *Review of Economic Studies*, 57:4 (1990), pp. 531– 53.

31. A. M. Brandenburger and W. S. Harborne, 'Valued-based Business strategy', *Journal of Economics and Management Strategy*, 5:1 (1996), p. 19.

32. J. J. Laffont, P. Rey and J. Tirole, 'Competition between Telecommunications Operators', *European Economic Review*, 41 (1997), p. 711.

33. R. Makadok, R., 'Can First-Mover and Early-Mover Advantages Be Sustained in an Industry with Low barrier to entry/imitation?', *Strategic Management Journal*, 7:19 (1998), pp. 683– 96.

34. J. Podolki and F. Scott Morton, 'Social Status, Entry and Predation: the Case of British Shipping cartels 1879– 1929', *The Journal of Industrial Economics*, 47 (1999), p. 42.

35. Ibid., p. 62.

36. A. McGahan, 'The Performance of US Corporations: 1981–1994', *Journal of Industrial Economics*, 47 (1999), pp. 373–98.

37. D. Fudenberg and J. Tirole, 'Pricing a Network Good to Deter Entry', *Journal of Industrial Economics*, 48: 4 (2000), p. 373.

38. R. Agarwal and D. Audretsch, 'Does Entry Size Matter?', pp. 21– 43.

39. http://www.usdoj.gov/atr/hmerger/11250.htm.

40. G. Stigler, 'Law and Economics?', *Journal of Law and Economics*, 35:2 (1992), pp. 455– 68, p. 458.

41. A. N. Kleit and M. B. Coate, 'Are Judges Leading Economic Theory? Sunk Costs, the Threat of Entry and the Competitive Process', *Southern Economic Journal*, 60:1 (1993), p. 104.

42. Ibid., p. 117.

43. S. Berry and A. Pakes, 'Some Applications and Limitations of Recent Advances in Empirical Industrial Organization: Merger Analysis', *American Economic Review*, 83:2 (1993), pp. 248.

44. Areeda and Turner, 'Predatory Pricing and Related Practices', p. 712.

45. Ibid., p. 733.
46. W. Baumol, 'Predation and the Logic of the Average Variable Cost Test', *Journal of Law and Economics*, 39 (1996), p. 49.
47. Ibid., p. 52.
48. Ibid., p. 56.
49. Ibid., p. 69.
50. P. Milgrom and J. Roberts, 'Predatory, Reputation and Entry Deterrence', *Journal of Economic Theory*, 27 (1982), pp. 280– 312.
51. J. A. Ordovez and G. Saloner, 'Predation, Monopolization and Antitrust', in R. Schmalensee and R. Willig, *Handbook of Industrial Organization,* vol. 1 (Amsterdam: Elsevier Science B.V., 2001), p. 565.
52. D. Deneffe and P. Wakker, 'Mergers, Strategic Investments and Antitrust Policy', *Managerial and Decision Economics*, 17: 3 (1996), pp. 236.
53. J. B. Baker and D. L. Rubinfeld, 'Empirical Methods in Antitrust Litigation: Review and Critique', *American Law and Economics Review,* 1:1 (1999), p. 387.
54. Ibid., p. 401.
55. Ibid., p. 419.
56. Ibid., p. 430.
57. Ibid., p. 430.
58. Kovacic and Shapiro, 'Antitrust Policy', p. 56.
59. D. Carlton, 'Does Antitrust Need to be Modernized?', p. 161.
60. R. G. Noll, 'Economic perspectives on the politics of regulation', in R. Schmalensee and R. Willig (eds.), *Handbook of Industrial Organization*, vol. 2 (Amsterdam: Elsevier Science B.V., 2001), p. 1261.
61. Ibid., p. 1272.
62. D. Evans, A. Nichols and R Schmalensee, 'An Analysis of the Government's Economic Case in US v. Microsoft', *Antitrust Bulletin*, 46:2 (2001), pp. 193.
63. Ibid., p. 195.
64. D. Evans and R. Schmalensee, 'Some Economic Aspects of Antitrust Analysis in Dynamically Competitive Industries', *Working Paper* (National Bureau of Economic Research, 8268, 2001), p. 28.
65. Carlton and Perloff, *Modern Industrial Organization*.
66. P. McAfee, H. Mialon and M. Williams, 'What is a Barrier of Entry? And Technical Appendix to', *American Economic Review*, 94:2 (2004), p. 465.
67. Carlton, 'Why Barriers to Entry are Barriers to Understanding', p. 466.

Conclusion

1. A. Smith, *An Inquiry into the Nature and Causes of the Wealth of Nations* (London: Printed for W. Strahan; and T. Cadell, in the Strand, 1776), I, vii, 27.
2. Ibid., I, x, c, 27.

WORKS CITED

Acs, Z. J., and D. B. Audretsch, 'Innovation, Market Structure and Firm Size', *Review of Economics and Statistics*, 69:4 (1987), pp. 567–74.

Agarwal, R., and D. B. Audretsch, 'Does Entry Size Matter? the Impact of the Life Cycle and Technology On Firm Survival', *Journal of Industrial Economics*, 49:1 (2001), pp. 21–43.

Aghion, P., and P. Bolton, 'Contracts as a Barrier to Entry', *American Economic Review*, 77:3 (1987), pp. 388–401.

Akerlof, G., 'Loyalty Filters', *American Economic Review*, 73:1 (1983), pp. 54–63.

Allen, B., 'Capacity Precommitment as an Entry Barrier for Price-Setting Firms', *International Journal of Industrial Organization*, 11 (1993), pp. 63–72.

Andreano, R. I., and S. I. Warner, 'Professor Bain and Barriers to New Competition', *Journal of Industrial Economics*, 7:1 (1958), pp. 66–76.

Ansoff, I., *Business Strategy: Selected Readings* (Harmondsworth: Penguin, 1969).

Archibald, G. C., 'Chamberlin versus Chicago', *Review of Economic Studies*, 29:1 (1961), pp. 2–28.

Areeda, P., and D. Turner, 'Predatory Pricing and Related Practices Under Section 2 of the Sherman Act', *Harvard Law Review*, 88 (1975), pp. 697–733.

Ariccia, G. Dell, Friedman, E. and Marquez, R. 'Adverse Selection as a Barrier to Entry in the Banking Industry', *RAND Journal of Economics*, 30:3 (1999), pp. 515–34.

Armstrong, M., and Porter, R. (eds), *Handbook of Industrial Organization* (Amsterdam: Elsevier, 2007).

Ayanian R., 'The Advertising Capital Controversy', the *Journal of Business*, 56:3 (1983), pp. 349–64.

Bagwell, K., 'Informational Product Differentiation as a Barrier to Entry', *International Journal of Industrial Organization,* 8 (1990), pp. 207–23.

—, 'The Economic Analysis of Advertising', in M. Armstrong and R. Porter (eds) *Handbook of Industrial Organization* (Amsterdam: Elsevier, 2007), *vol*. 3, pp. 1701–1844.

Bailey, E., 'Price and Productivity Change Following Deregulation: the US Experience', *Economic Journal*, 96 (1986), pp. 1–17.

Bain, J. S., 'Market Classifications in Modern Price Theory', *Quarterly Journal of Economics*, 56:4 (1942), pp. 560–74.

—, 'The Normative Problem in Industrial Organization', *American Economic Review*, 33:1 (1943), pp. 54–70.

—, *Literature and Price Policy and Related Topics, 1933–1947* (Berkeley, CA: University of California Press, 1947).

—, 'Output Quotas in Imperfect Cartels', *Quarterly Journal of Economics*, 62:4 (1948), pp. 617–33.

—, 'A Note On Pricing in Monopoly and Oligopoly', *American Economic Review*, 39:2 (1949), pp. 448–64.

—, 'Workable Competition in Oligopoly: Theoretical Considerations and Some Empirical Evidence', *American Economic Review*, 40:2 (1950), pp. 35–47.

—, *Price Theory* (1948; New York: Henry Holt and Company, 1952).

—, *Barriers to New Competition, their Character and Consequences in Manufacturing Industries* (Cambridge, MA: Harvard University Press, 1956).

—, *Industrial Organization* (1959; New York: Wiley, 1963).

—, 'The Impact On Industrial Organization', *American Economic Review*, 54:3 (1964), pp. 28–32.

—, 'The Comparative Stability of Market Structures', in J. Markham and G. Papanek, *Industrial Organization and Economic Development: Essays in Honour of Professor Edward S. Mason*. (Boston, MA: Houghton Mifflin, 1970).

Baker J. B., and Rubinfeld D. L. 'Empirical Methods in Antitrust Litigation: Review and Critique', *American Law and Economics Review*, 1:1 (1999), pp. 386–435.

Baron, D. P., 'Limit Pricing, Potential Entry and Barriers to Entry', *American Economic Review*, 63:4 (1973), pp. 666–74.

Baumol, W., *Economic Dynamics* (New York: the Macmillan Company, 1952).

—, 'On the Theory of Oligopoly', *Economica*, 99:25 (1958), pp. 187–98.

—, *Business Behavior, Value and Growth* (New York: Macmillan, 1959).

—, 'What Can Economic Theory Contribute to Managerial Economics?', *American Economic Review*, 51:2 (1961), pp. 142–6.

—, 'Reasonable Rules for Rate Regulation: Plausible Policies for an Imperfect World', in A. Phillips and O. Williamson (eds), *Prices: Issues in Theory, Practice, and Public Policy*. (Philadelphia, PA: University of Pennsylvania Press, 1964).

—, and R. Willing, 'Fixed Costs, Sunk Costs, Entry Barriers, and Sustainability of Monopoly', *Quarterly Journal of Economics*, 96:3 (1981), pp. 405–31.

—, 'Contestable Markets: an Uprising in the Theory of Industry Structure', *American Economic Review*, 72: 1 (1982), pp. 1–15.

—, J. Panzar and R. Willig, *Contestable Markets and the Theory of Industry Structure* (New York: Harcourt Brace Jovanovich, 1982).

—, J. Panzar and Willig, R., 'On the Theory of Perfectly-Contestable Markets', in J. Stiglitz and F. Matherwson (eds), *New Developments in the Analysis of Market Structure* (Cambridge, MA: Macmillan, 1986), pp. 339–65.

—, *Mercados Perfectos Y Virtud Natural* (1990; Madrid: Celeste, 1993).

—, 'Predation and the Logic of the Average Variable Cost Test', *Journal of Law and Economics*, 39 (1996), pp. 49–72.

—, *Growth, Industrial Organization and Economic Generalities* (Cheltenham: Edward Elgar, 2003).

Baxter, W., 'Posner's Antitrust Law: an Economic Perspective', *Bell Journal of Economics*, 8:2 (1977), pp. 609–19.

Bernheim, D. B., 'Strategic Deterrence of Sequential Entry Into an Industry', *RAND Journal of Economics*, 15: 1 (1984), pp. 1–11.

Bernheim, D. B., and M. D. Whinston, 'Multimarket Contact and Collusive Behavior', *Rand Journal of Economics*, 21:1 (1990), pp. 1–6.

Berry, C. H., 'Corporate Diversification and Market Structure', *Bell Journal of Economics and Management*, 5:1 (1974), pp. 196–204.

Berry, S., and A. Pakes, 'Some Applications and Limitations of Recent Advances in Empirical Industrial Organization: Merger Analysis', *American Economic Review*, 83:2 (1993), pp. 247–52.

Bondt, R. R. De, 'Limit Pricing, Uncertain Entry, and the Entry Lag', *Econometrica*, 44:5 (1976), pp. 939–46.

Boulding, K., 'The Theory of the Firm in the Last Ten Years', *American Economic Review*, 32:4 (1942), pp. 791–802.

—, 'In Defense of Monopoly', *Quarterly Journal of Economics*, 58:4 (1945), pp. 524–42.

—, *Análisis Económico* (1947; Madrid: Revista De Occidente, 1959).

Bork, R. H., 'Legislative Intent and the Policy of the Sherman Act', *Journal of Law and Economics*, 9 (1966), pp. 7–48.

—, 'Antitrust and Monopoly: the Goals of Antitrust Policy', *American Economic Review*, 57:2 (1967), pp. 242–53.

Braithwaite, D., 'The Economic Effects of Advertising', *Economic Journal*, 38:149 (1928), pp. 16–37.

Brandenburger A. M., and W. S. Harborne, 'Valued-Based Business Strategy', *Journal of Economics and Management Strategy*, 5:1 (1996), pp. 5–24.

Braudburd R. M., and D. R. Ross, 'Can Small Firms Find and Defend Strategic Niches? a Test of the Porter Hypothesis', *Review of Economics and Statistics*, 71:2 (1989), pp. 258–62.

Bresnahan, T., 'The Oligopoly Solution Concept Is Identified', *Economics Letters*, 10 (1982), pp. 87–92.

—, and R. Schmalensee, the *Empirical Renaissance in Industrial Economics* (New York: Basil Blackwell Published in Cooperation With *Journal of Industrial Economics*, 1987).

—, and P. Reiss, 'Do Entry Conditions Vary Across Markets', *Brookings Papers On Economic Activity*, 3 (1987), pp. 833–81.

—, and P. Reiss, 'Entry in Monopoly Markets', *Review of Economic Studies*, 57: 4 (1990), pp. 531–53.

—, 'Empirical Studies of Industries With Market Power', in R. Schmalensee and R. Willig (eds), *Handbook of Industrial Organization*, vol. 2. (Amsterdam: Elsevier Science B.V., 2001), pp. 1011–57.

Brock, W., and J. Scheinkman, 'Price Setting Supergames With Capacity Constraints', *Review of Economic Studies*, 52:3 (1985), pp. 371–82.

Bunch D. S., and R. Smiley, 'Who Deters Entry? Evidence On the Use of Strategic Entry Deterrents', *Review of Economics and Statistics*, 3:74 (1992), pp. 509–21.

Burke, A., and T. To, 'Can Reduced Entry Barriers Worsen Market Performance? a Model of Employee Entry', *International Journal of Industrial Organization*, 19 (2001), pp. 695–704.

Cabral, L., *Introduction to Industrial Organization* (Cambridge: the MIT Press, 2000).

—, *Readings in Industrial Organization* (Malden: Blackwell, 2000).

Cairns, R., and J. Galbraith, 'Artificial Compatibility, Barriers to Entry and Frequent-Flyer Programs', *the Canadian Journal of Economics*, 23:4 (1990), pp. 807–16.

Carlton, D., *Market Behavior Under Uncertainty* (New York: Garland Publishing, 1984).

—, 'The Theory and the Facts of How Markets Clear: Is Industrial Organization Valuable for Understanding Macroeconomics?', in R. Schmalensee and R. Willig, *Handbook of Industrial Organization*, vol. 1 (Amsterdam: Elsevier Science B.V., 2001), pp. 909–46.

—, 'Why Barriers to Entry Are Barriers to Understanding', *American Economic Review*, 94:2 (2004), pp. 466–70.

—, 'Barriers to Entry', *Working Paper* (National Bureau of Economic Research, 11645 (2005).

—, 'Does Antitrust Need to Be Modernized?', *Journal of Economic Perspectives*, 21:3 (2007), pp. 155–76.

Carlton, D., and J. Perloff, *Modern Industrial Organization* (New York: Harper Collins College Publishers, 1994).

Cassels, J. M., 'Excess Capacity and Monopolistic Competition', *Quarterly Journal of Economics*, 51: 3 (1937), pp. 426–43.

Caves, R., *La Industria Norteamericana: Estructura, Conducta Y Funcionamiento* (1964; México: Unión Tipográfica Editorial Hispano Americana, 1966).

—, J. Khalilzadeh-Shirazi, and M. Porter, 'Scale Economics in Statistical Analyses of Market Power', *Review of Economics and Statistics*, 57:2 (1975), pp. 133–40.

—, and Porter M., 'From Entry Barriers to Mobility Barriers: Conjectural Decisions and Contrived Deterrence to New Competition', *Quarterly Journal of Economics*, 91:2 (1977), pp. 241–62.

—, B. T. Gale, and M. Porter, 'Interfirm Profitability Differences: Comment', *Quarterly Journal of Economics*, 91:4 (1977), pp. 667–75.

—, 'Industrial Organization, Corporate Strategy and Structure', *Journal of Economic Literature*, 18:1 (1980), pp. 64–92.

—, 'Economic Analysis and the Quest for Competitive Advantage', *American Economic Review*, 74:2 (1984), pp. 127–32.

—, 'Mergers, Takeovers and Economic Efficiency (A Priori y a Posteriori)', *International Journal of Industrial Organization*, 7 (1989), pp. 151–74.

—, *Multinational Enterprise and Economic Analysis*, 2nd Edn (Cambridge: Cambridge University Press, 1996).

Chadwick, E., 'Results of Different Principles of Legislation and Administration in Europe, of Competition for the Field, as Compared With Competition Within the Field, of Service', *Journal of the Statistical Society of London*, 22:3 (1859), pp. 381–420.

Chamberlin, E. H., *The Theory of Monopolistic Competition* (Cambridge: Harvard University Thesis [1927], (1st Edn; Cambridge: Harvard University Press, 1933), (6th Edn; London: Geoffrey Cumberlege and Oxford University Press, 1949).

—, *Monopoly and Competition and their Regulation* (London: Mcmillan and Co LTD, 1954).

—, *Towards a More General Theory of Value* (New York: Oxford University Press, 1957).

Chappell, H. W., W. H. Marks and I. Park, 'Measuring Entry Barriers Using a Switching Regression Model of Industry Profitability', *Southern Economic Journal*, 49:4 (1983), pp. 991–1001.

Cheng, H., *Analysis of Panel Data* (Cambridge: Cambridge University Press, 2003).

Christensen, L. R., and R. Caves, 'Cheap Talk and Investment Rivalry in the Pulp and Paper Industry', *Journal of Industrial Economics*, 1:45 (1997), pp. 47–73.

Clark, J. B., and Clark, J. M., the *Control of Trusts* (New York: Augustus M Kelley. Publishers, 1912).

Clark, J. M., 'Toward a Concept of Workable Competition', *American Economic Review*, 30: 2 (1940), pp. 241–56.

—, 'Competition and the Objectives of Government Policy', in E. Chamberlin, *Monopoly and Competition and their Regulation* (London: Mcmillan and Co LTD, 1954), pp. 317–37.

Coase, R., 'The Nature of the Firm', *Economica*, 16: 4 (1937), pp. 386–405.

—, 'Industrial Organization: a Proposal for Research', *Working Paper* (National Bureau of Economic Research, 1972).

—, 'Marshall On Method', *Journal of Law and Economics*, 1: 18 (1975), pp. 25–31.

Coate, M., 'Merger Analysis in the Courts', *Managerial and Decision Economics*, 6:16 (1995), pp. 581–92.

—, 'Theory Meets Practice: Barriers to Entry in Merger Analysis', *Review of Law and Economics*, 4: 1 (2008), pp. 183–212.

Cohen, K. J., and Cyert, R. M., *Theory of the Firm: Resource Allocation in a Market Economy* (Englewood Cliffs, NJ: Prentice-Hall, 1965).

Cohen, J. L., and T. D. William, 'A Foundation for Behavioural Economics', *American Economic Review*, 92:2 (2002), pp. 335–8.

Comanor, W., and T. Wilson, 'Advertising Market Structure and Performance', the *Review of Economics and Statistics*, 49: 4 (1967), pp. 423–40.

—, 'The Effect of Advertising On Competition: a Survey', *Journal of Economic Literature*, 17: 2 (1979), pp. 453–76.

Corley, T. A. B., 'Emergence of the Theory of Industrial Organization, 1890–1990', *Business and Economic History*, 19 (1990), Pp.83–92.

Cubbin, J., 'Advertising and the Theory of Entry Barriers', *Economica*, 48: 191 (1981), pp. 289–98.

—, and P. Geroski, 'The Convergence of Profits in the Long Run: Inter-Firm and Inter-Industry Comparisons', *Journal of Industrial Economics*, 35:4 (1987), the Empirical Renaissance in Industrial Economics, pp. 427–42.

—, and S. Domberger, 'Advertising and Post-Entry Oligopoly Behaviour', *Journal of Industrial Economics*, 37: 2 (1988), pp. 123–40.

Cyert R. M., and J. G., March, *A Behavioral Theory of the Firm* (Englewood Cliffs, N.J.: Prentice-Hall, 1963), 2nd edn (Malden, MA: Blackwell Publishers, 1992).

—, and Ch. Hedrick, 'Theory of the Firm: Present, and Future, an Interpretation', *Journal of Economic Literature*, 10:2 (1972), pp. 398–412.

—, and G. Pottinger, 'Toward a Better Micro Economic Theory'. *Philosophy of Science*, 46, 2: (1979), pp. 204–22.

Davies, S. M., 'Dynamic Price Competition, Briefly Sunk Costs, and Entry Deterrence', *RAND Journal of Economics,* 22:4 (1991), pp. 519–30.

Davidson C. L., and R. Deneckere, 'Long-Run Competition in Capacity, Short-Run Competition in Price, and the Cournot Model', *RAND Journal of Economics,* 17:3 (1986), pp. 404–15.

Demsetz, H., 'Industry Structure, Market Rivalry and Public Policy', *Journal of Law and Economics*, 16:1 (1973), pp. 1–9.

—, 'Accounting for Advertising as a Barrier to Entry', the *Journal of Business*, 53:3 (1979), pp. 345–60.

—, 'Barriers of Entry', *American Economic Review,* 72:1 (1982), pp. 47–57.

Deneffe D., and P. Wakker, 'Mergers, Strategic Investments and Antitrust Policy', *Managerial and Decision Economics*, 17: 3 (1996), pp. 231–40.

Dickson, V. A., 'Sub-Optimal Capacity and Market Structure in Canadian Industry', *Southern Economic Journal*, 46:1 (1979), pp. 206–17.

Disney, R., J. Haskel and Y. Heden, 'Entry, Exit and Establishment Survival in UK Manufacturing', the *Journal of Industrial Economics*, LI: 1 (2003), pp. 91–112.

Dixit, A., 'A Model of Duopoly Suggesting a Theory of Entry Barriers', *Bell Journal of Economics,* 10:1 (1979), pp. 20–32.

—, 'The Role of Investment in Entry-Deterrence', *Economic Journal*, 90:357 (1980), pp. 95–106.

Djankov, S., R. La Porta, F. Lopez-De-Silanes and A. Shleiler, 'The Regulation of Entry', *Discussion Paper* (1904; Harvard Institute of Economic Research, 2000).

Duchesneau, T. D., 'Barriers to Entry and the Stability of Market Structures: a Note', *Journal of Industrial Economics*, 22: 4 (1974), pp. 315–20.

Dunne, T., M. Roberts, and L. Samuelson, 'Patterns of Firm Entry and Exit in U.S. Manufacturing Industries', *RAND Journal of Economics*, 19:4 (1988), pp. 495–515.

Easterbrook F. H., 'Antitrust and the Economics of Federalism', *Journal of Law and Economics*, 26: 1 (1983), pp. 23–50.

—, 'The Limits of Antitrust', *Texas Law Review*, 63:1 (1984), pp. 1–40.

Eaton, B. C. and R. G. Lipsey, 'Exit Barriers Are Entry Barriers: the Durability of Capital as a Barrier to Entry', *Bell Journal of Economics*, 11:2 (1980), 721–9.

—, and Ware, R., 'A Theory of Market Structure with Sequential Entry', *RAND Journal of Economics,* 18:1 (1987), pp. 1–16.

Edwards, H. R., 'Price Formation in Manufacturing Industry and Excess Capacity', *Oxford Economic Papers*, 7: 1 (1955), pp. 94–118.

Elberfeld, W., 'Market Size and Vertical Integration: Stigler's Hypothesis Reconsidered', the *Journal of Industrial Economics*, 50:1 (2002), pp. 23–42.

Evans, D., and R. Schmalensee, 'Some Economic Aspects of Antitrust Analysis in Dynamically Competitive Industries', *Working Paper* (National Bureau of Economic Research, 8268, 2001).

—, A. Nichols and R. Schmalensee, 'An Analysis of the Government's Economic Case in US V. Microsoft', *Antitrust Bulletin*, 46:2 (2001), pp. 163–242.

Farrell, J., 'Moral Hazard as an Entry Barrier', *RAND Journal of Economics*, 17:3 (1986), pp. 440–9.

—, and M. Katz, 'Competition or Predation? Consumer Coordination, Strategic Pricing and Price Floors in Network Markets', *Journal of Industrial Economics*, 53:2 (2005), pp. 203–31.

Fershtman C., and K. L. Judd, 'Equilibrium Incentives in Oligopoly', *American Economic Review*, 77: 5 (1987), pp. 927–40.

Fisher F. M., 'New Developments On the Oligopoly Front: Cournot and the Bain-Sylos Analysis', the *Journal of Political Economy*, 67:4 (1959). pp. 410–3.

Flaherty, M. T., 'Industry Structure and Cost-Reducing Investment', *Econometrica*, 48:5 (1980), pp. 1187–210.

—, 'Field Research On the Link Between Technological Innovation and Growth: Evidence for the International Semiconductor Industry', *American Economic Review*, 74:2 (1984), pp. 67–72.

Friedman, J. W., 'On Entry Preventing Behavior and Limit Price Models of Entry', in J. Gabszewicz and J.-F. Thisse (eds), *Microeconomic Theories of Imperfect Competition, Old Problems and New Perspectives* (Northampton: Edward Elgar Publishers, 1999).

Fudenberg, D., and J. Tirole, 'A "Signal-Jamming" Theory of Predation', *RAND Journal of Economics*, 17: 3 (1986), pp. 366–76.

—, 'Pricing a Network Good to Deter Entry', *Journal of Industrial Economics,* 48:4 (2000), pp. 373–90.

—, 'Noncooperative Game Theory for Industrial Organization: an Introduction and Overview', in R. Schmalensee and R. Willig. *Handbook of Industrial Organization* (Amsterdam: Elsevier Science B.V, 2001), vol. 1, pp. 259–327.

Gabszewicz, J. J., and Thisse, J. F., *Microeconomic Theories of Imperfect Competition, Old Problems and New Perspectives* (Northampton: Edward Elgar, 1999).

Gaskins, D. W., 'Dynamic Limit Pricing: Optimal Pricing Under Threat of Entry', *Journal of Economic Theory,* 3 (1971), pp. 306–22.

Gelfand, M., and P. Spiller, 'Entry Barriers and Multiproduct Oligopolies', *International Journal of Industrial Organization,* 5 (1987), pp. 101–13.

Geroski P. A., and R. T. Masson, 'Dynamic Market Models in Industrial Organization', *International Journal of Industrial Organization,* 5 (1987), pp. 1–13.

—, Masson, R. T., and J. Shaanan, 'The Dynamics of Market Structure', *International Journal of Industrial Organization,* 5 (1987), pp. 93–100.

—, and A. Jacquemin, 'The Persistence of Profits: a European Comparison', *Economic Journal,* 391:98 (1988), pp. 375–89.

—, and J. Schwalbach, *Barriers to Entry and Intensity of Competition in European Markets* (Commission of the European Communities, 1989).

—, *Markets Dynamics and Entry* (Cambridge: Blackwell, 1991).

—, 'Vertical Relations Between Firms and Industrial Policy', *Economic Journal,* 410: 102 (1992), pp. 138–47.

—, Gilbert, R., and A. Jacquemin, *Barriers to Entry and Strategic Competition* (New York: Harwood Academic Published, 1990).

Ghemawat, P., and B. Nalebuff, 'Exit', *RAND Journal of Economics,* 16:2 (1985), pp. 184–94.

—, 'Competition and Business Strategy in Historical Perspective', *Business History Review,* 76 (2002), pp. 37–74.

Gilbert, R., and X. Vives, 'Entry Deterrence and the Free Rider Problem', *Review of Economic Studies,* 53 (1986), pp. 71–83.

—, 'The Role of Potential Competition in Industrial Organization', *Journal of Economic Perspectives,* 3:3 (1989), pp. 107–27.

—, 'Mobility Barriers and the Value of Incumbency', in R. Schmalensee and R. Willig (Ed.), *Handbook of Industrial Organization,* vol. 1 (Amsterdam: Elsevier Science B.V., 2001), pp. 476–535.

Gorecki P. K., 'The Determinants of Entry By New and Diversifying Enterprises in the UK Manufacturing Sector 1958–1963: Some Tentative Results', *Applied Economics,* 7 (1975), pp. 139–47.

Green, C., 'Industrial Organization Paradigms, Empirical Evidence, and the Economic Case for Competition Policy', *Canadian Journal of Economics,* 20:3 (1987), pp. 482–505.

Greenwald B., and J. Kahn, *Competition Demystified* (New York: Porfolio, 2005).

Grossman, G. M. and H. Horn, 'Infant-Industry Protection Reconsidered: the Case of Informational Barriers to Entry', *Quarterly Journal of Economics*, 103:4 (1988), pp. 767–87.

Hall, R. L., and C. J. Hitch, 'Price Theory and Business Behaviour', *Oxford Economic Papers*, 2 (1939), pp. 12–45.

Harberger, A. C., 'Monopoly and Resource Allocation', *American Economic Review*, 44: 2 (1954), pp. 77–87.

Harrigan, K. R., 'Barriers to Entry and Competitive Strategies', *Strategic Management Journal*, 2 (1981), pp. 395–412.

—, 'Deterrents to Divestiture', *Academy of Management Journal*, 24:2 (1981), pp. 306–23.

Harrod, R. F., 'Doctrines of Imperfect Competition', *Quarterly Journal of Economics*, 48:3 (1934), pp. 442–70.

Haskel, J., and C. Martin, 'Capacity and Competition: Empirical Evidence on UK Panel Data', *Journal of Industrial Economics*, 42:1 (1994), pp. 23–44.

Hatten, K., and Katten M. L., 'Strategic Groups, Asymmetrical Mobility Barriers and Contestability', *Strategic Management Journal*, 8:4 (1987), pp. 329–42.

Hay, G. A. and D. Kelley, 'An Empirical Survey of Price Fixing Conspiracies', *Journal of Law and Economics*, 17 (1974), pp. 13–38.

Hicks, J. R., *Value and Capital: an Inquiry into Some Fundamental Principles of Economic Theory* (Oxford: Clarendon Press, 1939).

Hilke, J. C., 'Excess Capacity and Entry: Some Empirical Evidence', *Journal of Industrial Economics*, 33:2 (1984), pp. 233–40.

Hines, H. H., 'Effectiveness of "Entry" by Already Established Firms', *Quarterly Journal of Economics*, 71:1 (1957), pp. 132–50.

Hovenkamp, H., 'Antitrust Policy After Chicago', *Michigan Law Review*, 84:2 (1985), pp. 213–84.

—, 'Law and Economics in the United States: a Brief Historical Survey', *Cambridge Journal of Economics*, 19:2 (1995), pp. 331–52.

—, *The Antitrust Enterprise: Principle and Execution* (Cambridge: Harvard University Press, 2005).

—, 'The Neoclassical Crisis in U.S. Competition Policy, 1890–1955', *Http://Ssrn.Com/Abstract=1156927*, 2008.

Hsiao, Ch., *Analysis of Panel Data* (Cambridge: Cambridge University Press, 2003).

Hurdle, G., R. Johnson, A. Joskow, G. Werden and M. Williams, 'Concentration, Potential Entry, and Performance in the Airline Industry', the *Journal of Industrial Economics*, 38:2 (1989), pp. 119–39.

Ishibashi, I., 'A Note On Credible Spatial Entry Deterrence', *International Journal of Industrial Organization*, 21 (2003), pp. 283–9.

Jong H. W. De, 'Free versus Controlled Competition', in Carlsson, B. (Ed). *Industrial Dynamics*. (Boston, MA: Kluwert Academic Publishers, 1989), pp. 271–98.

Joskow, P., and A. Klevorick, 'A Framework for Analyzing Predatory Pricing Policy', *Yale Law Journal*, 89:2 (1979), pp. 213–70.

Kahn A. H., 'Discriminatory Pricing as a Barrier to Entry: the Spark Plug Litigation', *Journal of Industrial Economics*, 8:1 (1959), pp. 1–12.

Kaldor, N., 'The Economic Aspect of Advertising', *Review of Economic Studies*, 18:1 (1950–51), pp. 1–27.

—, 'Professor Chamberlin On Monopolistic and Imperfect Competition', *Quarterly Journal of Economics*, 52:3 (1938), pp. 513–29.

Kamien, M. I. and N. L. Schwartz, 'Uncertain Entry and Excess Capacity', *American Economic Review*, 62:5 (1972), pp. 918–27.

—, 'Cournot Oligopoly with Uncertain Entry', *Review of Economic Studies*, 42:1 (1975), pp. 125–31.

Katz, M., 'Recent Antitrust Enforcement Actions By the US Department of Justice: a Selective Survey of Economic Issues', *Review of Industrial Organization*, 21 (2002), pp. 373–97.

Kessides I., 'Towards a Testable Model of Entry: a Study of the US Manufacturing Industries', *Economica*, 57:226 (1990), pp. 219–38.

Kleit A. N., and M. B. Coate, 'Are Judges Leading Economic Theory? Sunk Costs, the Threat of Entry and the Competitive Process', *Southern Economic Journal*, 60:1 (1993), pp. 103–19.

Knight, F. H., *Risk, Uncertainly and Profits* (Boston, MA: Houghton Mifflin Company, 1921). 7th Impression (London: Replika Process, 1948).

—, *The Ethics of Competition and Other Essays* (London : G. Allen & Unwin, 1935), 2nd edn (New York : Harper & Brothers, 1936).

Kovacic, W. E., and C. Shapiro, 'Antitrust Policy: a Century of Economic and Legal Thinking', *Journal of Economic Perspectives*, 14:1 (2000), pp. 43–60.

Laffont, J. J., P. Rey and J. Tirole, 'Competition Between Telecommunications Operators', *European Economic Review*, 41 (1997), pp. 701–11.

Langinier, C., 'Are Patents Strategic Barriers to Entry?', *Journal of Economics and Business*, 56:5 (2004), pp. 349–61.

Lanning S. G., 'Cost of Maintaining a Cartel', *Journal of Industrial Economics*, 36:2 (1987), pp. 157–74.

Lerner, A. P., 'The Concept of Monopoly and the Measurement of Monopoly Power', *Review of Economic Studies*, 1:3 (1934), pp. 157–75.

Levin, R., 'Technical Charge, Barriers to Entry and Market Structure', *Economica*, 45:180 (1978), pp. 347–61.

Lieberman, M. B., 'Excess Capacity as a Barrier to Entry: an Empirical Appraisal', the *Journal of Industrial Economics*, 35:4 (1987), pp. 607–27.

—, 'Market Growth, Economies of Scale, and Plant Size in the Chemical Processing Industries', the *Journal of Industrial Economics*, 36:2 (1987), pp. 175–91.

Loescher, S. M., 'Intrafirm Grants and the New Legitimation of Coercive Competition: the Areeda-Turner Rule in Perspective', *Journal of Economic Issues*, 14:4 (1980), pp. 959–65.

Lustgarten, S. and S. Thomadakis, 'Mobility Barriers and Tobin's Q*', the *Journal of Business*, 60:4 (1987), pp. 519–37.

Lyons, B. R., 'The Welfare Loss Due to Strategic Investment in Excess Capacity', *International Journal of Industrial Organization*, 4 (1986), pp. 109–19.

Machlup, F., 'Marginal Analysis and Empirical Research', *American Economic Review*, 36:4 (1946), pp. 519–54.

—, 'Theories of the Firm: Marginalist, Behavioural, Managerial', *American Economic Review*, 57:1 (1967), pp. 1–33.

Makadok, R., 'Can First-Mover and Early-Mover Advantages Be Sustained in an Industry With Low Barrier to Entry/Imitation?', *Strategic Management Journal*, 7:19 (1998), pp. 683–96.

Mankiw, G., and M. Whinston, 'Free Entry and Social Inefficiency', *RAND Journal of Economics*, 17:1 (1986), pp. 48–58.

Mann, H. M., 'Seller Concentration, Barriers to Entry, and Rates of Return in Thirty Industries, 1950–1960', *Review of Economics and Statistics*, 48:3 (1966), pp. 296–307.

—, J. A. Henning and J. W. Meehan, 'Advertising and Concentration: an Empirical Investigation', the *Journal of Industrial Economics*, 16: 1 (1967), pp. 34–45.

Marin, P and Sicotte R., 'Exclusive Contracts and Market Power: Evidence from Ocean Shipping', the *Journal of Industrial Economics*, 51 (2003), pp. 193–213.

Martin, S., 'Advertising, Concentration, and Profitability: the Simultaneity Problem', *Bell Journal of Economics*, 10:2 (1979), pp. 639–47.

Marris, R. L., 'Why Economics Needs a Theory of the Firm', *Economic Journal*, 325:82 (1972), pp. 321–52.

Mascarenhas, B., and D. Aaker, 'Mobility Barriers and Strategic Groups', *Strategic Management Journal*, 10:5 (1989), pp. 475–85.

Mason, E. S., 'Monopoly in Law and Economics', *Yale Law Journal*, 47:1 (1937), pp. 34–49.

—, 'The Current Status of the Monopoly Problem in the United States', *Harvard Law Review*, 62:8 (1949), pp. 1265–85.

—, 'Market Power and Business Conduct: Some Comments', *American Economic Review*, 46:2 (1956), pp. 471–81.

—, *Economic Concentration and De Monopoly Problem* (Cambridge, MA: Harvard University Press, 1957).

—, and J. Shaanan, 'Optimal Oligopoly Pricing and the Threat of Entry', *International Journal of Industrial Organization*, 5 (1987), pp. 323–39.

Mathis S., and J. Koscianski, 'Excess Capacity as a Barrier to Entry in the US Titanium Industry', *International Journal of Industrial Organization*, 15 (1996), pp. 263–81.

Maurer, H., *Great Enterprise: Growth and Behavior of the Big Corporation* (New York: Macmillan, 1955).

Mcafee, P., H. Mialon, and M. Williams, 'What Is a Barrier of Entry? And Technical Appendix To', *American Economic Review*, 94:2 (2004), pp. 461–65.

Mcgahan, A., 'The Performance of US Corporations: 1981–1994', *Journal of Industrial Economics*, 47 (1999), pp. 373–98.

Mcgee, J. S., 'Predatory Price Cutting: the Standard Oil (N.J.) Case', *Journal of Law and Economics*, 1 (1958), pp. 137–69.

—, 'Predatory Pricing Revisited', *Journal of Law and Economics*, 23:2 (1980), pp. 289–330.

Merger Guidelines, *Http://Www.Usdoj.Gov/Atr/Hmerger/11247.Htm*, 1968.

—, *Http://Www.Usdoj.Gov/Atr/Hmerger/11249.Htm*, 1984.

—, *Http://Www.Usdoj.Gov/Atr/Public/Guidelines/2614.Htm*, 1984.

—, *Http://Www.Usdoj.Gov/Atr/Hmerger/11250.Htm*, 1992.

—, *Http://Www.Ftc.Gov/Bc/Docs/Horizmer.Htm*, 1992.

—, *Http://Www.Usdoj.Gov/Atr/Hmerger/11251.Htm*, 1997.

Milgrom P. and J. Roberts, 'Limit Pricing and Entry Under Incomplete Information: an Equilibrium Analysis', *Econometrica*, 50:2 (1982), pp. 443–59.

—, 'Predatory, Reputation and Entry Deterrence', *Journal of Economic Theory*, 27 (1982), pp. 280–312.

—, 'Informational Asymmetries, Strategic Behavior, and Industrial Organization', *American Economic Review*, 77:2 (1987), pp. 184–193.

Modigliani, F., 'New Developments On the Oligopoly Front', *Journal of Political Economy*, 66:3 (1958), pp. 215–32.

Mougeot, M. and F. Naegelen, 'Designing a Market Structure When Firms Compete for the Right to Serve the Market', *Journal of Industrial Economics*, 53 (2005), pp. 393–416.

Mueller, D. and J. E. Tilton, 'Research and Development Costs as a Barrier to Entry', *Canadian Journal of Economics*, 2:4 (1969), pp. 570–9.

—, *Profits in the Long Run* (Cambridge: Cambridge University Press, 1986).

Nachbar, J., B. Petersen and I. Hwangs, 'Sunk Costs, Accommodation, and the Welfare Effects of Entry', the *Journal of Industrial Economics*, 46 (1998), pp. 317–32.

Nagle, T. T., 'Do Advertising-Profitability Studies Really Show that Advertising Creates a Barrier to Entry?', *Journal of Law and Economics*, 24:2 (1981), pp. 333–49.

Nahata, B. and D. Olson, 'On the Definition of Barriers to Entry', *Southern Economic Journal*, 56:1 (1989), pp. 236–9.

Needham, D., 'Entry Barriers and Non-Price Aspects of Firms' Behavior', *Journal of Industrial Economics*, 25:1 (1976), pp. 29–43.

Nelson, R., 'Comments On a Paper By Posner', *University of Pennsylvania Law Review*, 127 (1978–79), pp. 949–52.

Neumann, J. Von and O. Morgenstern, *Theory of Games and Economic Behavior* (Princeton, NJ: Princeton University Press, 1944).

Newman, H., 'Strategic Groups and the Structure-Performance Relationship', *Review of Economics and Statistics*, 60:3 (1978), pp. 417–27.

Noll, R. G., 'Economic Perspectives On the Politics of Regulation', in R. Schmalensee and R. Willig (eds), *Handbook of Industrial Organization*, vol. 2 (Amsterdam: Elsevier Science B.V., 2001), pp. 1253–87.

Olson, M., and R. Zeckhauser, 'An Economic Theory of Alliances', *Review of Economics and Statistics*, 48:3 (1966), pp. 266–79.

Ordovez J. A., and G. Saloner, 'Predation, Monopolization and Antitrust', in R. Schmalensee and Willig R. *Handbook of Industrial Organization*, vol. 1 (Amsterdam: Elsevier Science B.V., 2001), pp. 537–96.

Orr, D., 'An Index of Entry Barriers and Its Application to the Market Structure Performance Relationship', the *Journal of Industrial Economics*, 23:1 (1974), pp. 39–49.

Osborne, D. K., 'On the Rationality of Limit Pricing', the *Journal of Industrial Economics*, 22:1 (1973), pp. 71–80.

Pagoulatos, E. and R. Sorensen, 'What Determines the Elasticity of Industry Demand?', *International Journal of Industrial Organization*, 4 (1986), pp. 237–50.

Pakes, A., 'Review: Mueller's Profits in the Long Run', *RAND Journal of Economics*, 18:2 (1987), pp. 319–32.

Peitz, M., 'The Pro-Competitive Effect of Higher Entry Cost', *International Journal of Industrial Organization*, 20 (2001), pp. 353–64.

Peltzman S., 'The Gains and Losses from Industrial Concentration', *Journal of Law and Economics*, 20:2 (1977), pp. 229–63.

Penrose, E., *The Theory of the Growth of the Firm* (Oxford: Basil Blackwell, 1959).

Peritz, R. J. R., 'Antitrust Policy and Aggressive Business Strategy: a Historical Perspective on Understanding Commercial Purposes and Effects', *Journal of Public Policy & Marketing*, 21:2 (2002), pp. 237–42.

Peteraf, M. and R. Reed, 'Pricing and Performance in Monopoly Airline Markets', *Journal of Law and Economics*, 37 (1994), pp. 193–213.

Phillips, A., 'A Theory of Interfirm Organization', the Quarterly Journal of Economics, 74:4 (1960), pp. 602–13.

—, and O. Williamson (eds), *Prices: Issues in Theory, Practice, and Public Policy* (Philadelphia, PA: University of Pennsylvania Press, 1964).

—, *Promoting Competition in Regulated Markets* (Washington, DC: the Brookings Institution, 1975).

—, 'Market Concentration and Performance: a Survey of the Evidence', *Notre Dame Law Review*, 61 (1986), pp. 1099–108.

Pigou, A., *The Economics of Welfare* (London: Macmillan and Co., 1920), 4th edn (Edinburgh : R. & R. Clark, 1932).

Podolki, J., and F. Scott-Morton, 'Social Status, Entry and Predation: the Case of British Shipping Cartels 1879–1929', the *Journal of Industrial Economics*, 47 (1999), pp. 41–67.

Porter, M. E., *Competitive Strategy: Techniques for Analyzing Industries and Competitors* (New York: The Free Press, 1980).

—, 'The Contributions of Industrial Organization to Strategic Management', *Academy of Management Review*, 6:4 (1981), pp. 609–20.

— and M. Spence, 'The Capacity Expansion Process in a Growing Oligopoly: the Case of Corn Wet Milling', in J. Mccall, *Economics of Information and Uncertainty*. (Chicago, IL: the University of Chicago Press, 1982), pp. 259–316.

Porter, R. H., 'Recent Developments in Empirical Industrial Organization', *Journal of Economic Education*, 25:2 (1994), pp. 149–61.

Posner, R. A., *Antitrust Law. an Economic Perspective* (Chicago, IL: Chicago University Press, 1976).

—, 'The Chicago School of Antitrust Analysis', *University of Pennsylvania Law Review*, 127 (1978–79), pp. 925–48.

Pyatt, G., 'Profit Maximization and the Threat of New Entry', *Economic Journal*, 81:322 (1971), pp. 242–55.

Qualls, D., 'Concentration, Barriers to Entry, and Long Run Economic Profit Margins', the *Journal of Industrial Economics*, 20:2 (1972), pp. 146–58.

Rhoades, S. A., 'Concentration, Barriers to Entry and Rates of Return: a Note', *Journal of Industrial Economics*, 19: 1 (1970), pp. 82–8.

—, 'Concentration, Barriers to Entry and Rates of Return Revisited', *Journal of Industrial Economics*, 20: 2 (1972), pp. 93–195.

Robinson, E. A. G., the *Structure of Competitive Industry* (1931; London: Nisbet & Co. Ltd, 1997).

Robinson, J., *Economics of Imperfect Competition* (1933; London: Macmillan and Co. Limited, 1942).

Rosen, S., 'George J. Stigler and the Industrial Organization of Economic Thought', the *Journal of Political Economy*, 101:5 (1993), pp. 809–17.

Rubinfeld D. L., 'Antitrust Policy', *International Encyclopaedia of Social and Behavioral Sciences*, 1 (2001), pp. 553–60.

Salingen, M., R. Caves and S. Peltzman, 'The Concentration-Margins Relationship Considered', *Brookings Papers On Economic Activity, Microeconomics* (1990), pp. 287–335.

Salop, S. C., 'Strategic Entry Deterrence', *American Economic Review*, 69:2 (1979), pp. 335–38.

—, and D. T. Scheffman, 'Raising Rivals' Cost', *American Economic Review*, 73:2 (1983), pp. 267–71.

Scheffman D. T., 'Antitrust Economics and Marketing', *Journal of Public Policy & Marketing*, 21:2 (2002), pp. 243–6.

Schelling, T., *The Strategy of Conflict* (1960; London: Oxford University Press, 1971).

Scherer, F. M., 'Firm Size, Market Structure, Opportunity and the Output of Patented Inventions', *American Economic Review*, 55: 5 (1965), pp. 1097–125.

—, *Industrial Market Structure and Economic Performance* (Chicago, IL: Rand Mcnally & Company, 1970).

—, 'The Causes and Consequences of Rising Industrial Concentration', *Journal of Law and Economics*, 22:1 (1979), pp. 191–208.

—, 'Professor Sutton's Technology and Market Structure', *Journal of Industrial Economics*, 48 (2000), pp. 215–23.

Schmalensee, R., 'Brand Loyalty and Barriers to Entry', *Southern Economic Journal*, 40:4 (1974), pp. 579–88.

—, 'On the Use of Economic Models in Antitrust: the Realemon Case', *University of Pennsylvania Law Review*, 127 (1979), pp. 994–1050.

—, 'Entry Deterrence in the Ready-to-Eat Breakfast Cereal Industry', *Bell Journal of Economics*, 9:2 (1978), pp. 305–27.

—, 'Economies of Scale and Barriers to Entry', *Journal of Political Economy*, 89:6 (1981), pp. 1228–38.

—, 'Antitrust and the New Industrial Economics', *American Economic Review*, 72:2 (1982), pp. 24–8.

—, *Handbook of Industrial Organization* (New York: Elsevier Science Pub, 1989).

—, 'Inter-Industry Studies of Structure and Performance', in R. Schmalensee and Willig R. (eds), *Handbook of Industrial Organization* (Amsterdam: Elsevier Science B.V., 2001) vol. 2, pp. 952–1009.

—, and R. Willig (eds), *Handbook of Industrial Organization* (Amsterdam: Elsevier Science B.V., 2001).

—, 'Sunk Costs and Antitrust Barriers to Entry', *American Economic Review*, 94:2 (2004), pp. 471–5.

Schmidt, I. and J. Rittaler, *Chicago School of Antitrust Analysis* (Boston, MA: Kluwer Academic Publishers, 1989).

Schwalbach, J., 'Entry By Diversified Firms Into German Industries', *International Journal of Industrial Organization*, 5 (1986), pp. 43–9.

Scott-Morton, F., 'Barriers to Entry, Brand Advertising and Generic Entry in the US Pharmaceutical Industry', *International Journal of Industrial Organization*, 18 (2000), pp. 1085–104.

Seade, J., 'On the Effects of Entry', *Econometrica*, 48:2 (1980), pp. 479–89.

Shaanan, J., 'Welfare and Barriers to Entry: an Empirical Study', *Southern Economic Journal*, 54:3 (1988), pp. 746–62.

Shaked A. and J. Sutton, 'Natural Oligopolies', *Econometrica*, 51:5 (1983), pp. 1469–83.

Shapiro, D. and Khemani R. S., 'The Determinants of Entry and Exit Reconsidered', *International Journal of Industrial Organization*, 5 (1987), pp. 15–26.

Shapiro, C., 'The Theory of Business Strategy', *RAND Journal of Economics*, 20:1 (1989), 125–37.

—, 'Theories of Oligopoly Behaviour', in R. Schmalensee and R. Willig (eds), *Handbook of Industrial Organization*. (Amsterdam: Elsevier Science B.V., 2001) vol. 1, pp. 329–414.

Shepherd, W. G., 'Causes of Increased Competition in the U.S. Economy, 1939–1980', the *Review of Economics and Statistics*, 64:4 (1982), pp. 613–26.

—, *The Economics of Industrial Organization: Analysis, Markets, Policies*, 4th Edn (Unpper Saddle River, NJ: Prentice Hall, 1994).

Sheshinski, E., and J. Dreze, 'Demand Fluctuations, Capacity Utilization, and Costs', *American Economic Review*, 66: 5 (1976), pp. 731–42.

Siegfried, J., and L. W. Weiss, 'Advertising, Profits and Corporate Taxes Revisited', the *Review of Economics and Statistic*, 56: 2 (1974), pp. 195–200.

Simon, H., 'New Developments in the Theory of the Firm', *American Economic Review*, 52:2 (1962), pp. 1–15.

— (Et. Al.), *Economics, Bounded Rationality and the Cognitive Revolution* (Aldershot: Elgar. 1992).

Smith, A., *An Inquiry Into the Nature and Causes of the Wealth of Nations* (London: Printed for W. Strahan; and T. Cadell, in the Strand., 1776) (Indianapolis, IN: *Liberty Fund, 1981*).

Smiley, R., 'Empirical Evidence on Strategic Entry Deterrence', *International Journal of Industrial Organization*, 6 (1988), pp. 167–80.

Spence, A. M., 'Entry, Capacity, Investment and Oligopolistic Pricing', *Bell Journal of Economics*, 8: 2 (1977), pp. 534–44.

—, 'Investment Strategy and Growth in a New Market', *Bell Journal of Economics*, 10:1 (1979), pp. 1–19.

—,'Strategic Entry Deterrence', *American Economic Review*, 69:2 (1979), pp. 335–38.

—, 'Notes of Advertising, Economies of Scale, and Entry Barriers', *Quarterly Journal of Economics*, 95:3 (1980), pp. 493–507.

—, 'Signaling in Retrospect and the Informational Structure of Markets', *American Economic Review*, 92:3 (2002), pp. 434–59.

Spier K., and M. Whinston, 'On the Efficiency of Privately Stipulated Damages for Breach of Contract: Entry Barriers, Reliance and Renegotiation', *RAND Journal of Economics*, 26:2 (1995), pp. 180–202.

Sraffa, P., 'The Laws of Returns Under Competitive Conditions', *Economic Journal*, 144:36 (1926), pp. 535–50.

Stenbacka R. L., 'Collusion in Dynamic Oligopolies in the Presence of Entry Threats', *Journal of Industrial Economics*, 34:2 (1990), pp. 47–154.

Stigler, G. J., *The Theory of Price: an Enlarged Edition of the Theory of Competitive Price* (1942; New York: Macmillan, 1946).

—, 'A Survey of Contemporary Economics', *Journal of Political Economy*, 57:2 (1949), pp. 93–105.

—, 'Monopoly and Oligopoly By Merger', *American Economic Review*, 40:2 (1950), pp. 23–34.

—, and J. S. Bain, 'Discussion', *American Economic Review*, 40:2 (1950), pp. 63–6.

—, 'Mergers and Preventive Antitrust Policy', *University of Pennsylvania Law Review*, 104 (1955–6), pp. 176–84.

—, 'Perfect Competition, Historically Contemplated', *Journal of Political Economy*, 65 (1957), pp. 1–17.

—, 'A Theory of Oligopoly', *Journal of Political Economy*, 72 (1964), pp. 44–61.

—, *The Organization of Industry* (Illinois: Richard D. Irwin, 1968).

—, 'Law and Economics?', *Journal of Law and Economics*, 35:2 (1992), pp. 455–68.

Sutton, J., 'Market Structure: Theory and Evidence', in M. Armstrong and R. Porter (eds), *Handbook of Industrial Organization.* (Amsterdam: Elsevier, 2007) vol. 3, pp. 2304–68.

Suzumura, K., and K. Kiyono, 'Entry Barriers and Economic Welfare', *Review of Economic Studies*, 54:1 (1987), pp. 157–67.

Sylos-Labini, P., *Oligopolio Y Progreso Técnico* (1956; Vilassar De Mar: Oikos-Tau, 1966).

Symeonidis G., 'In Which Industries Is Collusion More Likely? Evidence From the UK', *Journal of Industrial Organization*, 51 (2003), pp. 45–74.

Taylor, J., 'The Output Effects of Governemtn Sponsored Cartels during the New Deal', *The Journal of Industrial Organization*, 50 (2002), pp. 1–10.

Telser, L. G., 'Advertising and Competition', *Journal of Political Economy*, 72:6 (1964), pp. 537–62.

Tirole, J., *The Theory of Industrial Organization* (Cambridge, Mass: M.I.T., 1988).

Turner, D., 'Conglomerate Mergers and Section 7 of the Clayton Act', *Harvard Law Review*, 78 (1965), pp. 1313–95.

Tullock, G., 'Entry Barriers and Politics', *American Economic Review*, 55:1–2 (1965), pp. 458–66.

Vany, A. S. De, 'Capacity Utilization Under Alternative Regulation Restraints: an Analysis of Taxi Markets', the *Journal of Political Economy*, 83:1 (1975), pp. 83–94.

—, 'The Effect of Price and Entry Regulation On Airline Output, Capacity and Efficiency', the *Bell Journal of Economics*, 6:1 (1975), pp. 327–45.

Vernon, J. M., and R. E. M. Nourse, 'Profit Rates and Market Structure of Advertising Intensive Firms', *Journal of Industrial Economics*, 22:2 (1973), pp. 1–20.

Vives, X., 'Sequential Entry, Industry Structure and Welfare', *European Economic Review*, 32 (1988), pp. 1671–87.

—, 'Games With Strategic Complementarities: New Applications to Industrial Organization', *International Journal of Industrial Organization*, 23 (2005), pp. 625–37.

Waagstein, T., 'Fixed Cost, Limit Pricing and Investment in Barriers to Entry', *European Economic Review*, 17 (1982), pp. 75–86.

Wallace, D. H., 'Monopolistic Competition and Public Policy', *American Economic Review*, 26:1 (1936), pp. 77–87.

Ware, R., 'Inventory Holding as a Strategic Weapon to Deter Entry', *Economica*, 205:52 (1985), pp. 93–101.

Watkins, M. W., the Federal Trade Commission a Critical Survey', *Quarterly Journal of Economics*, 40:4 (1926), pp. 561–85.

Weiss, L. W., 'Factor in Changing Concentration', *Review of Economics and Statistic*, 45:1 (1963), pp. 70–7.

—, 'The Structure-Conduct-Performance Paradigm and Antitrust', *University of Pennsylvania Law Review*, 127:4 (1979), pp. 1104–40.

Weizsäcker, C. C. Von, *Barriers to Entry, a Theoretical Treatment* (Berlin: Springer Verlag, 1980).

—, 'A Welfare Analysis of Barriers to Entry', *Bell Journal of Economics*, 11:2 (1980), pp. 399–420.

Wenders, J. T., 'Excess Capacity as a Barrier to Entry', *Journal of Industrial Economics*, 20:1 (1971), pp. 14–9.

Whinston M., 'Antitrust Policy Toward Horizontal Mergers', in M. Armstrong and R. Porter (eds) *Handbook of Industrial Organization*, (Amsterdam: Elsevier, 2007), vol. 3, pp. 2369–440.

White, L., 'Business School Economics and Antitrust: What's Thought and What's Taught', *Journal of Public Policy & Marketing*, 21:2 (2002), pp. 254–6.

—, 'Economics, Economists, and Antitrust: a Tale of Growing Influence', in J. J. Siegfried (ed.), *Living Better Through Economics* (Cambridge: Harvard University Press, Forthcoming 2009).

Williamson, O. E., 'Selling Expense as a Barrier to Entry', *Quarterly Journal of Economics*, 77:1 (1963), pp. 112–28.

—, *The Economics of Discretionary Behavior Managerial Objectives in a Theory of the Firm* (Englewood Cliffs, NJ: Prentice-Hall, 1964).

—, 'A Dynamic Theory of Interfirm Behaviour', *Quarterly Journal of Economics*, 79:4 (1965), pp. 579–607.

—, 'Economies as an Antitrust Defense: the Welfare Tradeoffs', *American Economic Review*, 58:1 (1968), pp. 18–36.

—, 'Symposium On Antitrust Law and Economics', *University of Pennsylvania Law Review*, 127 (1978–1979), pp. 918–24.

—, 'Antitrust Enforcement: Where It Has Been; Where It Is Going', *Saint Louis University Law Journal*, 27 (1983), pp. 289–314.

—, *Antitrust Economics: Mergers, Contracting, and Strategic Behaviour.* (New York: Basil Blackwell Inc., 1987).

—, *Industrial Organization* (Vermont: Edward Elgar Publishing Limited, 1990).

—, 'The Lens of Contract: Private Ordering', *American Economic Review*, 92:2 (2002), pp. 438–43.

—, 'The Merger Guidelines of the U.S. Department of Justice-In Perspective', 2007, Http://Www.Usdoj.Gov/Atr/Hmerger/11257.Htm

Willig, R., S. Salop, and F. Scherer, 'Merger Analysis, Industrial Organization Theory, and Merger Guidelines', *Brookings Papers On Economic Activity: Microeconomics* (1991), pp. 281–332.

Wolfstetter, E., *Topics in Microeconomics: Industrial Organization, Auctions and Incentives.* (Cambridge: Cambridge University Press, 1999).

Woodward, J., *Industrial Organization, Theory and Practice* (1965; Oxford: Oxford University Press, 1980).

Working E. J., 'What Do Statistical "Demand Curves" Show?', *Quarterly Journal of Economics*, 41:2 (1927), pp. 212–35.

Yip, G. S., 'Diversification Entry: Internal Development versus Acquisition', *Strategic Management Journal*, 3:4 (1982), pp. 331–45.

INDEX

9 781138 663305